BACKCOUNTRY A

Mount Zirkel
WILDERNESS

A MOUNTAIN JAY™ ADVENTURE GUIDE

Text and Photography by
Raymond Ave

Mountain Jay Media LLC
mountainjaymedia.com

INTERNATIONAL STANDARD BOOK NUMBER: 0-9741755-2-8

PHOTOGRAPHY AND TEXT COPYRIGHT: Raymond Ave, 2003. All rights reserved.
MAP COPYRIGHT: Raymond Ave, Rebecca Finkel, 2003.
All rights reserved.

EDITOR: Patrick Shea
DESIGNER: Rebecca Finkel, F + P Graphic Design, Inc.

PUBLISHED BY: Mountain Jay Media LLC
P.O. Box 271893
Fort Collins, CO 80527
www.mountainjaymedia.com

PRINTED IN THE U.S.A. BY: Sheridan Books, Inc., Chelsea, MI
First Edition, First Printing.

PUBLISHER'S CATALOGING-IN-PUBLICATION DATA:
Ave, Raymond.
    Backcountry adventure guide to the Mount Zirkel Wilderness /
Raymond Ave. – 1st ed.
    p. cm. – (A Mountain Jay adventure guide)
    Includes bibliographical references and index.
    LCCN 2003107830
    ISBN 0-9741755-2-8
    1. Hiking – Colorado – Mount Zirkel Wilderness – Guidebooks.
    2. Hiking – Colorado – Routt National Forest – Guidebooks.
    3. Mount Zirkel Wilderness (Colo.) – Guidebooks. 4. Routt National
Forest (Colo.) – Guidebooks. I. Title.

    GV199.42.C62M687 2003   917.88'140434
       QBI03-200497

PLEASE NOTE: Backcountry adventure travel is an inherently dangerous activity. People are lost, injured, and sometimes killed while traveling in the backcountry. The information presented here is as accurate as possible. However, conditions in and around any wilderness are in a constant state of change, so it's impossible to guarantee that all the information presented here is completely accurate and up-to-date. People who choose to hike in or around any wilderness should possess sufficient backcountry navigation and survival skills and should be able to assess if their own abilities are sufficient for the situation they are facing before they choose when and where to enter a wilderness. Personal responsibility and self-reliance are essential to the wilderness experience, and the information presented in this book cannot change that. The author and publisher of this book disclaim any liability for accidents or injuries sustained by users of this book while engaged in activities described herein.

For my mom and dad,
Ray and Ramona Ave

Seven Lakes near the trail junction of Big Creek Trail and Buffalo Ridge Trail

Mount Zirkel Wilderness Overview

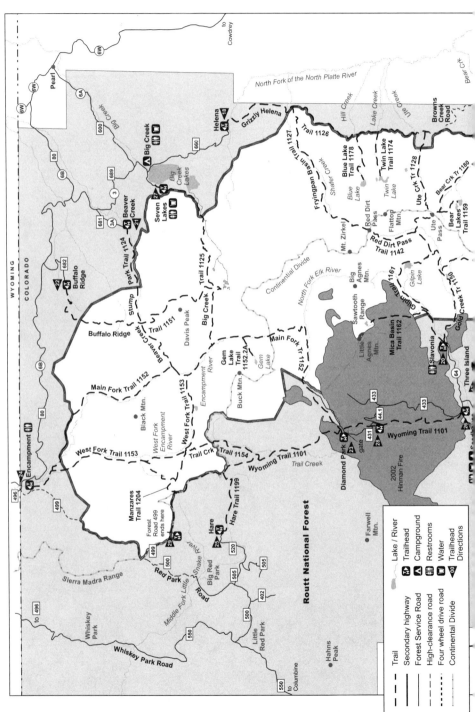

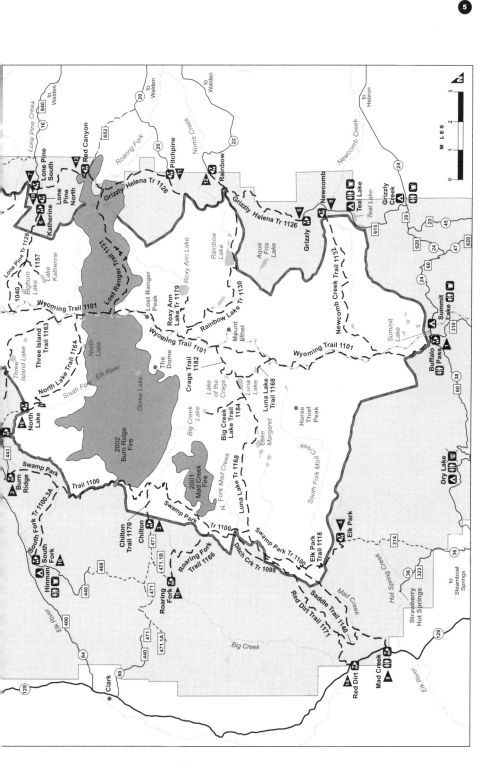

Table of Contents

Mount Zirkel Wilderness Overview. 4
Preface 8
Acknowledgements 10
Introduction 12
History of Northwest Colorado 13
  The Ute Indian Tribe 13
  Miners, Tie Hacks, and Settlers 15
  Historic Preservation on Public Lands 18
Natural Setting of the Mount Zirkel Wilderness 19
  Ecosystems in and around the Wilderness. 19
  Spruce Beetles and Fire in Spruce-fir Forest 20
  Geology of the Mount Zirkel Wilderness 25
When and How to Enjoy the Mount Zirkel Wilderness 31
  Wilderness Regulations and Travel Restrictions 31
  Leave No Trace, A National Outdoor Skills and Ethics Program 32
  The 10 Essentials. 33
  Strategies for Safer Swiftwater Crossings 33
  Hypothermia 37
  Acute Mountain Sickness and High Altitude Pulmonary Edema. 39
  Drinking Water Treatment 39
  Hazards in recently burned areas. 40
  Peak bagging safety and ethics 41
  Living with Wildlife in the Colorado Backcountry 41
  Colorado Outdoor Recreation Search and Rescue Card. 43
  Pack Stock Use on National Forest and Wilderness Lands. 43
  Seasons in the wilderness. 44
  Fishing in and around the Mount Zirkel Wilderness 45
  Hunting in and around the Mount Zirkel Wilderness 46
How to Use the Trail Descriptions 47

Southern Wilderness Overview. 50
  Southern Wilderness Trails At-a-Glance. 52
  Southern Wilderness Trailheads. 54
  Big Creek Lake Trail 1184. 62
  Bighorn Lake Trail 1040 64
  Chilton Trail 1170 66
  Crags Trail 1182 68
  Ditch Creek Trail 1099 70
  Elk Park Trail 1118. 72
  Grizzly Helena Trail 1126 — South of Lone Pine South Trailhead 74
  Lake Katherine Trail 1157. 80
  Lone Pine Trail 1129 82
  Lost Ranger Trail 1131 84
  Luna Lake Trail 1168. 87

Newcomb Creek Trail 1132   90
North Lake Trail 1164   94
Rainbow Lake Trail 1130   96
Red Dirt Trail 1171   99
Roaring Fork Trail 1166   102
Roxy Ann Lake Trail 1179   104
Saddle Trail 1140   106
South Fork Trail 1100.3A   108
Swamp Park Trail 1100   110
Three Island Trail 1163   117
Wyoming Trail 1101 — Southern Section   120

Central Wilderness Overview   127
Central Wilderness Trails At-a-Glance   128
Central Wilderness Trailheads   130
Bear Creek Trail 1180   132
Bear Lakes Trail 1159   134
Blue Lake Trail 1178   136
Fryingpan Basin Trail 1127   138
Gilpin Trail 1161   140
Gold Creek Trail 1150   142
Grizzly Helena Trail 1126 — North of Lone Pine North Trailhead   145
Mica Basin Trail 1162   150
Red Dirt Pass Trail 1142   152
Twin Lake Trail 1174   154
Ute Creek Trail 1128   156

Northern Wilderness Overview   158
Northern Wilderness Trails At-a-Glance   160
Northern Wilderness Trailheads   162
Beaver Creek Stump Park Trail 1124   166
Big Creek Trail 1125   168
Buffalo Ridge Trail 1151   171
Gem Lake Trail 1152.2A   176
Hare Trail 1199   178
Main Fork Trail 1152   180
Manzanares Trail 1204   185
Trail Creek Trail 1154   188
West Fork Trail 1153   190
Wyoming Trail 1101 — North of Seedhouse Road   193

Appendix A: Contact Information   198
Appendix B: Bibliography   199
Appendix C: Fishing Information   200

Preface

I hiked about 500 miles during the summers of 2001 and 2002 to gather the information for this book, experiencing all of the U.S. Forest Service trails in the Mount Zirkel Wilderness during the process. A couple of years earlier, I carried a pack 30 miles through this wilderness, which planted the seed for this project. After my more extensive experiences recently, I find that I love the Mount Zirkel Wilderness more than ever.

When I began the fieldwork for this book, I kept an open mind. I simply started hiking with my notebook, measuring wheel, and camera with the intention of letting the book write itself. It turns out that gathering the information for a hiking guide involves a lot of hard work. It was a labor of love though, and I wouldn't trade it for anything. With my mind open, I didn't have preconceived notions of the experience. Toward the end of my journey, I do think that I experienced some enlightenment of what wilderness means to me.

If there's one thing this experience has taught me, it may be something about control, or more accurately the illusion of control. In our daily lives, most of us feel a great level security in our surroundings. We live in a world largely created by man, and much of the work of man involves the struggle to control our environment. We dam rivers for flood control. We fight a war on disease from the Center for Disease Control. We spend our lives in a risk-reduced environment where it's easy to believe that we are "in control." But after all, control is an illusion. Despite constructing elaborate flood control schemes and investing in weather forecasting systems that reduce risk, people still die in floods. The world is undoubtedly a better place without polio and small pox, but the war against cancer rages on long after President Nixon committed our resources to eliminating it more than 30 years ago.

Glacially sculpted rocks near Beaver Creek Trailhead, Beaver Creek Stump Park Trail.

While we have had some success in our endeavor to control our world, it is important that we exercise some restraint in our efforts. Too much control can become detrimental. Consider the example of DDT. What was initially hailed as a magic bullet that would fight disease and hunger turned out to be a terrible mistake. We almost lost our national symbol, the bald eagle, to DDT. It's easy to lose perspective; if we're not careful, we can pursue the illusion of control at unreasonable costs. The existence of legally protected wilderness is at least in part recognition of the fact that the natural world needs to be protected from our zeal to control it.

In wilderness, we have the opportunity to surrender much of the control we take for granted in our day-to-day lives. We are given the opportunity to enter an environment largely untouched by man. We enter an environment populated by animals that have nothing to fear of a human without a firearm. In wilderness, rivers annually turn into flood-swollen torrents; weather can turn deadly at any time.

What can possibly be gained by entering such an environment? Maybe we can gain some perspective on the illusion of control. There's nothing like a fresh bear track to slay the illusion of control. We don't conquer wilderness; we only hope it will let us pass. In fact, it is through this surrender of control that the raw beauty of wilderness is revealed.

When we enter a realm where we do not have mastery, where we are only separate cogs in the machine, we appreciate the simple pleasure of just being. With this comes the realization that we live in a world that is truly full of wonder. The wonder and beauty of nature surpasses that of all the works of man. Yet, as part of this natural world, there is a measure of that wonder, that beauty that lies within us. That's where the best works of man originate.

When we become alienated from this best part of ourselves, we can stray to hubris and folly. By spending time in the natural world, we may get in touch with the part of ourselves that binds us to one another and the world around us. Perhaps we gain perspective on the illusion, learning that the pursuit of control can become detrimental rather than beneficial.

If you spend time in the natural world, your perception of it and relationship to it could change as well. But you can't gain any insight by staying home and reading a book, or watching a television program, or even driving around to marvel at the natural world through the windshield of your car. You have to get out there with the bugs and the bears, the spruce and mountain jays, and experience it yourself for it to affect you.

So get out and take a hike. Get in touch with the wonder and beauty of living. And when you've found a place that you love, a place that's special to you — fight to protect it from the illusion of control.

Acknowledgements

I'm grateful for the support of the many people that contributed to this book, and I want to thank them all for their help. However, if I have forgotten someone, I apologize. Please bring it to my attention, and I'll remember you in the next revision.

I'd like to begin by thanking the U.S. Forest Service employees who helped in the preparation of this book. The district rangers for the Hahns Peak/Bears Ears and Parks Ranger Districts of the Routt National Forest — Kim Vogel at Steamboat Springs and Chuck Oliver at Walden — helped by allowing their people to take the time to answer my questions and review sections of my manuscript.

Jon Halverson and Hal Wentz, the wilderness rangers from the Hahns Peak/Bears Ears and Parks Ranger Districts respectively, took many hours to answer my questions and carefully review the trail descriptions and the "When and How to Enjoy the Mount Zirkel Wilderness" sections of the manuscript. They both recommended changes and additions that made this a better book. Thanks also go to Win Dermody, Rich Levy, and Mike Castellini, who provided valuable input on field conditions in the wilderness.

Andy Cadenhead, a forester in the Steamboat Springs U.S. Forest Service office, patiently educated me about elementary forestry and spruce beetle epidemic details. He also took time to review and comment on these topics in the manuscript. Thanks to John Schmid (author of the definitive works on spruce beetles in the Rocky Mountains listed in the bibliography) who took the time to comment on the manuscript as well.

Dave McKee and Sue Struthers, U.S. Forest Service Archeologists formerly from the Hahns Peak / Bears Ears Ranger District, provided valuable information and resources for the "History of Northwest Colorado" section of the book.

Thanks to Diann Pipher and the information staff at the Steamboat Springs and Walden U.S. Forest Service offices for their help.

Ken Kehmeier and Kevin Rogers from the Colorado Division of Wildlife provided the fish stocking data presented in Appendix C.

My friends Dennis and Susan Snoddy helped me by editing and offering input for the geology section of the book.

Terry McShane, a Rescue3 International swiftwater rescue instructor, provided valuable insight for the "Strategies for Safer Swiftwater Crossings" section of the book.

My friend Ken Fantone took the time to review and make comments on the geology of the wilderness section.

My friend Reuben Luzano did some copy-editing on the manuscript when I was in a jam and needed help.

Lorraine Streckfus provided encouragement and editing during the early stages of the project.

Thanks to Paul Nielsen at Markham Photo Lab in Fort Collins who consistently provides film processing and service of exceptional quality.

I'd also like to thank Rebecca Finkel of F+P Graphic Design, Inc. who not only took my manuscript and made it into a book, but also provided invaluable guidance through the entire process. When working with Rebecca, it doesn't take long before it becomes obvious how she's earned the reputation of being among the best at what she does.

Thanks also to the many residents around Steamboat Springs and Walden who extended their kindness and hospitality while I was a guest in their area.

Meadow on the way to Mica Lake, Mica Basin Trail

Introduction

I love wilderness. I love spending my time hiking in wilderness, wandering alone in wide-open windswept spaces. I relish fresh bear tracks in the snow on cold windy fall days, afternoon thunderstorms in August, mountain skies choked with stars on crisp clear nights. Wilderness is a gourmet feast for the connoisseur of sensations: the sound of the wind in spruce, fir, and pines; the taste of cold, clear water from mountain streams; the smell of spruce forest after a rain; the way the shadows of clouds move over the mountains; and the warmth of the sun on bare skin.

A couple years ago I indulged in my love of wilderness by hiking all the trails in and around the Mount Zirkel Wilderness. This book is the result.

I could have chosen to hike lots of trails in different places, but instead I elected to hike all the trails in just this one place. (I prefer quality over quantity.) This guide covers all the trails in and around the Mount Zirkel Wilderness, giving you the information you need for choosing and planning your own hikes. To provide maximum accuracy, I used a calibrated measuring wheel to gather the distance information in the trail descriptions, and I provided the same level of detail in the directions to the trailheads themselves. Whether you're planning a day hike or preparing for a long backcountry visit, this book provides the details you need.

In addition to accuracy, this book features geology and history, as well as detailed information about ecosystems and the ongoing spruce beetle epidemic in the wilderness. The book also provides general information about backcountry safety, which adds to its utility on the trail.

Fires swept across the Mount Zirkel Wilderness during the summer of 2002. The fires affected Wyoming Trail, Swamp Park Trail, North Lake Trail, Lost Ranger Trail, Grizzly Helena Trail, Gilpin Creek Trail, Gold Creek Trail, Mica Basin Trail, and Main Fork Trail in varying degrees. The trail descriptions for these trails were written before the fires and therefore do not include current descriptions of the areas. However, you can consult a map of these areas affected by the fires on pages 4 and 5.

Printed on recycled paper in the United States, this book is black-and-white for a reason. Because of economics, full-color books are usually printed in Asia where recycled paper is not readily available and labor and environmental regulations are less restrictive. Instead, I chose to have this book's binding sewn, had it covered with more durable and weather-resistant Kivar, and had its corners rounded, so it will withstand the test of time and the rigors of riding in your pack.

However, the situation isn't merely black and white. If you want to view full-color pictures for choosing hikes, you can find them on my Web site, www.mountzirkelwilderness.com. A companion to my Web site and Trails Illustrated maps, the print version of this book is meant to be useful while actually on the trail or when planning a detailed itinerary.

I hope this book increases your enjoyment of the Mount Zirkel Wilderness. If you do take the time to indulge in your own love of wilderness, you may notice a difference in the way you view the natural world. You could come to realize that without wilderness, the world would be much diminished. You may even choose to get active and involved in public land management.

It all starts with getting out there. When you do that, you may get in touch with the wilderness inside yourself. If that happens, I think the rest will take care of itself.

History of Northwest Colorado

THE UTE INDIAN TRIBE

When John Charles Fremont entered North Park in Northwest Colorado on an exploratory expedition for the U.S. government in 1844, it was known to be the territory of the Ute Indian Tribe. These hearty mountain people bear the distinction of being the first Indian tribe to obtain the horse, from the Spanish in what is now New Mexico, as well as being one of the last Indian tribes forced onto reservations in the United States.

The earliest known Native American settlements in Colorado are in the southwest corner of the state. Mesa Verde National Park is the best known of these settlements and occupation of that site dates back to about the time of Christ. Around A.D. 1276, the people who inhabited the settlements in southwest Colorado abandoned their homes for reasons that are still unknown but may have been related to a 24-year drought that occurred then. Some of these people may have migrated north following game herds into the wetter high country of the Rocky Mountains, and this may have been the origin of the Ute tribe. The Utes share a similar language with the Hopi, Pima, and Papago Indians of Arizona, as well as the Shoshone tribe of Nevada and Wyoming, the Piute tribe of Utah, and the Comanche tribe of eastern Colorado, New Mexico, and Texas.

The Utes roamed the high country of Colorado on foot for at least 370 years, living as hunters that followed the game herds migrating in search of the best grasses. In about 1608, the Spanish were beginning to penetrate northward into Ute territory, and the two cultures began to interact. By 1640, the Utes had obtained horses from the Spanish, and this precipitated the start of a golden period in their history. On horseback, they easily followed the herds, and success in the hunts improved.

The Ute tribe was originally composed of seven bands: four northern and three southern. Each band was made up of several families divided into loose and somewhat independent groups. The bands would interact, usually during winter, and particularly to allow their children to court. The four northern and three southern bands of the tribe would interact with other bands within their respective geographic areas, but interaction between the northern and southern bands was less common.

The southern Ute bands included the Mouache band in south-central Colorado, the Capote band originally living in the San Luis Valley, and the Weeminuche band from the San Juan River valley and the San Juan Mountains. The Mouache and Capote bands currently reside on the Southern Ute Indian Reservation, while the Weeminuche band now lives on the Ute Mountain Reservation.

The four northern bands lived in river valleys closer to the current Mount Zirkel Wilderness. The Tabeguache (or Uncompahgre) band originally occupied the Gunnison and Uncompahgre River valleys, the Grand River (or Parianuc) band lived along the Colorado River, the Uintah band populated the Salt Lake valley, and the Yampa band lived along the Yampa and White Rivers. The northern bands currently reside in the Uintah and Ouray reservation in Utah.

It was the Yampa band of perhaps 500 to at most 1,500 people who called lands including the present day Mount Zirkel Wilderness and the Routt National Forest home. In a very real way, it is their stewardship that preserved the wilderness for centuries so that we can enjoy it as it is today. Near the headwaters of Gold Creek lies Ute Pass, which early settlers say bore tree markings indicating it was used by the Utes to cross the Park Mountain Range into their traditional hunting grounds in North Park.

The mastery of horses and the relative impenetrability of their mountain home allowed the Utes to hold onto their land after most other tribes either ceased to exist or were moved onto reservations. The Utes cultivated a friendly relationship with the U.S. government, negotiating a series of treaties protecting their homeland from invasion.

A treaty signed in 1868 set aside 16 million acres for the Utes on the west slope of Colorado and promised them a distribution of $60,000 a year in food, blankets, and clothing. The Mount Zirkel Wilderness and the Routt National Forest north of Steamboat Springs were not within the boundaries of the Ute Reservation defined by the treaty of 1868, although the Utes continued to hunt and trade in the area and remained the dominant Native American presence there. The 1868 treaty was guaranteed binding and "final forever." It lasted five years. In 1873 the Utes were forced to cede 4 million acres in the mineral-rich San Juan Mountains when miners began to invade that region.

The pressure of miners and settlers to open more Ute land to settlement continued to mount until the fall of 1879. At that time, Nathan Meeker was the Indian agent at the White River Agency, located near the present location of Meeker, Colorado, to distribute food and supplies to satisfy the 1868 and 1873 treaty obligations to the Yampa band of the Utes.

Having assumed the Indian Agent position only a year earlier, Meeker unilaterally moved the agency and began plowing the land used by the Yampa band as winter pasture for their beloved horses. Meeker also began talking of killing their horses and bringing soldiers onto the reservation if the Yampa Utes did not comply with his orders.

The number of horses a person owned largely determined that person's wealth and stature within the Ute community. One of the Indians confronted Meeker over plowing the pastureland and appeared to have assaulted him. Instead of defusing a still manageable situation, Meeker immediately requested protection from the U.S. Army, which was dispatched southward from Fort Steele in Wyoming.

When U.S. Army soldiers violated a treaty forbidding troops from entering onto the Ute's reservation (an agreement between the Indians and the Governor of Colorado), a battle between Ute warriors and the U.S. Army took place at the reservation boundary at Milk Creek. The battlefield is located about 11 miles northeast of Meeker, Colorado. Several soldiers and Indians lost their lives in this battle, and the Utes initially repelled the U.S. Army invaders.

The Yampa Utes reacted to the aggression by killing Meeker and all the male government employees at the reservation. Meeker's wife and daughter and the wife of another agency employee were taken by the Indians as they fled into the mountains. These hostages were later released. An inquiry was held to investigate the incident, but ultimately only one of the Utes was jailed for a short time and later released.

The Meeker incident ultimately led to the expulsion of all the northern Ute bands from the state of Colorado. These people currently reside on the Uintah and Ouray reservation in Utah. In the end, the U.S. Army was forced to hold back the rush of settlers into the homeland of the Utes until the Indians could be escorted out of the state in 1881.

MINERS, TIE HACKS, AND SETTLERS

When Fremont and his men entered North Park in 1844, they encountered immense herds of buffalo, deer, elk, and antelope. The group found a well-worn trace over the Park Range used by buffalo herds migrating between North Park and the Yampa valley. The trace was later converted to a wagon road, then a vehicle road, and the pass it crosses retains the name Buffalo Pass. There is now a trailhead near the southern edge of the Mount Zirkel Wilderness where the road still crosses the pass. Following Fremont's 1844 expedition through North Park, history shows a lull in white exploration of the area.

In 1859 miners began pouring into Colorado after reports began circulating back east about gold strikes near Pikes Peak. In 1860, Joseph Hahn led a prospecting expedition into the area surrounding the peak that would later bear his name. He returned with a group of miners in 1866 to mine the placer gold he found in the vicinity of the peak, forming the Hahns Peak Mining District. All the miners who accompanied Hahn in 1866 returned to the Front Range of Colorado that fall except for Hahn and another man, William Doyle, who may have fallen prey to gold fever. They decided to continue to work their claims through the winter and arranged for foodstuffs to be sent to their mining camp in October.

That fall while squirrels carefully cached pinecones and bears laid on fat for their coming winter slumber, Hahn and Doyle busied themselves building sluice boxes or scrutinizing the black sand in their gold pans. They were the first white men to winter in the region, so they were unaware they had chosen where the most snow typically falls each year in Colorado.

The food the men had arranged to be delivered that fall didn't come, but the snow did. The snow drove the game herds to lower elevations, isolating them from the miners. After surviving a bitter winter below Hahns Peak, the gaunt men began to make their way toward Empire, Colorado, in April of 1867 to secure supplies.

Hahn died of starvation and exposure along Muddy Creek, a tributary of the Colorado River, after a blizzard overtook the men in Middle Park. Doyle was rescued by men tending livestock in Middle Park and survived to tell the tale.

Mining activity fell silent in the Hahns Peak area for about seven years until enough miners made their way into the area to start a second Hahns Peak Mining District in 1874. One of the hamlets in the district, Poverty Flats, is presently the site of Hahns Peak Village, the oldest settlement in northwest Colorado. When Routt County was formed in 1877, residents chose the Hahns Peak District (at that time the largest settlement in the county) for the county seat.

The Hahns Peak Mining District continued to produce at a modest pace and remained the heart of the county until 1912 when the seat was moved to Steamboat Springs. Agricultural settlement into North Park and the Yampa valley had begun around 1879, and by the early part of the twentieth century agricultural pursuits had come to dominate the area.

Around 1900, a small mining operation was active near the confluence of Gold and Gilpin Creeks at the headwaters of the Elk River. The Slavonia Mine was so named for the Slavic miners who worked it. The mine was not in operation for long, and the remnants of cabins used by the miners remain hidden in the trees near the confluence of the creeks as well as above Gold Creek Lake.

At about the same time the Slavonia Mine was in operation, miners worked several small mines near Pearl, located along Big Creek on the east side of the Continental Divide. The remnants of a copper smelting operation that saw little or no use sits southeast of the few remaining houses near the crossroads of Jackson County Roads 6W and 6A. This mining operation also came and went quickly.

In 1902 the Carbon Timber Company established a large lumber camp of about 500 men based in Commissary Park, near the Wyoming State Line along the Encampment River. The company had contracts to supply railroad ties and lumber to the Union Pacific Railroad. The main lumber camp was located in the open meadow north of the Encampment Trailhead on the west side of the Encampment River, just north of the bridge over the river. The company floated about a half a million ties down the Encampment River, then the North Platte River, during the spring floods each year. The ties were recovered at the Union Pacific railhead at Fort Steele on the North Platte River in Wyoming.

The lumber camp was supplied from Grand Encampment Wyoming, now called Encampment, via what is now Forest Road 550. Farmers drove livestock from Big Red Park over the Sierra Madre Range to supply the lumber camp via what are now Forest Roads 499 and 500. The U.S. Forest Service has constructed an interpretive trail that begins about a mile east of the bridge over the Encampment River on Forest Road 80. You can read signs describing the lumber camps and the operations carried out there.

The camp lumberjacks, known as tie hacks, used hand tools such as an eight-foot measuring pole, a double-bladed axe, a *broadaxe,* a bark peeler, a one-man crosscut saw, and a *pickaroon* to hand-hew railroad ties from lodgepole pine trees in the area.

The tie hacks would begin by cutting a notch at the base of the tree on the side they wished it to fall. The tree was then sawed down with the one-man crosscut saw. An ideal lodgepole pine tree would be about 11 inches in diameter at breast height and would yield about six or seven ties. After felling the tree, the tie hack would remove limbs from the tree with his double-bladed axe, and then measure and mark an eight-foot length of the tree for each tie. Specifications in the late 1800s required each tie be at least seven inches by seven inches overall with at least five inches of hewn surface on each flat side. The sides of the tree not hewn flat were stripped of bark and left round.

Standing atop the felled tree, the tie hack would score each side of the tree with his double-bladed axe, roughly removing most of the wood to provide at least five inches of flat surface while leaving at least seven inches of width. He would then hew each flat side of the tie smooth with a *broadaxe,* a heavy straight-handled axe with a single blade about a foot long. So skilled were the tie hacks, it is said the finished tie was as smooth as if it were planed.

Using a *spud peeler* (basically a wood chisel mounted on a pole), workers peeled the bark from the top surface of the tie. With a one-man bucksaw, the tie hacks then cut the tie to length. Next, they peeled the bark from the other side of the tie, and the tie hack would mark each tie he cut (because he was paid piecemeal and wanted full credit).

With the *pickaroon,* which looked like a single-bladed pick, the tie hack hooked and dragged the tie to be stacked at the drag road for hauling. Most of the ties were cut in winter and then hauled on a horse-drawn sled — the horses wore snowshoes — to a landing near the river where they waited to be floated downstream each spring.

A tie hack could cut anywhere from 20 to 50 ties per day, depending on his abilities. The amount paid to the tie hacks per tie varied, but the men generally earned good wages for the time. Many of the tie hacks were of Scandinavian descent. These men worked hard six days a week at high altitude, judging by accounts of the food supplies required for them. Each man consumed about a pound and a half of meat per day as well as pancakes and eggs for breakfast, and potatoes, bread, pies or cakes, and vegetables with the other two meals.

Each spring the tie hacks would follow the ties down the flood-swollen river with pike poles, freeing logjams and shepherding the ties toward Fort Steele. The men would sleep in teepees as they drove the ties down the river, and they ate double their normal amount while doing this hard, cold, wet work.

After collecting their annual pay following the spring tie drive, the tie hacks (most were single) often imbibed and visited bordellos with understandable verve — although this would happen away from the lumber camps. Some tie hacks married and raised families in the camps, and some camps featured churches.

If you hike south from Encampment Trailhead along either Main Fork or West Fork Trails, you will travel through a lodgepole forest roughly 90 years old, having grown after the lumber camp was closed.

It was easier to turn a profit in the timber business before formation of what would become the National Forest in 1905. The Carbon Timber Company settled a trespass case with the government in 1907 for illegally harvesting timber, agreeing to pay $80,000 — half in cash and half in labor. To satisfy the labor portion of the settlement, the company built the Hog Park Guard Station near the Encampment Trailhead and cleared the Fireline Road along which Wyoming Trail follows the crest of the Sierra Madres from near the Wyoming State Line south to the trail junction with Hare Trail.

On December 8, 1911, the *Grand Encampment Herald* reported that the Carbon Timber Company logging camp would be shut down after the following spring tie drive. The newspaper was critical of U. S. Forest Service management of timber in the area stating, "The present government policy is to let it [the National Forest] stand for future generations or be consumed by forest fires, rather than let it be used to aid in the present prosperity and development of the country."[1] Some things never change. In fact, the demise of the Carbon Timber Company was brought about by a number of factors, including quality control problems, which led to it falling out of favor with the Union Pacific Railroad.

---

[1] Thybony, Scott, Rosenberg, Robert G., and Rosenberg, Elizabeth Mullett, *The Medicine Bows, Wyoming's Mountain Country,* The Caxton Printers, Caldwell Idaho, second printing, pp 67-68 (1985).

On June 12, 1905, the Park Range Forest Reserve was created on lands that included the Mount Zirkel Wilderness. In 1908, the forest reserve was renamed Routt National Forest in honor of former Colorado Governor John Routt.

Seedhouse Road got its name from a U.S. Forest Service building built along the road near the confluence of the North Fork and Middle Fork of the Elk River. Built in 1910, the building allowed workers to process seeds from lodgepole pine cones and Englemann spruce cones gathered from the surrounding forest. The cones were roasted over fires in the seedhouse to release their seeds, which were then packaged and sold. The seed-gathering operation only lasted about a year. The original building is gone, but the location was later used for a guardhouse and campground, and the name stuck.

The area now encompassing the Mount Zirkel Wilderness was managed as National Forest until the passing of the Wilderness Act. The United States government did something truly unique when it passed the 1964 Wilderness Act, creating the National Wilderness Preservation System. This act acknowledges the value and importance of retaining land in a wilderness state that offers solitude and enjoyment for everyone.

With the passing of the Wilderness Act in 1964, the Mount Zirkel Wilderness was created on 72,180 acres surrounding the peak. In 1980, the Mount Zirkel Wilderness was enlarged to 139,898 acres. Finally the Colorado Wilderness Bill of 1993 added 20,752 acres at the north end of the wilderness, bringing the total present size of the wilderness to 160,650 acres. The second and final additions include vital lower-elevation habitat that is under-represented in the Wilderness Preservation System.

HISTORIC PRESERVATION ON PUBLIC LANDS

Heritage resources are the physical remains and conceptual content or context of an area that provide a link to our past. Heritage resources include, but are not limited to, artifacts, Native American campsites, rock art, historic mines and logging camps, homesteads, ruins, landscapes, and structures. Heritage resources also include settings for legendary, historic, or prehistoric events. These connections to our past are excellent examples of a "non-renewable" heritage resource that should be protected and interpreted for the enjoyment of current and future generations.

Heritage resources are protected on federal land such as the Medicine Bow-Routt National Forest. A number of federal laws including the National Historic Preservation Act (NHPA) and the Archaeological Resource Protection Act (ARPA) provide for the protection of these resources from destruction by federal projects, unauthorized excavation, looting, artifact collecting, or vandalism. Destruction of fragile sites may be intentional or unintentional.

Please enjoy these links to our past, but preserve the site for the enjoyment of future generations. Members of the public can become active participants in Federal historic preservation programs and activities. To learn about preservation opportunities or to report vandalism to heritage resources, please contact the appropriate U.S. Forest Service office listed in Appendix A.

(Thanks to Dave McKee, archeologist for the U.S. Forest Service, for his contribution.)

Natural Setting of the Mount Zirkel Wilderness

ECOSYSTEMS IN AND AROUND THE WILDERNESS

The term ecosystem refers to the environment and living organisms (i.e., plants and animals) associated with a specific area. Temperatures drop with increasing elevation in the Rocky Mountains, so a variety of ecosystems are generally associated with their elevation.

When you follow trails from the base of the mountains to the summits, you'll pass through varying ecosystems generally named for the dominant plant species. The assortment of plants and animals that adapt to their environment are called a *community*.

These ecosystems are dynamic in nature, especially after disturbances such as fire, avalanche, and insect infestation. One forest dominated by a tree species may give way to other tree species following severe disturbances. *Succession* refers to the process of reforesting disturbed areas with temporary tree species that eventually are replaced by a *climax* or stable community. Naturalist's guides describe plant and animal communities in detail, some of which are listed in the bibliography of this book.

At the base of the mountain ranges, you'll find sagebrush shrublands up to an elevation of about 9,000 feet. Sagebrush and bunch grasses dominate these areas. In early summer, sage meadows reach a lush green color, even though they are generally associated with a desert climate. These meadows provide forage for livestock and wildlife.

You'll discover a variety of mountain wetland ecosystem types along the streams that descend the mountain slopes. Moose frequent the willow thickets along these streams, especially in spring. Higher in the mountains, dense grasses often line streams in areas such as Swamp Park.

In mountain areas where soil conditions don't favor forests, you'll find dry meadows instead. These subalpine meadows feature a carpet of grasses and wildflowers in early summer, and hummingbirds collect nectar from wildflowers in these high meadows.

Aspen forests thrive in adverse conditions between 7,000 and 10,000 feet. These forests can be found as successional communities, usually above about 9,000 feet, in previously disturbed areas (especially fire-affected areas). Aspens can also form climax communities, usually below 9,000 feet.

Also called quaking aspen, these trees make bright airy forests in summer, when the sound of their rustling leaves fills the air with the slightest breeze. Aspen trees send sprouts from their root systems, a process that creates large aspen groves populated by genetically identical trees called *clones*. This becomes obvious in fall when certain areas turn brilliant yellow while surrounding aspens from separate organisms, with different genetic code, change colors at different times. These inviting forests have a deep spicy aroma, especially during the fall. Aspens tend to populate south-facing slopes where snow melts away quicker because they are more drought-tolerant than neighboring lodgepole pines.

Between 7,000 and 9,000 feet, you'll find lodgepole pines, often on the damper north-facing slopes. Lodgepole pine forests are specifically adapted to exploit forest openings created by fire. The lodgepole seeds within pinecones are encased in chambers held together by pine resins. These cones can lie on the forest floor for long periods until the heat of a fire melts the resin and releases the seeds.

Lodgepole pine trees can form climax communities, along with aspen, below about 9,000 feet. Above 9,000 feet, they will often form successional communities after disturbances (for example fire in spruce-fir forest). Lodgepole forests are composed of ranks of mostly arrow-straight trees with a dense overstory and very little vegetation on the forest floor.

From 9,000 feet to treeline, forests dominated by Englemann spruce and subalpine fir form climax communities. These forests have a rich spruce scent, and trails are generally well shaded. Spruce and fir trees have shorter needles than lodgepole pine, and they are adapted for the heavy snowfall that blankets the mountains above 9,000 feet each winter. Spruce-fir forests are home to the grey or mountain jay.

Spruce-fir forests thrive in the cool damp conditions of the high country. Here, conditions conducive to wildfires are rare, which may be why they are not adapted to succeed after fire. The flames usually consume spruce cones and any seedlings. Fires usually move through spruce-fir forest in a mosaic pattern due to the relatively cool and damp conditions where they are found. Over time, they can re-establish themselves by spreading from the areas not affected by the fire.

Between 9,000 and 10,000 feet, aspen and lodgepole pine forests often succeed spruce-fir forests after fires because spruce and fir are shade-tolerant species, meaning their seedlings need the shade of other trees to protect them from direct sunlight. After lodgepoles and aspens become established, they provide enough shade for spruce and fir seedlings to become established adjacent to undisturbed spruce-fir stands. Eventually, after about 150 years following a fire, the spruce trees grow higher than the aspen and lodgepole forests and succeed these communities, forming climax communities once again. Luna Lake Trail travels through an area of mixed spruce-fir and aspen along the first couple miles east of Swamp Park Trail.

At timberline, Englemann spruce trees often form small clumps of trees that are twisted by the winds and heavy snows found in this harsh environment. These small clumps of trees are called *krummholz,* which in German means crooked woods.

Above timberline, you'll find alpine tundra. Grasses adapted to the harsh conditions dominate near the crest of the mountain ranges. These grasses withstand harsh winds and heavy bombardment by UV rays. This is also the home of the marmot or rock chuck.

SPRUCE BEETLES AND FIRE IN SPRUCE-FIR FOREST

As of the spring of 2003, a spruce beetle epidemic was spreading throughout the forests in and around the Mount Zirkel Wilderness. In the 1940s and early 1950s a spruce beetle epidemic wiped out more than 90% of the mature spruce in what is now the Flat Tops Wilderness. Barring an unusually cold winter, the present spruce beetle epidemic will also kill more than 90% of the mature spruce trees in the Mount Zirkel Wilderness over the next few years, drastically altering the forest.

During the summer of 2002, wildfires burned across the wilderness that had become more susceptible to fire because of the ongoing spruce beetle epidemic. At first impression, this sounds like a terrible disaster that will cause a major disruption to these spruce-fir forests, but these are natural events that have occurred periodically for millennia. Our life span is relatively short compared to a spruce tree's life, so we tend to view forests as static entities. In fact, forests are in a constant state of change, and fire and insect epidemics have always shaped them.

Spruce beetles live nearly their entire existence beneath the bark of spruce trees. The only time they aren't found there is during a brief period in summer when adult beetles emerge and fly to attack other spruce trees.

Adult spruce beetles are about ¼- to ³/₈-inch in length and are capable of flying at least 15 miles. Usually, adult spruce beetles attack fallen spruce trees. But during beetle epidemics they tend to attack standing, mature spruce trees greater than about eight inches in diameter.

These attacking adult beetles chew through the spruce bark and create tunnels called *galleries* just beneath the bark to lay their eggs. One of the tree's defenses is to push the beetle back out of its hole with sap, but spruce trees are not very effective in resisting beetle attack. The eggs hatch, and the beetle's larvae feed outward from the galleries before maturing into adults. The chewing and feeding actions by the beetle and their larvae can affect enough of the circumference of the tree to essentially girdle it.

Blue-stain fungus is also associated with spruce beetle attack. Adult beetles come into contact with the blue-stain fungus before they emerge from the gallery in which they were born, so they carry it on their body and deposit the fungus in the galleries they create in their new hosts. Once deposited, the blue-stain fungus grows in the egg galleries and interferes with the tree's ability to transfer nutrients, which leads to the death of its needles. The death of the spruce tree is finally caused by the combination of the girdling action of the galleries and the blockage of nutrient transfer due to the fungus.

After chewing through the bark of a standing tree and then vertically upward to make an egg gallery, the adult spruce beetle lays its eggs and dies. Spruce beetles can undergo a one-, two-, or three-year life cycle, depending on the environment. In northern Colorado, the two-year life cycle is the most common.

The eggs usually hatch and progress to a larval stage by the fall after they were laid. These larvae continue feeding on the inner bark of the tree. They then go dormant during winter.

The next summer, when they're about a year old, the larvae transform into adults. These adults usually emerge from standing trees and bore into the base of the same tree to hibernate during the following winter. This habit has survival value for the beetle, helping it endure harsh winter temperatures while avoiding predators. During normal snowfall years, a deep blanket of snow insulates the base of the tree and prevents access for predators like woodpeckers.

The woodpecker is the most significant spruce beetle predator, although other birds and insects also threaten the bugs. Perhaps the biggest threat is cold weather. Temperatures of −15° Fahrenheit kill all adults while -30° Fahrenheit temperatures kill all larvae.

The summer after transforming into adults (when they are two years old), beetles emerge from the tree in which they were born and fly to another tree. After they attack the new victim, they lay their eggs and eventually die. Thus the cycle begins anew.

In the 1940s, the spruce beetle epidemic in the Flat Tops Wilderness had spread to the Mount Zirkel Wilderness near Buffalo Pass. Extremely low temperatures in 1951 are often cited as a major factor ending that epidemic, although an extensive program of insecticide application by the U.S. Forest Service may have also contributed to its conclusion.

To combat the 1950s epidemic, U.S. Forest Service workers carried ortho-dichlorobenzene insecticide on the old jeep road that Wyoming Trail follows north of Buffalo Pass. After that epidemic ended, the beetles remained in the forest, although at greatly reduced population levels.

Spruce beetles are always present in spruce-fir forests. They are almost always at very low population levels, called *endemic,* subsisting on their preference for the occasional fallen tree. During this endemic phase, they rarely attack healthy standing trees.

Spruce beetles reach epidemic-sized populations, thousands of times greater than endemic levels, after *triggering events.* Triggering events usually involve a blowdown, avalanche, logging activity, or landslide that leaves a large number of spruce trees lying on or near the ground.

Fallen spruce trees provide optimum conditions for boosting beetle population. First, the trees soon die and are thus defenseless against the beetles. Also, woodpeckers and other predators cannot easily access the underside of fallen logs where the beetles bore their galleries and an insulating blanket of snow provides protection through the winter.

Upon reaching epidemic-sized populations after triggering events, the spruce beetles begin to attack large standing trees. In epidemic stage numbers, they have the ability to kill these large standing trees.

Epidemics can cycle through a few beetle generations until they have killed some large spruce trees in a relatively limited area or, when the weather and the composition of the spruce-fir forest are right, spruce beetle populations can continue to grow through several generations until they reach *pandemic* proportions. Pandemic beetle outbreaks spread over wide geographic areas and attack all mature trees.

Epidemics almost always begin and end due to weather-related events, so it's difficult to predict how severely a forest will be affected. Over time, spruce-fir forests tend to follow patterns as they experience these events. Pandemic beetle outbreaks occur periodically, separated by lower intensity epidemics.

Large-diameter spruce trees naturally come to dominate spruce-fir forests over time, which is the current situation in the Mount Zirkel Wilderness. Following a spruce beetle pandemic, the beetles have selectively killed off the large spruce trees so the forest becomes dominated by fir trees. It takes about 200 years before spruce trees achieve numerical superiority in the forest again.

After the spruce trees achieve dominance in the forest, their average diameter tends to continue to increase. The spruce trees in the recovering forest become vulnerable to another beetle attack at that point, but their average diameter then is not sufficiently large to support the development of a pandemic. Instead, a smaller scale epidemic would be expected after a triggering event (which tends to occur regularly in the Rocky Mountains).

As the average diameter of the spruce trees continues to increase, their ability to support the development of a pandemic beetle attack rises with it. Eventually the forest again becomes vulnerable to a spruce beetle pandemic after a triggering event. Research shows that pandemic beetle attacks occur about every 350 to 500 years.

Spruce beetle epidemics can cause spruce-fir forest to become more susceptible to fires. Newly killed standing spruce trees are vulnerable to fire until their needles have dropped off, which takes a couple years. About 50 years later, as dead spruce snags begin to fall and stack on the forest floor, the spruce-fir forest becomes vulnerable to fire once again until these downed trees rot.

With only a little more than 100 years of recorded history in the Rocky Mountains, foresters have to rely on other means to study past spruce beetle epidemics. Based on tree ring studies and other information, it appears that on average there have been half as many fires as beetle epidemics in some spruce-fir stands in the Rocky Mountains. Consequently, fires may be associated with roughly every other beetle epidemic in the long run.

In 1939, a blowdown triggered a spruce beetle epidemic in the Flat Tops Wilderness. The spruce-fir forests in the Flat Tops contained enough mature spruce stands to support the development of a pandemic. By the summer of 1949, researchers observed a layer of dead beetles six inches deep and six feet or more wide for about a mile along the eastern shore of Trappers Lake, located near the wilderness. By 1952, nearly all of the mature spruce trees in the Flat Tops Wilderness were dead.

The Routt Divide Blowdown triggered the current spruce beetle epidemic in the Mount Zirkel Wilderness. About 13,000 acres of trees were toppled by the strong winds on October 25, 1997. The spruce-fir forest in the Mount Zirkel Wilderness contains enough mature spruce-fir stands to support the development of a pandemic beetle outbreak similar to the Flat Tops pandemic of the 1940s. Pandemic spruce beetle populations can kill nearly all of the mature spruce trees over large areas, and the beetles have been known to attack lodgepole pine and even fence posts as the supply of mature spruce trees becomes exhausted. Most of the stands in the wilderness would be drastically affected over the next few years.

The progress of the spruce beetle epidemic after the Routt Divide Blowdown illustrates the effect of the epidemic on the forest, including the associated increase in fire danger. Using the assumption of a two-year life cycle for the beetles, and assuming that the blown-down trees remain suitable for propagation of beetles for about two years, the following model emerges for the progress of the beetle epidemic since the Routt Divide Blowdown in the fall of 1997 to the fall of 2002.

In 1998, the first wave of adult beetles attacked the wind-thrown trees, laid their eggs, and died.

In 1999, a second wave of adult beetles attacked the wind-thrown trees while the first wave reached adult stage in these trees.

In 2000, the first wave of adult beetles emerged from the wind-thrown trees and attacked standing trees and some remaining blowdown. The second wave of beetles in the wind-thrown trees matured to adults.

In 2001, the second wave of beetles emerged from the wind-thrown trees and attacked standing trees. Most of the wind-thrown trees had dried out and were no longer suitable for beetle attack. They had become a fire hazard instead. That year, the relatively small Mad Creek Fire burned near Swamp Park in blown-down timber but did not spread to the adjacent spruce-fir forest.

By the summer of 2002, the standing trees attacked by spruce beetles the previous year were dead and tinder dry but still green. They wouldn't begin turning the red color associated with beetle kill for another year. If you encounter them in the forest, these newly dead trees often rain down a shower of green needles when the wind blows, covering the forest floor below.

When these standing beetle-killed trees and the dried-out blown-down trees were exposed to one of the driest summers in Colorado on record, they were ready to burn. In July and August of 2002, lightning sparked large fires that burned through the spruce-fir forest in and around the wilderness. These fires affected approximately 30,000 acres, nearly 50 square miles of the forest. The 2002 fires burned about two-thirds of the blown-down timber from the Routt Divide Blowdown.

In contrast, in 2001 when the Mad Creek fire reached the still living and more fire-resistant standing spruce-fir forest adjacent to the blown-down timber, the flames did not propagate through the standing timber. By 2002, the beetles had killed standing timber adjacent to the blowdown, and when the fires reached the dead but still green and standing trees, the flames continued to spread.

The beetle epidemic continues to grow to pandemic proportions, so it is reasonable to expect an increased fire risk in the immediate future as the epidemic moves through the forest, especially with current moisture levels in the region.

During the next few years, you'll probably notice beneficial effects of the spruce beetle epidemic. This time should be a golden era for woodpeckers and other beetle predators in the forest. Woodpecker populations should increase several-fold as the epidemic progresses, and then subside once again after the beetles have died off.

Forage for livestock and wildlife, especially deer and elk, should increase because the forest floor will receive more light where the spruce canopy has been eliminated. Runoff from the streams leaving the wilderness should increase because more snow will make it to the ground, and the smaller forests will consume less water. A beetle epidemic is only catastrophic to the status quo — the forest lives on.

In about 350 to 500 years, after a series of lesser spruce beetle epidemics, the spruce-fir stands that were not burned during this pandemic may have matured and be susceptible to another pandemic. When a triggering event occurs, a spruce beetle pandemic will sweep through the forest once again. And thus the cycle continues.

GEOLOGY OF THE MOUNT ZIRKEL WILDERNESS

As I hiked along the eastern base of the Park Range on the Grizzly Helena Trail and looked down into the creek basin below, it was suddenly quite clear to me how the basin was formed. Massive rivers of ice had steadily and relentlessly ground away at the mountains above for thousands of years, then flowed down the side of the mountains and thrust a tongue of ice out onto the plains. The massive amounts of rock that the glacier carved out were deposited in a horseshoe shape, enveloping the park below me. I may have hiked through this area and not fully experienced it if I hadn't taken a little time to gain a basic understanding of the geology of the area before venturing into it.

The Park, Sawtooth, and Sierra Madre mountain ranges were formed along with most of the rest of the Rocky Mountains during the last mountain building episode, or *orogeny*, in this region. The Laramide Orogeny formed most of the mountain uplifts in the region from about 70 million to 40 million years ago.

In order to understand how these mountains were formed, it's first necessary to understand what a *fault* is. When stresses are applied to the earth's crust, they can cause the rock in the crust to split or fracture. When the rocks on each side of a fracture move relative to each other, the fracture becomes a fault.

The mountains within the Mount Zirkel Wilderness, as well as the Medicine Bow Range visible from the wilderness toward the east, were formed when two parallel faults created a solid block of rock between them that was thrust upward to relieve stresses within the crust.

The Rocky Mountains were eroded away by rain and wind as they rose above the surrounding landscape. This erosive action slowly buried the young mountains. What occurred next would finish the process of burying these mountain ranges to near the tops of their highest peaks with sediment and other debris.

Widespread volcanic eruptions occurred in the western United States, including Colorado, from about 40 million years ago until about 25 million years ago. To give an idea of the intensity of volcanic action during this period, a system of volcanoes where the San Juan Mountains are today are estimated to have spewed 5,400 cubic miles of ash and debris into the air. By comparison, Mount Saint Helens ejected a quarter of a cubic mile of ash and debris during its most recent eruption. The ash generated by the intense volcanic activity fell back to the earth and blanketed the landscape, further burying the mountains in the wilderness.

Near the end of this period of volcanic activity, between 33 and 23 million years ago, the nearby Rabbit Ears and Never Summer mountain ranges were formed. These mountain ranges are easy to see from within the wilderness, especially from trails in the southwest area.

The Rabbit Ears and Never Summer mountain ranges are the remains of *magma chambers* (magma is the molten rock below the crust of the earth) that fed volcanoes above them. If magma travels through the crust and reaches the surface, it's called lava when it reaches the earth's surface. The structures formerly above the magma chambers have since been eroded away, leaving only the magma that solidified, or crystallized, in the chambers that fed the volcanoes from below.

By the end of this period of volcanic activity, the Rocky Mountains were nearly buried under erosion sediments and volcanic debris. The area was a plain with only a few of the highest mountain peaks projecting through it. This would change with an event that would uncover the Rocky Mountains, an event known as a regional uplift.

Around 25 million years ago, the Colorado landscape began to rise in a series of pulses. During the last 10 million years alone, this area has risen more than 6,000 feet. Thus, the summit of Mount Zirkel was only about 6,000 feet above sea level before this most recent event. The regional uplift reactivated some of the faults and triggered the process that would lead to uncovering the mountain ranges created during the Laramide Orogeny.

As the land rose, the slow meandering streams on the volcanic ash-choked plains of Colorado began to flow faster, driven by the increasing gradient. The swifter streams began to carry away the accumulated sediments and volcanic debris that buried the Rocky Mountains, eventually reaching the much harder and erosion-resistant basement rocks of the mountain ranges buried below.

The erosion of the basement rocks that made up the mountain ranges was slower because the rocks are much harder. This left the unearthed mountain ranges relatively unaffected by the erosion process while the sediments that buried them were continually washed away. In this manner, the increased stream gradient resulting from a broad regional uplift uncovered the Rocky Mountains.

During the regional uplift between 10 and 12 million years ago, a broad area west of the wilderness experienced a period of volcanic activity. The Elkhead Mountains, visible to the west of the wilderness, are the remnants of the underground structures that fed these volcanoes. Hahns Peak marks the easternmost extent of this volcanic activity.

Hahns Peak is the remnant of a formerly subterranean structure that fed lava to a volcano above the site of the present peak. This type of structure is called a *volcanic plug*. Minerals tend to be deposited where the lava in the plug contacts the rock surrounding it. Such was the case with Hahns Peak, the site of intense mining activity in the past.

The finishing touches on the Rocky Mountains would be added relatively recently, in geologic terms, when glaciers sculpted the mountain ranges. Beginning about 1.8 million years ago, several distinct periods of colder climactic patterns formed ice in the Rocky Mountains. During these ice ages, the Park and Sawtooth Ranges were sculpted into their present shape by ice fields that descended from their summits and settled on the surrounding valley floors. The last of these ice ages ended only about 15,000 years ago.

These alpine glaciers are separate and distinct from the large continental ice sheets that covered portions of North America. The glaciers that sculpted the Rocky Mountains originated near the crestline of the ranges and flowed down toward the surrounding basins, ending at the foot of the mountain range.

Glaciers shape the land by two mechanisms: *plucking* and *abrasion*. Plucking refers to the action of incorporating rock loosened from along the sides and below the glacier into the moving mass of the glacier. The rock adjacent to a glacier is loosened by the freezing and thawing action of the water on cracks in the rocks.

Abrasion refers to the action of the rock embedded in the edges of the glacier on the rock below and along the sides of the glacier, as the mass of the glacier travels away from its source. Rocks embedded in glaciers leave behind grooves called striations that record the direction of the glacier's travels.

Glaciers carved features into the Park and Sawtooth Ranges whose names are familiar to most mountaineers. *Cirques* refer to the amphitheater-like basins formed at the origin of a glacier (semicircular basin elongated in the direction of the glacier's movement). This is where much of the material plucked and transported by the glacier originates. A bedrock lip usually exists where the glacier exited the cirque, and this lip often impounds a lake or *tarn*. In the case of the Park Range, cirques formed on each side of the Continental Divide, and glaciers radiated down to the east and west.

Lake Katherine and Bighorn Lake lie in glacial cirques on the east side of the Continental Divide. Mount Zirkel is flanked by three cirques you can see from the plateau near the summit (two cirques on the west side of the divide and one on the east). Twin and Blue Lakes sit at the bottom of two cirques nestled on the east side of Flattop Mountain, and a cirque between Big and Little Agnes Mountains in the Sawtooth Range created the Mica Basin. Luna Lake lies in a beautiful cirque on the west side of the Continental Divide. And you can find many more.

Most of the materials plucked from the mountains above are deposited where the glacier reaches its furthest extent in a landform known as a *moraine*. Moraines often contain rocks and boulders rounded by the abrasive effects of their transport.

Several well-preserved moraines extend along the base of the Park Range, especially on the east side of the range. Livingston Park lies encircled by the remains of a beautifully preserved moraine, the resting-place for the rock excavated from Rainbow Lake and its canyon. You'll catch your best view of this moraine from Grizzly Helena Trail as it climbs north of Norris Creek, a few miles south of Pitchpine Trailhead.

Just east of the junction of Jackson County Road 12W and 16, between Delaney Butte and Sheep Mountain, you'll discover another nice spot to see moraines deposited on the east side of the Park Range. The distinctive U-shape of Red Canyon shows how glaciers carved the canyon, and you can see the moraine below Red Canyon from this vantage point, forming a low sloping ridge that curves to the south. You can also see the moraines left at the base of Lone Pine Canyon and Bear Creek Canyon, which are joined together and separated by a medial ridge.

A glacial moraine impounds Big Creek Lakes near the northeast corner of the wilderness. A large glacier carved the valley that now contains Big Creek on the east side of the Continental Divide. Near Big Creek Falls along Big Creek Trail you can see sculpting of bedrock outcrops by this glacier. The creek has not washed away the moraine at the north edge of Big Creek Lake, so it still impounds Big Creek Lakes.

The moraines below Red Canyon and Norris Creek may also have impounded lakes for some time after the glaciers retreated, but these natural dams have been breached. Large rounded boulders are all that remain of Red Canyon's moraine near where Jackson County Road 20 crosses Roaring Fork Creek.

The moraines on the west side of the Continental Divide are harder to find and identify. A single glacier traveled down both sides of the Sawtooth Range (Gilpin Creek and North Fork of the Elk River Valleys) as well as the valleys containing Trail Creek, Gold Creek, and the South Fork of the Elk River and its tributaries. Ice from all these valleys fed the glacier that flowed down the present course of the Elk River, ending at a moraine near Hinman Park. You'll discover a good place to get an idea of the scale and direction of ice flows that fed the glacier that flowed down the Elk River along Wyoming Trail 1101, where it overlooks the Trail Creek drainage and beyond, a short distance south of Hare Trail.

Hinman Park features large rounded boulders, remnants of the moraine that was deposited there. Most of the moraine near Hinman Park was deposited south of the Elk River and the South Fork Trail travels over some of this material not far from the South Fork Trailhead.

South of the Elk River, the ice on the west side of the divide often ended in a maze of mountains and foothills, which makes well-preserved moraines difficult to find. One example of a nicely preserved moraine forms the south edge of Swamp Park, and Swamp Park Trail 1100 climbs this moraine just south of the park.

In fact, the uncovering of the Rocky Mountains and the shaping of the Park Range by glacial action continues today. Landslides can occur in the mountains as sediments continue to be stripped away. And an active rock glacier continues to shape the wilderness landscape east of Mount Zirkel in Fryingpan Basin.

Rock glaciers are accumulations of rocks usually found at the base of steep slopes. An ice core forms in the rock mass, and an active rock glacier flows downhill, forming arc-shaped ridges on its surface. Shafer Creek originates from the rock glacier in Fryingpan Basin.

Sometimes boulders being transported by a glacier don't make it to the moraine, dropping instead when the glacier retreats. These boulders, and the ones deposited in the moraines, are often conspicuous because they differ from the bedrock in the area.

You can view a geologic map of the wilderness at www.mountzirkelwilderness.com. This map identifies the rocks exposed at the surface. And four rock types make up much of the basement rocks of the mountain ranges in the wilderness.

Two of the rocks are *igneous rocks*. Igneous rocks originate as molten rock called magma that underlies the earth's crust. When a plume of magma rises into the crust without reaching the surface, this is called an *igneous intrusion*. If the molten rock reaches the surface of the earth, it becomes an *igneous extrusive* or volcanic rock.

When an igneous intrusive rock cools and solidifies within the crust, the cooling generally occurs slowly, and you can see large crystals in the rock with the naked eye. When these igneous intrusions become large, geologists call them *plutons.*

You might also witness *metamorphic rocks,* which begin as igneous, sedimentary, or other metamorphic rocks and change when heated or reheated. The heat comes either from burial or being in close proximity to an igneous intrusion.

Going from south to north in the wilderness, the first rock type you'll find is metamorphic shale rock, commonly visible in outcrops near Buffalo Pass. Formed about 1.8 billion years ago, this rock is mostly pink and exhibits beautiful bands.

About a mile north of Buffalo Pass Trailhead along Wyoming Trail, a nice outcrop of metamorphic shale rock also shows glacial sculpting, indicating this area was covered by an ice cap during recent ice ages. You can also find a nice, glacially sculpted outcrop of metamorphic shale rock along Newcomb Trail where it climbs away from Newcomb Creek toward the Continental Divide.

Traveling further north, you'll enter the broad band of the Mount Ethel Pluton where an intrusion of quartz monzonite occurred about 1.4 billion years ago. This pinkish grey rock stretches across the wilderness from west to east in a band about seven miles wide. This is the rock that gives Red Canyon its beautiful colors, and the large crystals in this rock are visible to the naked eye. It is a slightly softer rock than the metamorphic rocks that make up much of the range, so the effects of the glaciers on it are easier to see. Hikers can see glacial striations in this rock above Rainbow and Roxy Ann Lakes.

Rounded boulders from the Mount Ethel Pluton lie conspicuously throughout the wilderness, deposited by glaciers originating near the peak. You can see large rounded boulders of quartz monzonite (transported by glaciers) on the metamorphic shale bedrock along Newcomb Creek Trail, and several also settled along Mad Creek.

Further north in the wilderness, beginning just south of Lost Ranger Peak, a broad band of metamorphic volcanic rock begins. This is probably the most common rock type in the wilderness. It is charcoal gray in color and can contain quartz bands with flecks of mica embedded in the rock, which was formed roughly 1.8 billion years ago.

Metamorphic volcanic rock gives Bear Mountain its teeth. Bear Lakes, Lake Katherine, and Bighorn Lake lie nestled in cirques carved from this type of rock. You might see rounded boulders of this rock type where Lost Ranger Trail crosses Roaring Fork Creek in Red Canyon. These boulders were plucked by glaciers in the Roaring Fork basin north of Red Canyon and deposited onto the quartz monzonite bedrock in Red Canyon.

Near Seven Lakes along Big Creek Trail, an igneous intrusion of quartz monzonite will look familiar to anyone who has hiked over the Mount Ethel Pluton, although it was formed during a separate event about 400 million years earlier. Glaciers sculpted the shallow depressions that make up Seven Lakes.

Other rocks are present on the surface of the wilderness, and with the aid of the geologic map and a little time and effort, you can learn to identify these rocks too.

The story of what happened before the Laramide Orogeny goes back more than two billion years instead of 70 million. It's a story of continents being built and broken apart, mountain ranges being built and worn away, seas advancing and receding, and many other natural wonders. It's also a long story, much too long to be covered in this book. But if you want to know what happened before the Laramide Orogeny, get a copy of Audrey DeLella Benedict's *A Sierra Club Naturalist's Guide: The Southern Rockies,* listed in the bibliography section at the end of this book.

Knowing the story of the formation of the landscape that makes up the Mount Zirkel Wilderness can add to your enjoyment of the area. The mountain ranges in the wilderness were formed about 70 million years ago, only to be buried in their own erosion debris and volcanic ash. They were exhumed, over the last 25 million years, by increased stream gradients brought about by a broad regional uplift. The erosion-resistant mountain ranges that were buried in sediments and volcanic ash have remained after the debris that buried them was carried away by erosion.

Glaciers sculpted the crestline spires of the Sawtooth Range as well as the cirques in the Park Range, and you can find lakebeds excavated in the cirques. The debris removed by the glaciers has been deposited in moraines at the base of the mountains. Visitors will find preserved cirques and their corresponding moraines along the east side of the Park Range where several glaciers terminated near the floor of North Park.

By learning to identify a few of the common rocks that form the backbone of the mountain ranges in the wilderness, you can gain insight into where boulders deposited along trails may have originated. This can give you clues of ice movements through the canyons in the wilderness during recent ice ages.

The uncovering of the Rocky Mountains and shaping of these mountains by glaciers continues today. For example, you can witness a rock glacier in Fryingpan Basin east of Mount Zirkel, and landslides continue to uncover the crystalline core of the mountain ranges in the wilderness.

When and How to Enjoy the Mount Zirkel Wilderness

WILDERNESS REGULATIONS AND TRAVEL RESTRICTIONS

Before venturing into the wilderness, it's important to know what wilderness is and what regulations are in effect there. The U.S. Forest Service is tasked with managing the wilderness to preserve the area's wild character and provide for solitude. The Wilderness Act of 1964 defines wilderness as follows: "A wilderness, in contrast with areas where man and his works dominate the landscape, is an area where the earth and its community of life are untrammeled, where man is a visitor who does not remain." Inherent in the Wilderness Act are regulations that limit our recreation to primitive means. Wilderness is meant to be a place to escape from the crowds and the works of man, where you can experience the peace and solitude of the backcountry.

These rules and recommended practices are meant to protect our wilderness resource. We must all work together to protect the wilderness characteristics of these areas for present and future generations. A backcountry ethic that respects the wilderness and recognizes its fragility and need for protections, combined with the use of Leave No Trace practices, is essential to preserve the beauty, solitude, and challenge we seek. The following regulations apply within the Mount Zirkel Wilderness:

1. Possessing or using any motorized or mechanized equipment, including chain saw, bicycle, motorcycle, hang glider, or cart is prohibited. This includes game carts. Primitive methods are a basic part of the wilderness experience.

2. No camping or campfires within 100 feet of any lake, stream, or trail, or within ¼-mile (1,320 feet or 440 yards) of Gilpin, Gold Creek, or Three Island Lakes. This regulation is designed to protect water quality and fragile wet areas, provide for solitude, and allow heavily used areas to recover. Evidence of prior use does not necessarily mean a campsite is acceptable. Wilderness rangers strictly enforce these camping restrictions with no exceptions.

3. Pets must be under immediate physical or visual and voice control at all times. The goal of this restriction is to prevent harassment of wildlife or disturbance of other wilderness users and their property.

4. Group size is limited to a combination of 25 people and livestock, with a maximum number of 15 people in any group. The impacts of people and stock multiply in large groups. Smaller groups help to promote the feeling of solitude.

5. Hobbling, tethering, or allowing livestock to graze within 100 feet of any lake, stream, or trail is prohibited. With the goal of protecting water quality and fragile wet areas, this restriction also provides for solitude. Pack stock users should be careful not to allow their stock to graze in re-vegetation sites undergoing recovery.

6. Possessing or transporting any unprocessed stock feed (including weed-free hay) is prohibited within the wilderness. This helps prevent the introduction and spread of non-native plants and noxious weeds. When non-native plants become established, they can seriously disrupt natural plant communities.

7. National Forest land in Colorado and Wyoming outside of the wilderness is closed to the use of hay or straw that has not been certified as noxious weed-free. Its orange and blue twine or galvanized wire identifies certified weed-free hay.

8. Camping is limited to a maximum of 14 days.

9. Caching or storing of equipment, personal property, or supplies on National Forest land is prohibited. All equipment brought onto National Forest lands must be taken out when you leave.

LEAVE NO TRACE, A National Outdoor Skills and Ethics Program
Leave No Trace is not just a set of rules defining appropriate behavior in the wilderness; it is an attitude, a land ethic that respects the wilderness, recognizes its fragility (and the need to protect it). In years past we spoke of people's ability to survive the wilderness. Now, we speak of wilderness and the land's capability of surviving human use. The best way that you can help the land to survive is to make the least possible impact on the environment. The principles of Leave No Trace are:

• **Plan ahead and prepare.** This book can help you do this. Know the area and what to expect when packing. Give yourself time at the end of each day's travel to find a suitable camp. Find a dry, screened area away from the trail. It is required that you camp at least 100 feet away from lakes and streams to prevent pollution from dishwater, human waste, and manure.

• **Camp and travel on durable surfaces.** Whenever possible, choose an established site that will not show signs of additional use. Avoid any heavily used campsites that have been posted as re-vegetation sites. This will allow these areas to heal. Pack a portable water jug to carry water to camp, thereby reducing trips to lakes and streams.

• **Dispose of waste properly.** Pack it in; pack it out. Before leaving camp, take one last look around. Have you packed all of your trash and left your site in its natural condition? Scatter wastewater away from camp and water sources. To protect water quality, bury human waste at least six inches deep and at least 200 feet from any water source. Use biodegradable soap.

• **Leave what you find for others to enjoy.** Camp lightly and take only pictures. Examine, but do not touch, or disturb historic structures and artifacts. Avoid introducing or transporting non-native species. Refrain from outdated practices such as trenching around tents, building structures, putting nails into trees, and collecting from the forest. Your site should need no modification. Good campsites are found, not made.

• **Minimize use and impacts of fire.** Use a gas stove instead of building a fire. Campfires leave permanent scars on the land. If you must have a fire, use an existing rock fire ring (if available) or build a mound fire. Do not build new fire rings.

• **Respect wildlife.** It's important to appreciate the vital role wilderness preservation plays in protecting wildlife habitat and biological diversity. The animals that live in the wilderness often struggle for survival, and any additional stress due to human contact can make the difference between life and death, especially during winter. Avoid contact with wildlife, particularly during sensitive times when they're mating, nesting, and raising their young. Minimize the stress you cause to animals by observing them from a distance. Never feed wild animals; this alters their natural behavior and can expose them to predators or other dangers. Control your pets if you bring them into the forest, or leave them at home.

• **Be considerate of other visitors.** Respect other visitors and protect the quality of their experience. Be courteous. For example, yield to other users on the trail. Step to the downhill side of the trail when encountering pack stock. Take breaks and set up camp away from trails and other visitors. Let nature's sounds prevail. Avoid loud voices and noises.

To learn more about Leave No Trace, you can visit the Leave No Trace Web site at www.lnt.org.

The Mount Zirkel Wilderness is located on the Medicine Bow-Routt National Forests of the U.S. Forest Service. The district ranger offices listed in Appendix A in this book are responsible for management of the wilderness and adjoining national forest lands in their respective jurisdictions. You can call their information staff to ask questions about using the wilderness and surrounding National Forest land.

THE 10 ESSENTIALS

The ten essentials are the items that you should always carry on your person when venturing into the backcountry. In general, I always carry enough equipment when venturing out to be able to spend a night in the backcountry, if necessary. The ten essentials include:

1. Waterproof fire-starting materials (e.g., waterproof matches, lighter, and striker)

2. Knife

3. Emergency shelter (e.g., a space blanket, poncho, or tarp)

4. Extra food and water

5. First aid kit (available at most outdoor stores)

6. Signaling device, such as a mirror or whistle

7. Map and compass (and the ability to use them)

8. Sun protection for your eyes (sunglasses) and skin (sunscreen)

9. Extra clothing, enough to survive overnight temperatures

10. Flashlight with extra batteries and bulbs

In addition to taking along the 10 essentials each time you go into the backcountry, it's also important that someone knows where you are going and when you plan to return. Fill out the trailhead register as you enter the backcountry. If you don't return as scheduled, your contact should call the appropriate county sheriff's department (listed in Appendix A) to report that you are late in returning.

STRATEGIES FOR SAFER SWIFTWATER CROSSINGS

You may have been there once yourself. You're halfway across a stream swollen with spring runoff, rocks the size of eggs are tumbling down the stream bed and pelting your shins, and you realize you may have bitten off more than you can chew. In that moment comes the realization that the power of the stream you are crossing and the danger it poses is greater than you realized when you started across. With luck, we may make it to the safety of one side or the other and subsequently approach these situations with a newfound respect.

In fact, all swiftwater drownings can be traced to one of two fundamental errors: either the victim has underestimated the situation they faced, or they have overestimated their ability to deal with the situation. Knowing how to evaluate and make safer swiftwater crossings is especially important when hiking during spring runoff season in and around the Mount Zirkel Wilderness. The wilderness receives some of the heaviest snowfall in the state of Colorado, and the streams leaving it become flood-swollen torrents during normal precipitation years.

The first step you should take when assessing the crossing of a running stream is to determine if the ford you are attempting qualifies as a swiftwater crossing. The question you need to ask here is: Can I sit on the bottom of the stream at the most difficult point of this crossing (deepest, swiftest, or both)? If you cannot easily sit down at this point, you are facing a swiftwater crossing.

Usually far away from help, swiftwater crossings can be the most dangerous things we attempt in the backcountry. The danger of hypothermia setting in due to a violent swim in a cold mountain stream is very real. In general, if you doubt your ability to safely cross a stream, simply turn back and plan to return when the flow is likely to be less.

Mountain streams are fed by snowmelt during the spring thaw, so their flow varies throughout the day with the heat of the sun. At high elevations, the flow will be at a minimum early in the morning, and as the heat of the day begins to melt the snow, a surge of water will move down the stream and reach lower elevations later in the day. It's best to plan a swiftwater crossing to correspond with the minimum flow of the stream you plan to cross, depending on your elevation. In general, plan a crossing early in the day, so if an unplanned swim occurs, you will have more hours of sunshine to warm a potential hypothermia victim.

In addition to planning when to attempt a swiftwater crossing, these stream crossings should be approached with a strategy that reduces risk by following a few basic swiftwater crossing safety rules.

Rule 1: Always have a backup plan

In a situation where a trail crosses a swift and deep stream, this usually means you should be prepared to swim. Don't bet your life that you will not lose your footing. If you do lose your footing and you have not already planned a self-rescue strategy, you are needlessly risking your own life and potentially those of your companions who may try to rescue you. Look at the stream below where you will attempt your crossing for two types of hazards: rocks and *strainers*.

If the stream below your crossing is strewn with boulders and violent whitewater, you probably don't want to swim it. Drownings frequently result from simple trauma and the resulting loss in consciousness in these situations. If there is a violent rapid immediately below where you will cross, try to find another spot. If in doubt, turn back.

Strainers are obstructions that allow the water to pass — but not you. A common example of a strainer is a fallen tree across the stream. Unfortunate swimmers who are swept into strainers have a 95% chance of drowning. If you notice any obstructions below your crossing that can be considered a strainer, do not attempt the crossing. Again, either find another spot to cross downstream of the obstruction or (if in doubt) turn back.

Now, let's assume you have found an acceptable spot to attempt a swiftwater crossing, and the downstream stretch is free from obstructions and strainers. We now come to the second rule of swiftwater crossing.

Rule 2: Unbuckle your waist and chest straps and loosen your shoulder straps

Before you attempt the crossing, you must loosen and unbuckle all your pack straps so that you can easily get out of your pack during a swim. The first thing you will want to do is free yourself from your pack. This brings us to the next rule.

Rule 3: Plan on losing your pack

The idea here is that during a difficult swim, you may have to let your pack go down the stream in order to save yourself. Think about what basic survival gear you will need after a swim, and make sure that it stays either in a secure pocket on your body or small waist pack. Your survival gear should include waterproofed materials for starting a fire, a basic shelter such as a space blanket, a waterproofed map, a compass, and a signal mirror and whistle at a minimum. It's also a good idea to put on any spare insulation and windproof shells in your pack at this point, both to protect you from hypothermia during a potential swim, and to get it on your body where it can't be lost.

Now you are ready to attempt the crossing. When crossing swiftwater alone, the most stable position to assume is facing upstream, leaning upstream on a stout hiking staff or branch that provides a third point of contact with the stream bottom. As you move sideways across the stream, keep two points of contact on the stream bottom at all times, moving the third.

If your party includes plenty of other people, you can secure added stability by standing in line facing upstream with each person grasping the pack shoulder straps of the person in front. The furthest person upstream should be the largest person in the group and should use a hiking staff or branch for stability.

If at any point during the crossing a person loses footing and begins to be swept downstream by the current, that person should self-rescue swim for the bank that offers the quickest and surest means of exiting the stream. This brings us to the fourth swiftwater safety rule.

Rule 4: Never try to stand up while swimming in swift water

The hazard of attempting to stand in swiftwater is that you could get your foot caught in rocks or debris on the bottom of the stream – a situation called *foot entrapment* – which would allow the force of the current to push your body underwater and drown you. When forced to swim in swiftwater, you should immediately remove your pack, try to hang on to it, and assume the swiftwater self-rescue swimming position.

The self-rescue position is a reclined position on your back with your feet pointed downstream, toes pointed toward the sky. From this position, you can use your arms to swim toward one bank or the other, or roll onto your belly to swim to shore. Your legs serve as shock absorbers for any obstructions you may hit on your way downstream.

The one exception to using the self-rescue position during a swim is if you would encounter a strainer that cannot be avoided. If you are being swept into a strainer that you realize cannot be avoided, your best chance for survival is to roll over onto your belly and swim head first as hard as you possibly can to try to climb up and over the strainer. With a 5% chance of survival, the best way to deal with strainers is to avoid them altogether.

When is it safe to attempt to stand when you reach the shore? The simple answer is when your butt is dragging bottom and you are no longer moving. This is also the basis for judging when you are facing a swiftwater crossing situation, discussed above. If you can sit on the bottom of the stream, it is safe to stand, and you should immediately move a safe distance from the stream where you can rest and evaluate your next move.

After a swim in an icy cold mountain stream, hypothermia is probably your greatest threat, and you should deal with it immediately by getting on dry clothes (if possible) and building a roaring fire to warm the affected person. The next section deals with hypothermia diagnosis, prevention, and treatment.

When you're in a group attempting a swiftwater crossing, it's important to keep the following hierarchy in mind when someone is forced to swim:

1. Your own safety comes first
2. The safety of the people in your group second
3. The safety of others third

You have to realize that by trying to save someone you could make matters worse. There could be two or more people drowning instead of one. Again, the key here is personal responsibility.

When attempting to aid a person swimming in swiftwater, you should try to rescue the person while minimizing the danger to yourself. The method used to rescue someone should be prioritized as follows:

1. If possible, reach the person from shore and pull them to safety
2. If the person is beyond your immediate reach, a rope or branch can be used to extend your range from shore
3. Only attempt to swim out to rescue someone if you have been trained in rescue swimming techniques. People have been drowned when someone they are attempting to rescue climbs on top of them during the rescue. Your first priority is for your own safety. If you are interested in learning swiftwater rescue techniques, including rescue swimming, Rescue3 International offers multi-day swiftwater rescue training courses that are tailored to whitewater boaters and emergency rescue personnel. This training includes rescue swimming instructions. You can find the contact information for Rescue3 International in Appendix A.

HYPOTHERMIA

Hypothermia is the most common emergency situation visitors face in the backcountry. The term hypothermia refers to a lowering of the body's core temperature below 95° Fahrenheit. Knowing the causes, symptoms, and corrective actions to address this illness are absolutely essential backcountry skills.

Hypothermia actually refers to two different diseases. *Chronic* hypothermia occurs over a period of hours or even days when a person's equipment fails to maintain the body's core temperature. *Acute* or *immersion* hypothermia is generally caused by immersion in cold water and occurs over a period of minutes. Treatment of this most common life-threatening wilderness hazard depends on the type of hypothermia encountered.

Treating chronic hypothermia

The best way to deal with the risk of chronic hypothermia is to avoid its onset. Stay warm, rested, and well hydrated. The two factors that affect your ability to stay warm are the equipment you have to retain your body heat, and your body's ability to replenish lost body heat. Always bring extra insulating layers and dry clothes when venturing into the backcountry. Bring along a rain- and wind-resistant shell to help you stay dry. Afternoon thunderstorms are daily occurrences during summer in the Rocky Mountains, so plan accordingly. Snow is always a possibility in the high country, even during summer. Avoid cotton clothing, especially next to your skin.

Remember: cotton kills. The increased heat loss from wet cotton next to your skin can overwhelm your body's ability to maintain its core temperature. Cotton fibers are *hydrophilic,* which means they absorb water and remove heat from your body as the water evaporates. Synthetic fabrics such as polyester are *hydrophobic,* meaning they hold less water and dry quicker when they become wet. Like wool, synthetic pile insulating layers such as polyester fleece retain their ability to insulate your body when wet.

In addition to minimizing heat loss, it is important to maintain your body's ability to replace lost heat. Don't overexert yourself. Drink plenty of water when hiking, and eat plenty of high-energy foods. Take frequent rest breaks. Know your limits, and be careful not to exceed them. When hiking in a group, always let the slowest or weakest hiker set the pace. Always monitor yourself and your companions for exhaustion, and be careful to protect your body from heat loss while recovering from exhaustion.

After you have done all you can to avoid hypothermia, you have to be able to recognize its onset and know how to treat it. This is especially true because mental confusion often accompanies hypothermia. People suffering from hypothermia often deny their condition, which makes your ability to diagnose this disease critical.

The first sign of chronic hypothermia is exhaustion. Pay attention so you can distinguish between common fatigue and hypothermic exhaustion. The next sign of the onset of hypothermia is mental confusion and loss of muscle coordination (for example, an inability to walk 30 feet — 9 meters — in a straight line).

Once you diagnose the problem, you treat hypothermia in the following ways:

1. Prevent further heat loss
If possible, replace wet clothing with dry clothing. If replacing wet clothing is not possible, cover it with a wind- and weather-resistant shell, and add more insulation over it.

2. Treat dehydration
All people suffering from chronic hypothermia are dehydrated. Drink lots of water, at least three quarts in the first hour. If you have a stove, warm the water to prevent further heat loss.

3. Treat the person gently
Severely hypothermic persons are at risk for cardiac rhythm problems.

4. Add heat
If a hypothermic person can stand, build a fire. And drink hot beverages, if possible. Water containers such as bladders or bottles can be filled with warm water and placed next to the body of the hypothermia victim. But be careful not to burn a hypothermia victim with hot water packs by first testing the water temperature on a non-hypothermic person's skin. A hypothermic person is less sensitive to pain and can easily be burned.

5. Avoid *rewarming shock*
A severely hypothermic person who cannot stand may go into shock if re-warmed too quickly and face a significant risk of death. So you have to be careful adding heat. One or two companions lying in a sleeping bag with a severely hypothermic victim may be the only safe method of adding heat.

6. Avoid adding cold
If possible, warm the fluids before giving them to a hypothermic person. Remove wet clothing in a sheltered area, and replace them with dry clothing (if you can).

7. Allow rest
Since persons suffering from chronic hypothermia are usually suffering from exhaustion, they need rest. If they are adequately insulated from further heat loss and have been well hydrated and re-warmed, they can be allowed to sleep.

Left untreated, chronic hypothermia will lead to a coma and worse. This degree of hypothermia requires evacuation for medical treatment. Wrap the person to prevent further heat loss, and continue adding heat. If one or two persons not suffering from hypothermia can join the victim in a sleeping bag, this can rewarm the victim.

Treating acute hypothermia
Treatment for acute hypothermia differs slightly from chronic hypothermia treatment. In the case of acute hypothermia brought on by prolonged immersion in cold water, the victim's energy stores may be adequate, but the outer body temperature has been lowered to dangerous levels. This leads to a phenomenon known as *afterdrop* in which a person's core temperature continues to drop after being removed from the water as the blood carries the heat from the warm torso to the much colder extremities. While afterdrop also comes into play when treating chronic hypothermia, its effect can be more pronounced in acutely hypothermic persons and can lead to death if not adequately addressed.

The ideal treatment for acute hypothermia is immersion in 110° Fahrenheit water. I am unaware of any hot springs within the Mount Zirkel Wilderness, so the best backcountry remedy for acute hypothermia is a roaring fire. Know how to start a fire, and carry waterproof fire-starting equipment where you won't lose them if inadvertently you take a cold swim. Your life may depend on your ability to start a fire. If a dry sleeping bag is available, the technique of sharing it with non-hypothermic person(s) may also help restore lost body heat in the acutely hypothermic person.

In the case of both chronic and acute hypothermia, prevention is the best course. Be sure you can recognize the early signs and symptoms of hypothermia, which include uncontrolled shivering, decreased mental acuity, and loss of fine motor skills. And take corrective actions as early as possible to prevent development of a serious situation.

ACUTE MOUNTAIN SICKNESS AND HIGH ALTITUDE PULMONARY EDEMA

Acute Mountain Sickness can strike when traveling above 9,000 feet, and symptoms include dizziness, loss of appetite, and body aches. It is best to allow a few days for getting acclimated at elevations between about 5,000 feet to 8,000 feet before venturing above about 9,000 feet. It's important to take frequent rest breaks when traveling above 9,000 feet, eat plenty of carbohydrates, and drink plenty of fluids (avoiding alcoholic beverages). Aspirin can help treat the symptoms of altitude sickness, but the only sure treatment for altitude sickness is to retreat to lower elevation.

High Altitude Pulmonary Edema (HAPE) is a rare but potentially fatal disease caused by leakage of blood plasma into the lungs, inhibiting the air sacs' ability to transfer oxygen and carbon dioxide between the air and blood. This disease rarely strikes healthy individuals below 9,000 feet elevation. The average elevation of onset is about 12,000 feet.

The early symptoms of HAPE resemble pneumonia, although it is not associated with an infection nor accompanied with fever. Within 12 to 36 hours of reaching high altitude, the HAPE victim experiences extreme weakness, shortness of breath, nausea, vomiting, very rapid pulse (120-160), *cyanosis* (bluish color), and "noisy" breathing that progresses to moist crackling and irritative coughing that produces frothy white or pink sputum and later blood.

If untreated, the HAPE victim looses consciousness with bubbles in the mouth or nose. If the victim is not immediately given oxygen or moved to a lower elevation, he or she will die. All of the early symptoms of this disease may be mistaken for Acute Mountain Sickness or fatigue or may go unnoticed during the night. The most effective first aid for this rare disease is rapid evacuation to lower elevation or constant administration of oxygen.

DRINKING WATER TREATMENT

You should treat drinking water collected from mountain streams and pools to prevent infection by intestinal parasites. Colorado surface waters are infested with *Giardia Lambia* bacteria, but you can eliminate this potentially harmful intestinal bug by boiling the water, using water purification filters, or chemically treating the water. *Cryptosporidia* bacteria are also a common contaminant in surface waters, although generally at lower levels than Giardia Lambia. Water filters and purifiers remove Cryptosporidia cysts from water, and although boiling is also effective in deactivating them, chemical methods are not effective. Viruses such as hepatitis are also a potential contaminant of surface waters, although this would be unusual in the Colorado mountains. Viruses can only be removed by boiling or chemical treatment methods.

Boiling water in the United States for five minutes kills all potential disease-carrying bacteria and viruses. If you choose to utilize this method, you will have to carry extra fuel for your stove to process your drinking water, and you will have to set up your stove each time you need more drinking water.

Iodine-based purification tablets kill viruses and giardia bacteria in water when used properly, but they are ineffective against Cryptosporidia bacteria. When gathering water from areas used for livestock grazing or with potential human waste contamination, iodine probably isn't the best option because of the potential presence of Cryptosporidia. Also, iodine could take an hour or more to render water safe for drinking, so be sure to follow manufacturer's instructions carefully when using iodine tablets, being aware of their limitations when treating very cold or murky waters.

Another drawback with iodine tablets is the potential for unpleasant tastes and odors. Drink mixes can mask these tastes and odors *after* the iodine has had sufficient time to disinfect the water, and some iodine tablet manufacturers sell kits containing additional tablets (ascorbic acid or vitamin C) to mask the iodine taste in chemically treated water.

Water filters remove bacterial cysts such as Giardia Lambia and Cryptosporidia, and they produce the tastiest drinking water, but filters alone are not effective in removing viruses. Some water filters, also called water purifiers, are equipped with iodine resins in their filter cartridges. These devices that incorporate both filtration and chemical treatment are effective against both bacteria and viruses.

Your level of comfort determines your decision to use water purification, as well as which purification technique you'll use. If you find yourself in the backcountry for an extended period of time without water purification means, it's still important to remain hydrated to maintain mental clarity and ward off hypothermia. If you have no other choice, drink untreated water to keep strong and hydrated until you reach safety.

HAZARDS IN RECENTLY BURNED AREAS

The fires of 2002 burned about 50 square miles of forests in and around the Mount Zirkel Wilderness. Trails affected include Wyoming Trail, Swamp Park Trail, North Lake Trail, Lost Ranger Trail, Grizzly Helena Trail, Gilpin Creek Trail, Gold Creek Trail, Mica Basin Trail, and Main Fork Trail. Usually, when fires move through a forest, most burned trees remain standing for some time before finally falling. U.S. Forest Service sawyers and fallers have removed obviously hazardous trees along trails, but in order to render trails completely safe, a 300-foot wide swath of trees would have to be cut down along each path, which is neither practical nor aesthetically desirable. For these reasons, it's important to understand that trees in these areas will continue to fall during coming years. The trick, of course, is not being in the path of a tree when it does fall.

When traveling through areas recently affected by fires, be aware of snags along the trail and take your time, looking up as you move down a trail, especially on windy days. Avoid recently burned areas during windy periods if possible. Always be careful where you choose to pitch your tent, avoiding areas where falling trees could pose hazards.

PEAK-BAGGING SAFETY AND ETHICS

Mount Zirkel, Lost Ranger Peak, and Davis Peak are popular destinations for peak-bagging hikers. If you choose to climb these or other peaks, you should observe some basic safety rules and ethics to protect yourself and the delicate ecosystem you cross.

Thunderstorms are common in the Rocky Mountains during summer, and lightning occasionally kills people hiking on exposed areas above timberline. Plan your visit to mountain peaks so that you can be back off the summit by noon, when afternoon thunderstorms become likely. If you see a storm approaching, get off the peak to a less exposed area as soon as possible.

If caught above timberline in an electrical storm, avoid ridgelines, cliffs, and open areas where you are the highest point. Crouching in a boulder field above timberline is better than being in the open. If you have an insulating pad, kneel on it to provide some insulation from the ground. If possible, retreat below timberline and crouch in a forest where it is safer than above timberline.

Don't slide or "ski" down scree slopes, both for your own safety and to protect these delicate high-country areas from potential erosion damage. Use extra care when crossing large boulder fields to avoid being trapped or crushed by shifting boulders. Avoid scree slopes and boulder fields when possible.

The Leave No Trace guideline for traveling on durable surfaces is especially important when traveling above timberline. Alpine tundra is very fragile, and once it's damaged, it takes many years to recover, if ever. Whenever possible, travel on durable surfaces above timberline and avoid the delicate plants that survive there. When traveling in a group, avoid walking in single file off trail, especially above timberline.

LIVING WITH WILDLIFE IN THE COLORADO BACKCOUNTRY

Deaths due to wildlife attack are rare in the Colorado backcountry, but it's good to know a few basic rules if you encounter potentially dangerous wildlife such as mountain lion and black bear.

Mountain lion attacks are rare but potentially deadly, especially for small women and children who make easier prey than larger persons do. When hiking in the backcountry, it is very important to keep close tabs on children, always keeping them in sight.

If you encounter a lion, remain calm, stop, move slowly, and give it room to escape. Mountain lions are usually shy creatures, and the encounter may be unintentional. If you are hiking with small children, bring them close to you and pick them up if necessary to prevent them from running away.

If the lion does not move on, back away from it slowly without turning your back or running away. Running away could trigger the predatory instinct in the animal and provoke an attack. Talk loudly and firmly to the lion while backing away and try to appear as large as possible, spreading your arms and opening your jacket if you are wearing one.

If the lion behaves aggressively, and you can gather rocks or sticks without bending down to pick them up, throw them to attempt to drive it away. Convince the lion that you are not prey and are instead a threat to it.

If a lion attacks, you fight back. Do all you can to stay on your feet to fend off the animal's attack. People have used hiking sticks, binoculars, articles of clothing, even bare hands to drive off attacking mountain lions.

Black bear attacks in Colorado are even more rare than mountain lion attacks. The recommended reaction to a bear encounter varies slightly from that for a mountain lion. Instead of reacting aggressively, you should adopt a passive posture with a bear, trying not to provoke it or appear threatening. Bears rarely attack people unless they feel threatened or provoked.

If you see a bear, remain calm and talk aloud to let it know you are there. Stop and back away slowly while facing the bear, giving it wide berth. Avoid eye contact as this may make the bear feel threatened. If the bear moves toward you drop a hat or bandana if possible to attempt to distract it while you continue to back away slowly.

Bring children close to you, and pick them up if necessary to prevent them from running away. As with a lion, running away could provoke a predatory response in the bear. You cannot outrun or out-climb a black bear.

If a bear raises onto his back legs and moves toward you, it could be trying to catch your scent to identify you. This isn't necessarily a sign of aggression. Once it identifies you, a bear may leave the area or try to intimidate you by charging within a few feet of you before leaving.

As with a mountain lion, if a bear attacks you, try to stay on your feet and fight back. Black bears have been driven away with rocks, sticks, binoculars, and bare hands.

Report encounters with mountain lions or bears to the Colorado Division of Wildlife. The numbers are listed in Appendix A.

When setting up a campsite in the backcountry, it's necessary to take some precautions to avoid attracting a black bear to your camp. Set up your camp so your tent, cooking area, and a tree where you hang your food are points on a triangle separated from each other by at least 100 feet. Maintain a clean camp, collecting and securing food and garbage at all times.

Before turning in for the night, remove all garbage, cooking utensils, food items, and other items with food odors, such as toothpaste or other toiletries, from your pack and your kitchen area and carry along a rope and bag to hang them from a tree branch. Attach food items to a rope tossed over a tree branch and hoist them at least 10 feet off the ground and at least five feet from the trunk of the tree before tying the rope off.

Your pack likely has food odors on it, so it too should be placed at least 100 feet away from your tent. Unzip all the compartments on the pack so mice don't chew through it to investigate food odors. Do all you can to keep your tent free of food odors.

If a mountain lion visits your camp during the night, it probably isn't interested in what's hanging from the tree.

COLORADO OUTDOOR RECREATION SEARCH AND RESCUE CARD

If someone gets into a situation where a search and rescue operation has to be mounted to recover them, he or she could be held liable for the cost incurred in the effort. If, for example, a helicopter evacuation is required, the cost of the rescue operation could be considerable. You can avoid the potential expense of a search and rescue if you purchase a Colorado Outdoor Recreation Search and Rescue Card before venturing into the backcountry. Monies from search and rescue card contributions go to the Colorado Search and Rescue Fund, which reimburses local governments for the costs of search and rescue operations and training.

A $0.25 contribution to the Search and Rescue Fund is included in the fee for a hunting or fishing license in Colorado. You also make an automatic $0.25 contribution to the fund when you register a boat, snowmobile, or off-road vehicle in Colorado. If you contribute to the fund in these ways, you do not need to purchase an Outdoor Recreation Search and Rescue Card for your search and rescue expenses to be covered.

Backcountry users who don't otherwise contribute to the Search and Rescue Fund should purchase a Colorado Outdoor Recreation Search and Rescue Card ($3 for one-year contribution or $12 for a five-year contribution). The Colorado Local Affairs Department administers the Search and Rescue Fund program. Appendix A has information for contacting the Local Affairs office to purchase a card via mail or to find where the cards are available locally, as well as where the proceeds of the fund are used.

PACK STOCK USE ON NATIONAL FOREST AND WILDERNESS LANDS

Because of the additional impact of pack stock on National Forest land, it's important to observe some simple rules to responsibly manage your animals.

1. Use lightweight camping equipment to minimize the number of stock needed for the group.

2. Plan your trip to avoid heavily used areas, congested trails like those leaving the Slavonia Trailhead, and wet seasons when the ground is especially fragile. Keep your animals in single file on the trail to prevent excessive damage.

3. Secure pack stock well away from lakes, streams, and trails to prevent damage to fragile wet areas and protect water quality. Use a highline, picket lines, electric fence, or hobbles to keep stock from affecting trees and other vegetation. Relocate stock frequently to avoid excessive damage.

4. Pack sufficient processed feed into areas where good natural forage is unavailable. This prevents introducing weeds and overgrazing, and it helps keep pack stock healthy. Unprocessed feeds, including certified weed-free hay, are not permitted in the wilderness. It's a good idea to feed your pack stock weed-seed-free hay for a few days prior to entering the National Forest or wilderness to allow weed seeds from their native pasture to work through their digestive system.

5. If you are not familiar with the area where you are going, you can call one of the district ranger offices listed in Appendix A to inquire about the area's suitability for pack stock use and the availability of forage.

SEASONS IN THE WILDERNESS

Winter comes early and stays late in the Rocky Mountains. Most of the precipitation that falls on the mountains comes in the form of snow, and it can snow any time of the year. The Mount Zirkel Wilderness receives some of the highest snowfall amounts in the state of Colorado. When spring thaw triggers the annual runoff of mountain precipitation, the streams leaving the wilderness become flood-swollen torrents.

Spring thaw usually begins in mid-May and lasts through mid-July during average snowfall years. The mountzirkelwilderness.com Web site has links to other Web sites where snowpack depths for various river basins in Colorado are tabulated and compared against historical norms. The information on this Web site can be used to estimate the magnitude and duration of the spring runoff from the wilderness. The mountzirkelwilderness.com Web site also has links to U.S. Geological Survey (USGS) river-gauging stations that provide real-time stream flows for rivers flowing from the wilderness. The USGS sites also have historical data available so that you can get an idea of how the runoff compares to historical spring floods. You can also contact the U.S. Forest Service office where your visit is planned, listed in Appendix A, to get up-to-date reports on stream flows and hazards in the wilderness.

Stream crossings can be deadly during the spring runoff if you don't use proper techniques to evaluate and make these crossings. In general, if you have any doubt about your ability to make a crossing, you should turn back and return after spring thaw when crossings are easier. Refer to the "Strategies for Safer Swiftwater Crossings" section.

The thaw begins at lower elevations and works its way up toward the peaks above. The snow tends to cover the higher elevations in the wilderness until early July during normal years, although during recent drought years the high country snowpack has receded earlier, and in heavy snow years it recedes later. The snow can make travel difficult or even impossible without proper gear, including snowshoes or cross-country skis and proper winter clothing. Again, if in doubt contact the U.S. Forest Service office where you plan to visit, listed in Appendix A.

After the spring thaw, the wilderness high country remains saturated with water usually through the end of July. These marshy conditions coupled with warm summer temperatures make for optimum conditions for mosquitoes to breed and flourish. Mosquito populations in the Mount Zirkel Wilderness can be quite extraordinary until the high country dries out, which usually happens by early August but can occur earlier during drought years. Insect repellant is a must during this time, and you may prefer hikes such as a tour along the crest of mountain ranges (for example, Wyoming Trail north of Buffalo Pass or along Buffalo Ridge Trail) because prevailing winds there tend to blow away mosquitoes. Backcountry travelers who brave the mosquitoes are rewarded with plentiful wildflowers in mountain meadows.

August and September tend to be good months to plan trips into the wilderness with minimal mosquito populations and pleasant weather. Expect large crowds during summer holiday weekends such as Labor Day and Independence Day.

September often marks the beginning of firearm hunting seasons that last through the end of the year. You'll find hunting regulations and the dates of seasons posted on the Colorado Division of Wildlife Web site, which you can access via mountzirkelwilderness.com. Wearing an orange vest and hat during any firearm big game hunting season is a good idea whether you are hunting or not. You can buy hunter-orange vests and hats at outdoors stores in the area for reasonable prices, a potentially lifesaving investment. Pet owners often tie brightly colored bandanas around their animal's neck to prevent confusion for hunters. Pack stock users may put hunter-orange on their animals as well. It's the responsibility of hunters to identify their targets, but it's better to be safe than sorry.

Snow can fall any time of the year in the mountains, but these snows are unlikely to stay for extended periods between early July and the end of September. With the coming of October it becomes important to keep a close watch on weather forecasts when venturing into the mountains; early storms can result in a heavy and persistent snowpack. During recent drought years, roads into the National Forests adjacent to the wilderness have remained open into December, but this is exceptional. Always be wary of changing weather conditions in the fall, and be cognizant of the fact that early snows can persist into winter, which can make getting vehicles out difficult or even impossible. Tire chains provide an extra measure of security during this time of year.

Winter recreation in the Mount Zirkel Wilderness is limited because the roads providing access to it are often closed several miles from the wilderness boundary.

FISHING IN AND AROUND THE MOUNT ZIRKEL WILDERNESS

The lakes in and around the wilderness are popular destinations for fishermen. Fishing any-where in the state of Colorado requires a valid Colorado fishing license. The www.mountzirkelwilderness.com Web site provides links to the Colorado Division of Wildlife Web site where you can find fishing regulations and information about obtaining a license.

The Colorado Division of Wildlife periodically stocks some lakes in and around the wilderness. Appendix C contains a table that tells when the lakes were stocked and what types of fish are present in the lakes. You can also check the mountzirkelwilderness.com Web site for the most up-to-date information about Colorado Division of Wildlife fish stocking activities in and around the wilderness.

HUNTING IN AND AROUND
THE MOUNT ZIRKEL WILDERNESS

Hunting within the Mount Zirkel Wilderness, as anywhere in the state of Colorado, requires a valid Colorado hunting license, and hunting information is also available on the Colorado Division of Wildlife Web site (accessible via mountzirkelwilderness.com). You'll also find useful telephone numbers for hunters, including the numbers of local sheriff's offices and the Colorado Division of Wildlife, in Appendix A.

If your family needs to contact you with an emergency message while you are out of telephone contact **during hunting season,** they can do so through the Buckskin Network. To have a message broadcast in the area, call the Buckskin Network / Colorado State Patrol at (970) 824-6501. To hear emergency messages, tune into the Buckskin Network on KBCR-FM 96.9, KBCR-AM 1230, KRAI-FM 93.7, or KRAI-AM 550 at 6 a.m.

MOUNT ZIRKEL WILDERNESS
USGS 7.5' QUADRANGLE INDEX

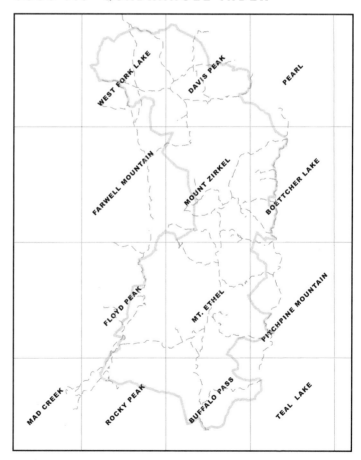

How to Use the Trail Descriptions

OVERVIEW

It was my ultimate goal when creating this book that you would include it in your pack when hiking in the wilderness. Every attempt has been made to fill this book with valuable information that you may need at some point on the trail, so it's worth the weight in your pack.

I have also avoided the practice of combining more than one trail into a single "hike." Instead, this book moves from south to north with detailed trail descriptions for all 42 trails in and adjacent to the Mount Zirkel Wilderness. How you choose to combine those trails is up to you, likely based on your own preferences and physical and time constraints. This means you have to know your own abilities and limitations. A wilderness area is no place to learn your capabilities.

Each section begins with detailed driving directions to all the trailheads within that section. The detailed trail descriptions tell you which trails are accessed by the trailheads, and when trails are not directly accessed by trailheads, the trail descriptions include the routes and distances to the nearest trailheads.

When planning your trip to the Mount Zirkel Wilderness, the tools associated with this book include:

- National Geographic Trails Illustrated series of maps. Two of these Trails Illustrated maps cover the entire wilderness area and provide a good scale for backcountry navigation. These maps cover larger areas that may be necessary to identify landmarks beyond the boundaries of United States Geologic Survey (USGS) topographic maps.

- If you prefer more detail or wish to make notations on your maps, this book also lists the USGS topographic quadrangle maps that cover each trail. The USGS maps provide more detail than the Trails Illustrated maps, but the scale on the USGS maps is finer than the Trails Illustrated maps so more maps will probably be required for your trip. Also, be aware that the USGS maps are not as up-to-date or as weather-resistant as the Trails Illustrated map series.

- It's a good idea to call the nearest U. S. Forest Service office for your trip in addition to checking my Web site (see below), especially if you do not live near the wilderness. You'll find the address and phone numbers for the U. S. Forest Service offices in Walden and Steamboat Springs in Appendix A. Before you leave, call the office to receive the most up-to-date information from information staff regarding temporary closures or ongoing activities and conditions that may affect your visit.

- I designed www.mountzirkelwilderness.com to work in conjunction with this book. The photos on this site can help you select a trail or combination of trails. Other resources help you during the planning stages and allow you to reflect on visits when you return as well. My goal is to provide current weather, trail, and road conditions online and to post updates and any changes to the text of this book. Essentially live feeds of conditions can help you make appropriate decisions when departing for your visit to the area.

- This book contains detailed trail descriptions, water source locations, trail sections with suitable campsites, and other relevant information. Landmarks described in the book allow you to monitor your progress.

Scope of detail for each trail

Each of the 42 trail descriptions in this book provides information organized into the following categories:

• Difficulty

Criteria for Below Average, Average, and Above Average ratings include the condition of the trail, the elevation range and gradient of the trail, and the relative difficulty of trail navigation. Be aware that this is only a relative rating, and ultimately each hiker faces unique limits. You are responsible for knowing your limitations and taking care not to exceed them when you enter the wilderness.

• Total Length

This gives the length of the trail to the nearest tenth of a mile.

• Scenery

Using the same scale used for the Difficulty rating, I rated the quality of the scenery along the trail. I loved hiking all of the trails in and around the wilderness and found they are all worth hiking, so this was the most difficult rating to assign. Nevertheless, by focusing on the quantity and quality of scenic panoramic views along the trails, I determined what I hope is a meaningful rating.

• Usage

I rated the relative density of user population Light, Moderate, or Heavy, based on information received from the U. S. Forest Service and my own experiences traveling the various trails.

• Allowed Uses

The U. S. Forest Service manages the National Forest lands where the wilderness is located, allowing only certain types of activities on trails in accordance with federal laws and the agency's own management policies. Hikers and pack stock are allowed on all trails, both inside the wilderness boundary and outside it. Pets must be under immediate physical or voice control at all times on National Forest land. Only specific trails outside of the wilderness boundary allow mountain bikes, as well as single- and double-track motorized vehicles, which include dirt bikes and all-terrain vehicles (ATVs or four-wheelers).

• Access

When possible, this section lists the trailheads providing vehicle access to the trail. If the trail cannot be directly accessed at a trailhead, I provide the locations of the nearest trailheads.

• Maps

The National Geographic Trails Illustrated and USGS topographic maps that show the trail being described are listed here.

• Waypoints

These listings of distances to selected landmarks along the trail give you a quick way to find distances otherwise buried in the trail descriptions. In order to insure the accuracy of the location of the landmarks along the trails, I walked each trail with a calibrated measuring wheel and measured off the feet. I checked the accuracy of these values by measuring a few trails twice and found a variance of less than 1%. This approach has insured the accuracy and reliability of the distances presented in this book.

Remember that the federal law prohibits the use of game carts in the wilderness in order to preserve the primitive nature of the area. A measuring wheel is not considered a cart by U. S. Forest Service regulations and is thus allowed in the wilderness.

• Elevation Profile

This functions as a quick visual representation of the elevations and gradients you'll encounter along the trail.

• Trail Descriptions

In addition to the above categories, each trail description includes water and campsite locations along the way. But, wilderness areas are notoriously in constant flux, so trail markings like cairns and signs may change following the publication of this book. You can communicate these errors via the wilderness forum on my Web site, which will be incorporated for the next revision. Always carry suitable topographic maps and a compass, and be confident in your ability to navigate with them before venturing into the wilderness.

Southern Wilderness Overview

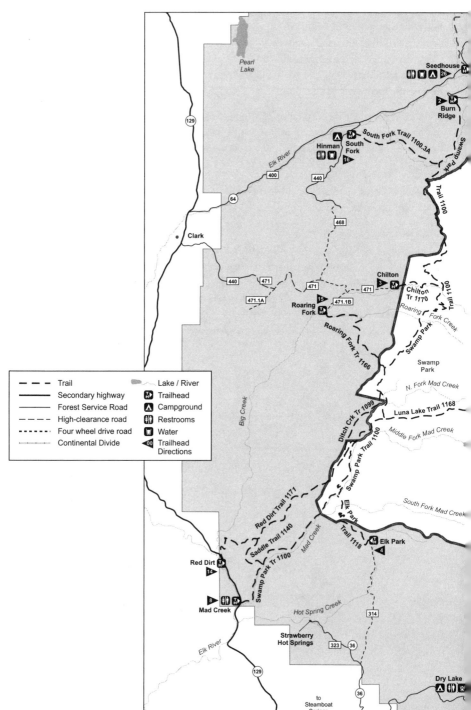

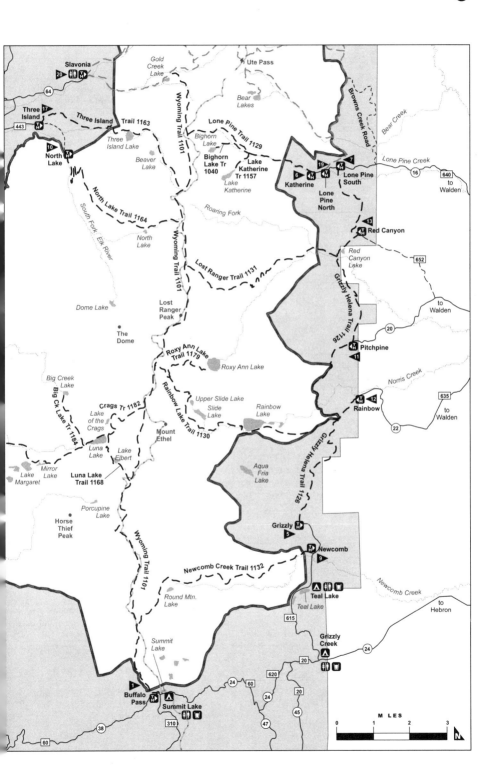

Southern Wilderness Trails At-a-Glance

Name	USGS Quads (Colorado)	National Geographic Trails Illustrated Maps (Colorado)
Big Creek Lake Trail 1184	Mount Ethel	#117 Clark Buffalo Pass
Bighorn Lake Trail 1040	Mount Zirkel	#116 Hahns Peak Steamboat Lake
Chilton Trail 1170	Floyd Peak	#117 Clark Buffalo Pass
Crags Trail 1182	Mount Ethel	#117 Clark Buffalo Pass
Ditch Creek Trail 1099	Floyd Peak, Rocky Peak	#117 Clark Buffalo Pass
Elk Park Trail 1118	Rocky Peak	#117 Clark Buffalo Pass
Grizzly Helena Trail 1126—Southern Section	Pitchpine Mountain, Teal Lake	#117 Clark Buffalo Pass
Lake Katherine Trail 1157	Mount Zirkel, Mount Ethel	#116 Hahns Peak Steamboat Lake, #117 Clark Buffalo Pass
Lone Pine Trail 1129	Pitchpine Mountain, Boettcher Lake, Mount Zirkel	#116 Hahns Peak Steamboat Lake, #117 Clark Buffalo Pass
Lost Ranger Trail 1131	Pitchpine Mountain, Mount Ethel	#117 Clark Buffalo Pass
Luna Lake Trail 1168	Mount Ethel, Floyd Peak	#117 Clark Buffalo Pass
Newcomb Creek Trail 1132	Buffalo Pass, Teal Lake	#117 Clark Buffalo Pass
North Lake 1164	Mount Zirkel, Mount Ethel	#116 Hahns Peak Steamboat Lake, #117 Clark Buffalo Pass
Rainbow Lake Trail 1130	Pitchpine Mountain, Mount Ethel	#117 Clark Buffalo Pass
Red Dirt Trail 1171	Floyd Peak, Rocky Peak, Mad Creek	#117 Clark Buffalo Pass
Roaring Fork Trail 1166	Floyd Peak	#117 Clark Buffalo Pass
Roxy Ann Lake Trail 1179	Pitchpine Mountain, Mount Ethel	#117 Clark Buffalo Pass
Saddle Trail 1140	Rocky Peak, Mad Creek	#117 Clark Buffalo Pass
South Fork Trail 1100.3A	Floyd Peak	#117 Clark Buffalo Pass
Swamp Park Trail 1100	Farwell Mountain, Floyd Peak, Rocky Peak, Mad Creek	#116 Hahns Peak Steamboat Lake, #117 Clark Buffalo Pass
Three Island Trail 1163	Mount Zirkel, Mount Ethel	#116 Hahns Peak Steamboat Lake, #117 Clark Buffalo Pass
Wyoming Trail 1101—Southern Section	Buffalo Pass, Mount Ethel, Mount Zirkel	#116 Hahns Peak Steamboat Lake, #117 Clark Buffalo Pass

Difficulty	Scenery	Usage	Total Length (miles)	Page Number
Below Average	Below Average	Light to Moderate	1.6	62
Above Average	Above Average	Light	1.3	64
Below Average	Average	Light to Moderate	1.4	66
Above Average	Average	Light	1.9	68
Below Average	Below Average	Light to Moderate	2.2	70
Above Average	Above Average	Light	2.8	72
Below Average	Average	Moderate	15.2	74
Average	Average	Moderate	0.9	80
Above Average	Average	Moderate to Light	4.0	82
Above Average	Average	Light	5.8	84
Average	Above Average	Light to Moderate	8.4	87
Average	Average	Light	6.8	90
Above Average	Below Average	Heavy	5.4	94
Average	Average	Heavy	8.7	96
Average	Above Average	Light to Heavy	6.7	99
Above Average	Below Average	Light	3.3	102
Above Average	Average	Light	1.7	104
Average	Average	Moderate to Heavy	1.1	106
Below Average	Average	Moderate	3.0	108
Average	Average	Light to Moderate	21.3	110
Average	Below Average	Heavy	6.2	117
Below Average	Above Average	Moderate to Heavy	20.3	120

Southern Wilderness Trailheads

Buffalo Pass Trailhead from the east (approximately 21 miles from the start)

 Starting at the Hebron Crossroads on Colorado State Highway 14, turn west onto Jackson County Road 24 (CR 24) and follow it about 12 miles until it meets FR 620. *Notes:* Hebron Crossroads is approximately 13 miles southwest of Walden on Colorado State Highway 14. The blacktop on CR 24 ends 7.3 miles west of Hebron. You'll pass the Grizzly Creek Ranger Station 11.0 miles west of SH14, where CR 24 becomes FR 20 and winter road maintenance ends. FR 20 passes Grizzly Creek Campground and the intersection with FR 615 before reaching FR 620.

Bear right onto FR 620 and continue west on FR 620 about two miles until it meets FR 60. *Note:* FR 620 is the continuation of CR 24.

Bear to the right onto FR 60 and continue west on FR 60 about 7 miles to Buffalo Pass Trailhead at the Buffalo Pass summit. *Note:* FR 60 is the continuation of CR 24. You'll find room for several vehicles at Buffalo Pass Trailhead, as well as additional parking for vehicles towing trailers a short distance south of the trailhead.

Buffalo Pass Trailhead from the west (Steamboat Springs)
(17.1 miles from the start)

 Starting at the stoplight on US 40 at the east edge of Steamboat Springs (Third and Lincoln), turn north onto Third Street and go one block (0.1 miles) to Fish Creek Falls Road.

Turn right (east) onto Fish Creek Falls Road and drive 0.3 miles to the intersection with Amethyst.

Turn left (northwest) onto Amethyst and follow it 2.5 miles north (out of Steamboat Springs) until it meets CR 38. *Note:* Amethyst becomes Routt County Road (CR) 36 outside Steamboat Springs.

Turn right (east) onto CR 38 and drive 10.9 miles to Buffalo Pass Trailhead. *Notes:* CR 38 becomes FR 60 upon entering the National Forest. You'll pass Dry Lake Campground, which marks the end of winter road maintenance, 3.3 miles after turning onto CR 38. You'll find room for several vehicles at the trailhead, as well as additional parking for vehicles with a trailer a short distance to the south.

Burn Ridge Trailhead (28.6 miles from the start)

Starting at the stoplight on US 40 just west of the Steamboat Springs city limits (US 40 and Elk River Road), turn north onto Routt County Road 129 (CR 129 or Elk River Road) and drive 17.5 miles to the intersection with FR 400 (Seedhouse Road). *Note:* Seedhouse Road intersects CR 129 past the Clark Store at Glen Eden, just after crossing the Elk River.

Turn right (east) onto FR 400 and follow it 9.4 miles to the intersection with FR 443. *Note:* Winter maintenance on FR 400 ends about 5.5 miles east of CR 129, just past where FR 440 intersects it.

Turn south onto FR 443 and travel 1.7 miles to the Burn Ridge Trailhead. *Note:* You'll see parking for about 10 vehicles and two vehicles with horse trailers at the trailhead.

Chilton Trailhead (24.7 miles from the start)

3 *Important note:* A high-clearance four-wheel drive vehicle is required to reach Chilton Trailhead.

Starting at the stoplight on US 40 just west of the Steamboat Springs city limits (US 40 and Elk River Road), turn north onto Routt County Road 129 (CR 129 or Elk River Road) and drive 16.6 miles to the intersection with CR 60 (Greenville Mine Road). *Note:* CR 60 intersects CR 129 just south of the Clark Store.

Turn east onto CR 60 and drive 2.7 miles to where CR 60 / FR 440 meets FR 471. *Note:* CR 60 becomes FR 440 at the Forest Service boundary.

Continue east on FR 471 where it meets FR 440 (which goes north and is gated-closed), and drive 4.1 miles until you meet FR 471.1B. *Notes:* FR 471 requires a high-clearance vehicle. You'll pass the FR 468 intersection 2.7 miles west of FR 440. FR 468 provides alternate access to FR 471 from Hinman Park and FR 440, but traveling east from Clark on FR 440 and then FR 471 is a better choice. A high-clearance four-wheel drive vehicle is required beyond the intersection with FR 468, and the road is not suitable for vehicles with trailers. The U.S. Forest Service does not recommend traveling this section when it is wet. When FR 471 turns south into the Big Creek valley, the descent is steep, treacherous, and rocky.

Turn left (northeast), staying on FR 471 where it meets FR 471.1B, and drive 1.3 miles (following Big Creek upstream) to the Chilton Trailhead. *Note:* You'll find parking for several vehicles west of the trailhead on the north side of the creek.

Elk Park Trailhead (9.2 miles from the start)

4 *Important note:* A high-clearance four-wheel drive vehicle is required to reach Elk Park Trailhead.

Starting at the stoplight on US 40 at the east edge of Steamboat Springs (Third and Lincoln), turn north onto Third Street and go one block (0.1 miles) to Fish Creek Falls Road.

Turn right (east) onto Fish Creek Falls Road and drive 0.3 miles to the intersection with Amethyst.

Turn left (northwest) onto Amethyst and follow it 4.8 miles north out of Steamboat Springs (toward Strawberry Hot Springs) to FR 314 (Elk Park Trail Road). *Notes:* Amethyst becomes Routt County Road CR 36 outside Steamboat Springs. The intersection with Elk Park Trail Road is marked with a sign.

Turn right (east) onto Elk Park Trail Road and follow it 4.0 miles north to the Elk Park Trailhead. *Notes:* The first few tenths of a mile along Elk Park Road is in good condition until you pass the last house, where Elk Park Road begins a steep, treacherous, 4.0-mile climb (with loose rocks and deep ruts) toward Elk Park. A high-clearance four-wheel drive vehicle is a necessity on this road, but you should still expect to scrape a few things (that's if you are lucky and take the right lines). Expect to smell your brakes heating up

on the way back down. This road is definitely the worst road described in this book and is not suitable for vehicles with trailers. A beaver pond (at least 18 inches deep) covers the road where it crosses Hot Springs Creek 2.4 miles after turning off CR 36 (this is the second creek crossing). The road continues past the crossing 1.6 miles to the Elk Park Trailhead. You'll find room for parking eight to 10 vehicles at the trailhead.

Grizzly Trailhead (16.6 miles from the start)

Starting at the Hebron Crossroads on Colorado State Highway 14, turn west onto Jackson County Road 24 (CR 24) and follow it 11.1 miles to FR 615. *Notes:* Hebron Crossroads is approximately 13 miles southwest of Walden on Colorado State Highway 14. The blacktop on CR 24 ends 7.3 miles west of Hebron. You'll pass the Grizzly Creek Ranger Station 11.0 miles west of SH14, where CR 24 becomes FR 20 and winter road maintenance ends. FR 20 passes Grizzly Creek Campground immediately before reaching FR 615.

Turn right (north) onto FR 615 and drive 5.5 miles to the end of FR 615 and Grizzly Trailhead. *Notes:* Along the way, you'll pass Teal Lake Campground about 3 miles north of FR 20, then Newcomb Trailhead at the 3.9-mile mark. The Grizzly Trailhead area provides plenty of room to park several vehicles and vehicles with trailers.

Katherine Trailhead (20.3 miles from the start)

Starting at Walden, drive 0.6 miles west on Colorado State Highway (SH) 14/125 to the intersection with Jackson County Road (CR) 12W.

Turn west onto Jackson County Road (CR) 12W and drive 5.1 miles until it meets CR 18.

Turn north where CR 18 meets CR 12W and continue 6.8 miles (north then west) on CR 12W until it meets CR 16 between Sheep Mountain and Delaney Butte. *Note:* CR 12W meets CR 18 at a T intersection where CR 12W turns to the north and CR 18 continues straight ahead.

Turn left (south) onto the gravel CR 16 and drive 7.8 miles west on CR 16 to the Katherine Trailhead. *Notes:* Winter road maintenance ends at Lone Pine Ranch, 2.2 miles west of the intersection of CR 12W and CR 16. CR 16 becomes FR 640 at the U.S Forest Service boundary (where you'll find a fence and parking area), 5.1 miles west of the intersection of CR 12W and CR 16. If you're towing a trailer, you may want to leave it here to scout turnaround and parking opportunities further along FR 640, especially during holiday weekends. You'll pass Lone Pine South Trailhead 1.2 miles west of the U.S. Forest Service boundary and Lone Pine North Trailhead 0.5 miles further west. Katherine Trailhead is 1.0 miles beyond Lone Pine North Trailhead and provides parking for about six vehicles as well as room for a few vehicles with trailers.

Lone Pine South Trailhead (18.8 miles from the start)

7 **Starting at Walden,** drive 0.6 miles west on Colorado State Highway (SH) 14/125 to the intersection with Jackson County Road (CR) 12W.

Turn west onto Jackson County Road (CR) 12W and drive 5.1 miles on CR 12W to where it meets CR 18.

Turn north where CR 18 meets CR 12W and continue 6.8 miles (north then west) on CR 12W until it meets CR 16 between Sheep Mountain and Delaney Butte. *Note:* CR 12W meets CR 18 at a T intersection where CR 12W turns to the north and CR 18 continues straight ahead.

Turn left (south) onto the gravel CR 16 and drive 6.3 miles west on CR 16 to the Lone Pine South Trailhead. *Notes:* Winter road maintenance ends at Lone Pine Ranch, 2.2 miles west of the intersection of CR 12W and CR 16. CR 16 becomes FR 640 at the U.S Forest Service boundary, 5.1 miles west of the intersection of CR 12W and CR 16 (where you'll find a fence and parking area). If you're towing a trailer, you may want to leave it here to scout turnaround and parking opportunities further along FR 640, especially during holiday weekends. Lone Pine South Trailhead has parking for only three or four vehicles and no room for vehicles towing trailers. Lone Pine North Trailhead offers similar opportunities to park 0.5 miles west of Lone Pine South Trailhead while Katherine Trailhead provides parking for about six vehicles as well as room for vehicles with trailers, 1.0 miles past Lone Pine North Trailhead on FR 640.

Mad Creek Trailhead (5.4 miles from the start)

8 **Starting at the stoplight on US 40** just west of the Steamboat Springs city limits (US 40 and Elk River Road), turn north onto Routt County Road 129 (CR 129 or Elk River Road) and drive 5.4 miles to Mad Creek Trailhead. *Note:* You'll find parking for several vehicles and vehicles with horse trailers at Mad Creek Trailhead.

Newcomb Trailhead (14.0 miles from the start)

9 **Starting at the Hebron Crossroads** on Colorado State Highway 14, turn west onto Jackson County Road 24 (CR 24) and follow it 11.1 miles to FR 615. *Notes:* Hebron Crossroads is approximately 13 miles southwest of Walden on Colorado State Highway 14. The blacktop on CR 24 ends 7.3 miles west of Hebron. You'll pass the Grizzly Creek Ranger Station 11.0 miles west of SH14, where CR 24 becomes FR 20 and winter road maintenance ends. FR 20 passes Grizzly Creek Campground immediately before reaching FR 615.

Turn right onto FR 615 and drive 3.9 miles to the Newcomb Trailhead. *Notes:* You'll pass Teal Lake Campground about 3 miles north of FR 20. Grizzly Trailhead is at the end of FR 615, 1.6 miles past Newcomb Trailhead. You'll find plenty of parking for vehicles and trailers at Newcomb Trailhead.

North Lake Trailhead (31.7 miles from the start)

10 *Important note:* A high-clearance four-wheel drive vehicle is required to reach North Lake Trailhead.

Starting at the stoplight on US 40 just west of the Steamboat Springs city limits (US 40 and Elk River Road), turn north onto Routt County Road 129 (CR 129 or Elk River Road) and drive 17.5 miles to the intersection with FR 400 (Seedhouse Road). *Note:* Seedhouse Road intersects CR 129 past the Clark Store at Glen Eden, just after crossing the Elk River.

Turn right (east) onto FR 400 and follow it 9.4 miles to the intersection with FR 443. *Note:* Winter maintenance on FR 400 ends about 5.5 miles east of CR 129, just past where FR 440 intersects it.

Turn south onto FR 443 and travel 4.8 miles to the North Lake Trailhead at the end of FR 443. *Notes:* You'll pass Burn Ridge Trailhead 1.7 miles after turning onto FR 443, and Three Island Trailhead 3.1 miles after turning onto FR 443. A high-clearance four-wheel drive vehicle is required for the final 1.7 miles on FR 443 (after passing Three Island Trailhead). You'll discover plentiful parking for vehicles and vehicles towing trailers at the North Lake Trailhead.

Pitchpine Trailhead (17.9 miles from the start)

11 **Starting at Walden,** drive 0.6 miles west on Colorado State Highway 14/125 to the intersection with Jackson County Road 12W (CR 12W).

Turn west onto CR 12W and drive 5.1 miles to where it meets CR 18. *Note:* CR 12W meets CR 18 at a T intersection where CR 12W turns to the north and CR 18 continues straight ahead.

Continue straight west onto CR 18, driving 4.4 miles until CR 18 ends where it meets CR 5 at a T intersection. *Note:* CR 18 meets CR 5 just south of Delaney Buttes Lakes.

Turn north on CR 5 and drive 0.7 miles to the intersection with CR 20.

Turn west onto CR 20 and drive 7.1 miles to Pitchpine Trailhead, located at the end of CR 20. *Notes:* Winter road maintenance on CR 20 ends where FR 652 intersects it 4.2 miles west of CR 5. You'll find plenty of parking for vehicles and trailers at Pitchpine Trailhead.

Rainbow Trailhead (17.9 miles from the start)

12 **Starting at Walden,** drive 0.6 miles west on Colorado State Highway 14/125 to the intersection with Jackson County Road 12W (CR 12W).

Turn west onto CR 12W and drive 5.1 miles to where it meets CR 18. *Note:* CR 12W meets CR 18 at a T intersection where CR 12W turns to the north and CR 18 continues straight ahead.

Continue straight (west) onto CR 18, driving 4.4 miles until CR 18 ends where it meets CR 5 at a T intersection. *Note:* CR 18 meets CR 5 just south of Delaney Buttes Lakes.

Turn left (south) onto CR 5 and drive 1.8 miles until it meets CR 22.

Continue straight onto CR 22 (where CR 5 bears left or south) and drive 7.2 miles to Rainbow Trailhead, located at the end of CR 22. *Notes:* Winter maintenance on CR 22 ends at the large rock with "slow" painted on it, 6.0 miles after leaving CR 5. You'll find room for about 12 vehicles and two vehicles with trailers at the Rainbow Trailhead.

Red Canyon Trailhead (18.0 miles from the start)

13 *Important note:* A high-clearance four-wheel drive vehicle is required to reach Red Canyon Trailhead.

Starting at Walden, drive 0.6 miles west on Colorado State Highway 14/125 to the intersection with Jackson County Road 12W (CR 12W).

Turn west onto CR 12W and drive 5.1 miles to where it meets CR 18. *Note:* CR 12W meets CR 18 at a T intersection where CR 12W turns to the north and CR 18 continues straight ahead.

Continue straight west onto CR 18, driving 4.4 miles until CR 18 ends at a T intersection where it meets CR 5. *Note:* CR 18 meets CR 5 just south of Delaney Buttes Lakes.

Turn north on CR 5 and drive 0.7 miles to the intersection with CR 20.

Turn west onto CR 20 and drive 4.2 miles to where FR 652 meets it. *Notes:* FR 652 meets CR 20 between several oil tanks and an irrigation ditch. Winter road maintenance on CR 20 ends where FR 652 intersects it.

Turn northwest onto FR 652 and drive about 3 miles to Red Canyon Trailhead. *Notes:* A high-clearance four-wheel drive vehicle is required on FR 652, and it's not suitable for vehicles towing trailers. You'll find parking for two or three vehicles at Red Canyon Trailhead.

Red Dirt Trailhead (6.6 miles from the start)

14 **Starting at the stoplight on US 40** just west of the Steamboat Springs city limits (US 40 and Elk River Road), turn north onto Routt County Road 129 (CR 129 or Elk River Road) and drive 6.6 miles to Red Dirt Trailhead. *Note:* You'll find parking for several vehicles and vehicles towing trailers at Red Dirt Trailhead.

Roaring Fork Trailhead (24.7 miles from the start)

15 *Important note:* A high-clearance four-wheel drive vehicle is required to reach Roaring Fork Trailhead.

Starting at the stoplight on US 40 just west of the Steamboat Springs city limits (US 40 and Elk River Road), turn north onto Routt County Road 129 (CR 129 or Elk River Road) and drive 16.6 miles to the intersection with CR 60 (Greenville Mine Road). *Note:* CR 60 intersects CR 129 just south of the Clark Store.

Turn east onto CR 60 and drive 2.7 miles to where CR 60 / FR 440 meets FR 471. *Note:* CR 60 becomes FR 440 at the Forest Service boundary.

Continue east on FR 471 where it meets FR 440 (which goes north and is gated-closed), driving 4.1 miles until meeting FR 471.1B. *Notes:* FR 471 requires a high-clearance vehicle. You'll pass the FR 468 intersection 2.7 miles west of FR 440. FR 468 provides alternate access to FR 471 from Hinman Park and FR 440, but traveling east from Clark on FR 440 then FR 471 is a better choice. A high-clearance four-wheel drive vehicle is required beyond the intersection with FR 468, and the road is not suitable for vehicles with trailers. The U.S. Forest Service does not recommend traveling this section when it is wet. When FR 471 turns south into Big Creek valley, the descent is steep, treacherous, and rocky.

Turn right (southwest) onto FR 471.1B and drive about 1.3 miles to Roaring Fork Trailhead. *Notes:* FR 471.1B fords Big Creek about 0.1 miles before reaching the trailhead, making it a bad choice during periods of high flow. Don't make the mistake of entering private property through a gate to the southwest of the trailhead where trespassing is considered punishable by rifle fire. You'll find room for several vehicles at the Roaring Fork Trailhead.

South Fork Trailhead (23.1 miles from the start)

16 **Starting at the stoplight on US 40** just west of the Steamboat Springs city limits (US 40 and Elk River Road), turn north onto County Road 129 (CR 129 or Elk River Road) and drive 17.5 miles to the intersection with FR 400 (Seedhouse Road). *Note:* Seedhouse Road intersects CR 129 past the Clark Store at Glen Eden, just after crossing the Elk River.

Turn right (east) onto FR 400 and follow it 5.4 miles to the intersection with FR 440. *Note:* FR 440 leads to the Hinman Park Campground.

Turn right (south) onto FR 440 and drive about 0.2 miles to the South Fork Trailhead. *Notes:* You'll reach South Fork Trailhead just after crossing the Elk River. Hinman Campground is about 0.3 miles past the trailhead on FR 440. You'll find ample parking for vehicles and trailers at South Fork Trailhead.

Three Island Trailhead (30.0 miles from the start)

17 **Starting at the stoplight on US 40** just west of the Steamboat Springs city limits (US 40 and Elk River Road), turn north onto Routt County Road CR 129 (CR 129 or Elk River Road) and drive 17.5 miles to the intersection with FR 400 (Seedhouse Road). *Note:* Seedhouse Road intersects CR 129 past the Clark Store at Glen Eden, just after crossing the Elk River.

Turn right (east) onto FR 400 and follow it 9.4 miles to the intersection with FR 443. *Note:* Winter maintenance on FR 400 ends about 5.5 miles east of CR 129, just past where FR 440 intersects it.

Turn south onto FR 443 and travel 3.1 miles to the Three Island Trailhead. *Notes:* You'll find room for parking about four to six vehicles without trailers at the North Lake Trailhead. You'll pass Burn Ridge Trailhead 1.7 miles after turning onto FR 443. You'll find North Lake Trailhead at the end of FR 443 (1.7 miles past Three Island Trailhead), but high-clearance four-wheel drive vehicles are required on this section.

Burn Ridge fire (with firefighters in the foreground)

Big Creek Lake Trail 1184

Big Creek Lake Trail 1184 runs south to north from its intersection with Luna Lake Trail 1168 to its terminus at Big Creek Lake. This trail offers one-way access to a beautiful mountain lake in a cirque at the headwaters of Big Creek.

DIFFICULTY
Below Average, 400-foot climb in 1.3 miles

TOTAL LENGTH
1.6 miles

SCENERY
Below Average, with beautiful lake and heavily glaciated landscape

USAGE
Light, Moderate during hunting season

ALLOWED USES
Hikers and pack stock only are allowed on this trail.

ACCESS
This trail begins at Luna Lake Trail just west of Luna Lake, 6.0 miles east of Swamp Park Trail 1100.

MAPS
Trails Illustrated: # 117 Clark Buffalo Pass
USGS 7.5' Quadrangle: Mount Ethel

WAYPOINTS
Luna Lake Trail marks the beginning of the trail at 0 miles
Trail crests saddle into Big Creek drainage — 1.4 miles
Big Creek Lake marks the end of the trail at 1.6 miles

TRAIL DESCRIPTION
Big Creek Lake Trail 1184 begins at its junction with Luna Lake Trail and heads north towards Big Creek Lake. You'll travel through alpine meadow and spruce-fir forest.

The way to the lake begins by descending toward the North Fork of Mad Creek. You can find campsites that meet U.S. Forest Service regulations and Leave No Trace guidelines where the trail crosses the bottom of the creek valley.

At 0.3 miles, the path crosses the North Fork of Mad Creek where it meanders through its valley, entrenched in thick meadow. The path begins to climb north here toward a saddle separating the North Fork of Mad Creek from Big Creek.

At 0.4 miles, the path enters a spruce-fir forest, climbing to the west of the stream that drains the saddle. The trail soon leaves the forest at 1.0 miles and continues to climb west of the stream across alpine meadows.

ELEVATION PROFILE

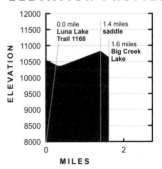

At 1.1 miles, two cairns mark the path going around the west side of a bedrock outcropping west of the stream. You'll continue north across the meadow toward the obvious saddle ahead.

At 1.4 miles, where the trail crests the saddle separating the two creek basins, you'll be able to see Big Creek Lake ahead through the trees.

At about 1.6 miles, the trail ends at Big Creek Lake. Although you can find camping opportunities in the vicinity of the lake, choose sites with care because the meadows near the lake are often wet and unsuitable.

Bighorn Lake Trail 1040

Bighorn Lake Trail 1040 runs east to west from where it meets Lone Pine Trail 1129 to its conclusion at Bighorn Lake. The trail intersects Lone Pine Trail 1.3 miles west of the Katherine Trailhead. Bighorn Lake Trail 1040 generally follows the course of the Lone Pine Creek valley for the first 0.8 miles before crossing the creek and climbing the steep lip of the glacial cirque containing the lake. The trail climbs 800 feet in 1.3 miles.

A glacier filled the Lone Pine valley during the last ice age, originating in glacial cirques near the Continental Divide. One of these cirques contains Bighorn Lake. You can appreciate the work of the glacier on the rocks from the lake and from above it at the rim of the cirque not far from Wyoming Trail.

DIFFICULTY
Above Average, 800-foot climb in 1.3 miles; easy to follow

TOTAL LENGTH
1.3 miles

SCENERY
Above Average, with views of beautiful glacial cirque, Lone Pine valley, and Rawah Peaks beyond

USAGE
Light

ALLOWED USES
Hikers and pack stock only are allowed on this trail.

ACCESS
This trail begins at Lone Pine Trail, 1.3 miles west of the Katherine Trailhead, page 56.

MAPS
Trails Illustrated: #116 Hahns Peak Steamboat Lake
USGS 7.5' Quadrangle: Mount Zirkel

WAYPOINTS
Lone Pine Trail junction marks the beginning of the trail at 0 miles
Bighorn Lake marks the end of the trail at 1.3 miles

TRAIL DESCRIPTION
Bighorn Lake Trail 1040 begins where it meets Lone Pine Trail 1129 and heads west towards its terminus at Bighorn Lake, primarily through spruce-fir forest.

A sign pointing the way to the Continental Divide marks the trail junction of Bighorn Lake Trail 1040 and Lone Pine Trail 1129. The way to the Divide is the continuation of the Lone Pine Trail 1129. The trek to Bighorn Lake on Trail 1040 begins here, to the southwest. About 100 feet after the junction with Lone Pine Trail 1129, Katherine Lake Trail 1157 intersects Bighorn Lake Trail 1040. Here a sign points left to Katherine Lake and right to Bighorn Lake, and Bighorn Lake Trail 1040 continues to the right.

For the next 0.8 miles, the trail follows along the north side of Lone Pine Creek, crossing one or two smaller tributaries along the way. You can find campsites that meet U.S. Forest Service regulations and Leave No Trace guidelines along this initial trail section.

At 0.8 miles, you'll cross Lone Pine Creek and begin a 400-foot climb that accelerates appreciably over the next 0.3 miles. At 1.1 miles, you'll conclude the worst of the rocky climb. Take the time to enjoy the views of Lone Pine Creek valley and North Park and the Rawah Peaks beyond.

ELEVATION PROFILE

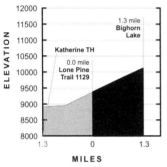

At 1.3 miles, Bighorn Lake comes into view. Spur trails to the north lead to campsites that meet U.S. Forest Service regulations and Leave No Trace guidelines.

Chilton Trail 1170

Chilton Trail 1170 runs west to east from the Chilton Trailhead to Swamp Park Trail. This trail provides access from Forest Road 471 to Swamp Park Trail 1100 via the Big Creek drainage.

Chilton Trail can be combined with Swamp Park Trail 1100, Roaring Fork Trail 1166, and Forest Roads 471 and 471.1B to make a 11.4-mile loop hike with about 1,400 feet of elevation gain and loss.

DIFFICULTY
Below Average, relatively flat and easy to follow, trail travels across wet marshy terrain

TOTAL LENGTH
1.4 miles

SCENERY
Average, travels up Big Creek valley

USAGE
Light, Moderate during hunting season

ALLOWED USES
Hikers and pack stock only are allowed on this trail.

ACCESS
◀3 The trail begins at Chilton Trailhead, page 55.

MAPS
Trails Illustrated: #117 Clark Buffalo Pass
USGS 7.5' Quadrangle: Floyd Peak

WAYPOINTS
Chilton Trailhead marks the beginning of the trail at 0 miles
North Fork of Big Creek — 0.9 miles
Swamp Park Trail marks the end of the trail at 1.4 miles

TRAIL DESCRIPTION
Chilton Trail 1170 travels north of Big Creek on its way to intersecting Swamp Park Trail 1100. The path travels up the floor of Big Creek valley, passing through willow thickets and spruce-fir forest.

ELEVATION PROFILE

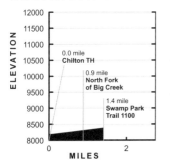

The path begins close to the north edge of the valley with the creek only a short distance to the south. A sign marks the Mount Zirkel Wilderness boundary at 0.1 miles. You'll see plenty of blowdown timber on the south wall of the canyon as the trail proceeds east.

At 0.4 miles, you can find campsites that meet U.S. Forest Service and Leave No Trace guidelines as the trail moves away from the creek and a patch of forest develops between the trail and creek. In fact, campsites are never far away from this point to the end of the trail.

At 0.9 miles, the path crosses the North Fork of Big Creek soon after entering the forest in an aspen grove. The trail continues east of the crossing in spruce-fir forest.

At 1.4 miles, the trail ends when it intersects Swamp Park Trail 1100. The trail junction is marked with a sign in a small clearing with aspen trees on the north edge and spruce-fir forest the rest of the way around.

Crags Trail 1182

Crags Trail 1182 runs west to east from its junction with Luna Lake Trail 1168 to its terminus at Wyoming Trail 1101 near the Continental Divide. This trail offers a way to sheltered campsites for Wyoming Trail through hikers who can descend from Wyoming Trail to the sheltered campsites around Luna Lake, or Lake Elbert, via Luna Lake and Crags Trails.

Luna Lake Trail connects Wyoming Trail with Swamp Park Trail 1100. Three Island Lake and North Lake Trails also connect Wyoming and Swamp Park Trails, so you can combine these trails to form loops between the Continental Divide and the western base of the Park Range.

DIFFICULTY
Above Average, 1,100 feet descent in 1.9 miles, easy to follow

TOTAL LENGTH
1.9 miles

SCENERY
Average, with beautiful lake and heavily glaciated landscape

USAGE
Light

ALLOWED USES
Hikers and pack stock only are allowed on this trail.

ACCESS
The trail begins at Luna Lake Trail, 6.7 miles east of Swamp Park Trail 1100.

MAPS
Trails Illustrated: # 117 Clark Buffalo Pass
USGS 7.5' Quadrangle: Mount Ethel

WAYPOINTS
The east edge of Luna Lake marks the beginning of the trail at 0 miles
Lake of the Crags — 0.6 miles
Wyoming Trail marks the end of the trail at 1.9 miles

TRAIL DESCRIPTION
Crags Trail 1182 begins where a sign marks its intersection with Luna Lake Trail and heads east toward its terminus at the Continental Divide. It's difficult finding campsites that meet U.S. Forest Service regulations and Leave No Trace guidelines along this trail. The trail travels through primarily spruce-fir forest as it climbs from Luna Lake to Lake of the Crags. The path then travels in alpine meadow and glacially sculpted bedrock along the way to Wyoming Trail.

At 0.1 miles, you'll discover the ruins of an old cabin. Luna Lake served as headquarters for an organization called the Rocky Mountain Trout Club during the early 1900s. The organization was formed to sell lots for cabins, only one of which was built. This may be the ruin of that cabin. Remember it is illegal to disturb archeological sites on National Forest. The path continues to climb toward the lake.

You'll reach Lake of the Crags at 0.6 miles. The trail travels along the east shore of the lake, and as you head away from the lake the path begins to rise once again toward the Continental Divide, traversing alpine meadows.

ELEVATION PROFILE

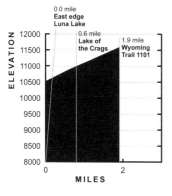

At 1.9 miles, a sign marks the trail's conclusion where it intersects Wyoming Trail 1101.

Ditch Creek Trail 1099

Ditch Creek Trail 1099 runs south to north from Red Dirt Trail to Swamp Park Trail at Swamp Park. This trail provides a relatively flat way to reach Swamp Park from Red Dirt Trail. Ditch Creek Trail also provides a path to Swamp Park that is about 0.2 miles shorter than the combination of Red Dirt Trail and Swamp Park Trail.

DIFFICULTY
Below Average, relatively flat

TOTAL LENGTH
2.2 miles

SCENERY
Below Average, some nice views initially, mostly travels through spruce-fir or aspen groves

USAGE
Light, Moderate during hunting season

ALLOWED USES
Hikers and pack stock only are allowed on this trail.

ACCESS
Ditch Creek Trail begins where it intersects Red Dirt Trail, 6.4 miles east of Red Dirt Trailhead.

MAPS
Trails Illustrated: #117 Clark Buffalo Pass
USGS 7.5' Quadrangle: Floyd Peak, Rocky Peak

WAYPOINTS
Red Dirt Trail junction marks the beginning of the trail at 0 miles
Irrigation ditch met — 0.3 miles
Irrigation ditch departed — 1.7 miles
Swamp Park marks the end of the trail at 2.2 miles

TRAIL DESCRIPTION
Ditch Creek Trail 1099 follows the ridge above Mad Creek on its way to Swamp Park, following an irrigation ditch much of the way. The path travels along the ridge to the west of Mad Creek through spruce-fir and aspen forests.

A sign marks the beginning of Ditch Creek Trail 1099 where it meets Red Dirt Trail 1171. The path immediately begins northward, traversing the ridge west of Mad Creek. The trail passes some outcroppings as it heads north.

At 0.3 miles, the path crosses an irrigation ditch. The trail follows this ditch nearly all the way to Swamp Park. At about 0.6 miles, the path encounters a number of user trails. Some trails head to the west while others go southeast. If in doubt, head east toward the irrigation ditch and follow it north until you find the tread once again. The path then heads north, following the course of the irrigation ditch. You can find campsites meeting U.S. Forest Service regulations and Leave No Trace guidelines in the aspen groves here.

At 1.2 miles, the trail crosses to the east side of the ditch. The path becomes slightly harder to follow as it picks its way through boulders and aspen trees. This marks the end of camping opportunities along the trail.

At 1.4 miles, the path comes beside the ditch once again and continues following it. At 1.7 miles, the trail crosses the ditch for the final time and turns northward, away from the ditch, toward Swamp Park. The path climbs slightly through spruce-fir and aspen forests here.

ELEVATION PROFILE

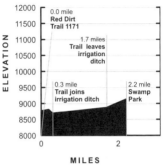

You'll reach a sign marking the Mount Zirkel Wilderness boundary at 2.0 miles in a spruce-fir forest. The trail continues north toward Swamp Park. At 2.2 miles, a sign marks the trail junction with Swamp Park Trail at the south edge of Swamp Park.

Elk Park Trail 1118

Elk Park Trail runs south to north from the Elk Park Trailhead to the trail junction with Swamp Park Trail 1100. This trail, in conjunction with Swamp Park Trail, provides access from points on the west side of the wilderness to the system of trails in the southern portion of the wilderness via Luna Lake Trail 1168.

After a hard day hiking Elk Park Trail, you can savor a unique treat only two miles north of the intersection of Forest Road 314 and CR 36. Located at the end of CR 36, Strawberry Hot Springs provides an opportunity to soothe your aching muscles after a long hike.

You'll notice sculpting from the glacier that flowed down Mad Creek when you reach an excellent vista as the trail descends into the Mad Creek drainage.

DIFFICULTY
Above Average

TOTAL LENGTH
2.8 miles

SCENERY
Above Average, with nice views into Mad Creek's canyon

USAGE
Light

ALLOWED USES
Hikers and pack stock only are allowed on this trail.

ACCESS
◄ This trail begins at Elk Park Trailhead, see page 55

MAPS
Trails Illustrated: #117 Clark Buffalo Pass
USGS 7.5' Quadrangle: Rocky Peak

WAYPOINTS
Elk Park Trailhead marks the beginning of the trail at 0 miles
Mount Zirkel Wilderness boundary (the start of a steep descent into Mad Creek Valley)
    — 1.3 miles
Swamp Park Trail near Mad Creek marks the end of the trail at 2.8 miles

TRAIL DESCRIPTION

Elk Park Trail 1118 travels through aspen groves on the way to the edge of Mad Creek valley. Soon after passing the Mount Zirkel Wilderness boundary, the trail begins a scenic descent into the Mad Creek drainage, near where the South Fork of Mad Creek meets the main fork. You won't find opportunities to camp along this trail until it reaches the floor of the Mad Creek valley.

The path climbs from the trailhead, soon entering aspen groves that prevail along the first 1.3 miles of the trail. At 0.5 miles, the trail crests a ridge and begins a short descent into a shallow depression. A faint trail goes off to the left in this area, but Elk Park Trail continues ahead on the right branch of the fork.

The path climbs out of the shallow depression and tops another ridge at 0.7 miles. After topping this second ridge, the trail begins the long descent toward Mad Creek, initially gentle through an aspen grove.

At 1.0 miles, you'll catch nice views down Mad Creek to the Elk River valley beyond. You'll reach the Mount Zirkel Wilderness boundary sign at 1.3 miles. The gentle portion of the descent ends soon after passing the wilderness boundary, and the trail begins a steeper drop through a series of switchbacks.

The views up Mad Creek valley are quite nice as the trail descends through a well-designed and maintained series of switchbacks. The South Fork of Mad Creek comes into the drainage just north of here. Look for glacial sculpting on the walls of the valley here.

ELEVATION PROFILE

At 2.2 miles, the path reaches the floor of Mad Creek valley in an aspen grove with thick bracken fern undergrowth. The trail climbs out of this first shallow depression and then descends to cross the South Fork of Mad Creek at 2.4 miles.

Soon after crossing the South Fork of Mad Creek, you'll notice ample opportunities for camping near the trail as you continue to the junction with Swamp Park Trail.

You'll cross a broad rocky creek bed at 2.6 miles, and the path soon enters a small clearing. A sign marks the trail junction with Swamp Park Trail 1100 at 2.8 miles.

Grizzly Helena Trail 1126
South of Lone Pine South Trailhead

The southern section of the Grizzly Helena Trail 1126 runs south to north from the Grizzly Trailhead to the Lone Pine South Trailhead. The northern section of the Grizzly Helena Trail begins at the Lone Pine North Trailhead 0.4 miles west of the Lone Pine South Trailhead on Forest Road 640. Lone Pine Trail 1129 begins at the Katherine Trailhead 1.0 miles west of the Lone Pine North Trailhead on Forest Road 640. Newcomb Trailhead is 1.6 miles south of Grizzly Trailhead on Forest Road 615.

Along the way north from Grizzly Trailhead, Rainbow Trail 1130 and Lost Ranger Trail 1131 intersect Grizzly Helena Trail 1126 and provide access to Wyoming Trail 1101 at the Continental Divide. These trails may be combined for loop hikes back to Grizzly Helena Trail. Newcomb Trail 1132 and Lone Pine Trail 1129 also provide access to Wyoming Trail 1101. These trails begin at trailheads a short distance from the beginning and end of Grizzly Helena Trail, so they also provide opportunities for loop hikes to the Continental Divide and back.

Aqua Fria Trail 630 also intersects the southern section of Grizzly Helena Trail 1126. Trail 630 provides one-way access to Aqua Fria Lake and is an ATV trail outside of the wilderness boundary, so it is not described in this book.

DIFFICULTY
Below Average, relatively small elevation gains, easy to follow

TOTAL LENGTH
15.2 miles

SCENERY
Average, nice views of North Park, Rabbit Ears Range, and Rawah Peaks

USAGE
Moderate

ALLOWED USES
Hiking, pack stock, mountain bikes, and single-track motorized vehicles are allowed all along the trail. Double-track motorized vehicles are allowed from Grizzly Trailhead north to the trail junction with Aqua Fria Trail only.

ELEVATION PROFILE

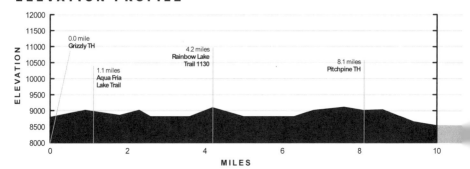

ACCESS

This trail begins at Grizzly Trailhead (see page 56) and ends at Lone Pine South Trailhead (see page 57). The trail can be accessed 8.1 miles north of Grizzly Trailhead at Pitchpine Trailhead (see page 58) and 12.4 miles north of Grizzly Trailhead at Red Canyon Trailhead (see page 59).

You can also access Grizzly Helena Trail 4.2 miles north of Grizzly Trailhead via Rainbow Trailhead (see page 58) and the first 0.6 miles of Rainbow Lake Trail 1130.

MAPS

Trails Illustrated: #117 Clark Buffalo Pass

USGS 7.5' Quadrangles: Pitchpine Mountain, Teal Lake

WAYPOINTS

Grizzly Trailhead at the end of Forest Road 615 marks the beginning of the trail at 0 miles

Trail to Aqua Fria Lake separates from Grizzly Helena Trail — 1.1 miles

Rainbow Lake Trail 1130 — 4.2 miles

Pitchpine Trailhead — 8.1 miles

Lost Ranger Trail 1131 — 11.3 miles

Red Canyon Trailhead — 12.4 miles

Lone Pine South Trailhead marks the end of the trail description at 15.2 miles

TRAIL DESCRIPTION

Grizzly Helena Trail 1126 passes along the base of the east side of the Park Range. Relatively flat and easy to follow, the trail works its way along the base of the mountains and travels through a variety of terrains ranging from forests to sagebrush meadows and willow thickets. You'll pass through forests of aspen, lodgepole pine, Englemann spruce, and mixed fir. These forests are separated by subalpine meadows or willow thickets found on valley floors adjacent to streams. Because this trail lies outside the wilderness boundary, ORVs and mountain bikes are welcome along specific sections. Campsites that meet U.S. Forest Service regulations and Leave No Trace guidelines are plentiful along several sections of this trail.

The Grizzly Helena Trail begins at the Grizzly Trailhead and treks north. Soon after leaving the trailhead, the trail crosses Beaver Creek. The trail ford is deep and presents a swiftwater drowning hazard during periods of high flow. A log crosses the creek just to the west of the trail ford, and some rocks in the creek bed are exposed at low water a short distance west of the log.

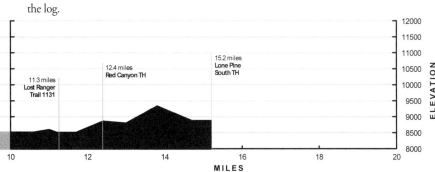

After crossing Beaver Creek, you'll find campsites that meet U.S. Forest Service regulations and Leave No Trace guidelines (but only for a short distance). At 0.3 miles, such campsites become scarce until you near the junction with Rainbow Lake Trail at 3.6 miles.

As the trail continues north, it rises over glacial till through a mixed forest of lodgepole pine, Englemann spruce, and fir. At 0.9 miles, the **road to Agua Fria Lake** merges with the Grizzly Helena Trail from the east. A sign marks the continuation of Grizzly Helena Trail 1126 to the south. The two trails share the double-track path until they separate at 1.1 miles.

A sign marks the point where Grizzly Helena Trail separates, becoming a single-track multi-use trail to the north. Four-wheel-drive ATVs are not allowed on Grizzly Helena Trail north of the trail to Aqua Fria Lake. The point where the trails separate is easy to miss. If you find yourself on a long steep climb, you may have missed the split in the trails and be on your way to Agua Fria Lake.

After separating from Agua Fria Lake Trail, the path soon enters an aspen stand. The trail spends most of its time in aspen groves as it travels north from here until it passes Pitchpine Trailhead. At 1.8 miles, the trail crosses Butler Creek and soon begins a hillside hike at the foot of the mountains.

The path reaches a wire gate in a barbed wire fence at 2.3 miles. This marks the point where the trail begins traversing a short section through private property. Respect private property. Don't stray from the path, and don't hunt in the sagebrush meadow here without permission. The views are quite spectacular. Feel free to take them but leave everything else. The path leaves private property through a barbed wire fence at 2.6 miles.

The trail crosses two small streams within the mile following your return to National Forest land north of the second wire gate. At 3.6 miles, the trail passes a small stand of pines to the west where you can find campsites meeting U.S. Forest Service regulations and Leave No Trace guidelines. This marks the beginning of camping opportunities near the trail junction with Rainbow Lake Trail.

The trail meets with **Rainbow Lake Trail 1130** on a ridgetop at 4.2 miles, and then begins to descend toward Livingston Park. At 4.4 miles, campsites that meet U.S. Forest Service regulations and Leave No Trace guidelines become hard to find, marking the end of dry camping opportunities in the vicinity of Rainbow Lake Trail.

The trail keeps dropping toward Livingston Park. At 4.8 miles as you traverse the valley floor, you'll find plenty of acceptable campsites. Soon the trail parallels Norris Creek and begins following it upstream. You'll cross Norris Creek at 5.5 miles, which could present a swiftwater drowning hazard during periods of high flow, especially when strainers clustered a short distance below the crossing. The trail turns to follow the stream in the downstream direction north of the crossing.

The trail passes by two pools of water after crossing Norris Creek before beginning to climb out of the valley. At 6.3 miles, the path enters a stand of aspens and begins climbing out of Livingston Park. You won't find campsites that meet U.S. Forest Service regulations and Leave No Trace guidelines where the path rises out of the valley.

The views of the Livingston Park are quite spectacular as the path climbs out of the valley. The moraines left by the Livingston Glacier look like giant arms encircling and embracing the park below. Beaver make themselves at home in the pools scattered throughout the park. North Park and Rawah Peaks form the backdrop for this beautiful scene.

At 6.8 miles, the path turns to the north and begins to traverse the ridgetop north of Livingston Park. You'll easily discover campsites that meet U.S. Forest Service regulations and Leave No Trace guidelines as the path continues north. The trail crosses two seasonal streams, but don't count on a water supply here in late summer.

The path enters a sagebrush meadow at 7.3 miles and soon climbs a low hill on the north side of the meadow. At 7.6 miles, the trail tops the low ridge. You'll cross a stream as the path descends toward Pitchpine Trailhead.

The trail reaches **Pitchpine Trailhead** at 8.1 miles where information bulletin boards mark the trailhead. The trail begins to climb from the trailhead toward a ridgetop to the north. As the path rises, you'll have a challenge finding campsites that meet U.S. Forest Service regulations and Leave No Trace guidelines. You'll cross a road about 400 feet from the trailhead. The path continues north through sagebrush meadows that soon give way to forest. You can see old mine works on the hillside west of the trail here.

The path crests the ridge soon after passing a wire gate in a fence line at 8.6 miles. Look for dry camping according to U.S. Forest Service regulations and Leave No Trace guidelines near the top of the ridge.

After topping the ridge, the path begins a long gentle descent into the valley of the Roaring Fork. The path travels through a gate in a fence at 8.8 miles. Signs here indicate that the trail enters U.S. Forest Service property north of the fence. You'll enter a stand of lodgepole pine as the trail continues onto National Forest property. The path exits the lodgepole pines at 9.3 miles when you encounter a road. The trail continues through sagebrush meadows and thin forest for a short distance here. You'll cross a small stream soon after you reach the road, and you'll pass a wire gate in a fence soon after the stream. It may be possible to locate campsites meeting U.S. Forest Service regulations and Leave No Trace guidelines in the sagebrush meadow near the stream, or along the trees that border the meadow.

The path continues descending into the Roaring Fork valley after entering the forest once again. At 10.1 miles, the path nears the valley floor. The landscape favors finding campsites here, but this section of the trail is on private property. Avoid camping and hunting on private property.

The trail continues across the valley floor until it begins to climb toward the mouth of Red Canyon at 10.6 miles. The trail crosses onto National Forest property once again as it climbs out of the valley.

As the trail rises toward the entrance of Red Canyon, it approaches the shear walls adjacent to the canyon. The path skirts the bottom of a large boulder field with a shear wall above. At 11.0 miles, the trail passes to the east of a series of small pools. You'll have luck finding campsites that meet U.S. Forest Service regulations and Leave No Trace guidelines in the small forested bench west of these pools.

After passing the series of pools to the west of the trail, the path soon begins to descend toward the Roaring Fork. As the path nears the stream, you can hear the falls at the mouth of the canyon.

Difficult to see, the falls drop in a deep, narrow chute cut through the bedrock at the canyon entrance. Contrast the glacial erosion that carved the U-shaped canyon with the stream erosion that carved the narrow chute through the bedrock at the mouth of the canyon since the glaciers have receded.

Grizzly Helena Trail meets with the **Lost Ranger Trail** at 11.3 miles, a short distance after it fords Roaring Fork. This crossing may present a swiftwater drowning hazard during periods of high flow. Anyone swept off their feet making this crossing would quickly find themselves in the narrow chute of the falls below the crossing where self-rescue would be impossible.

The trail then begins a climb to the top of the moraine left by a glacier that filled Red Canyon located to the north of the mouth of the canyon. Initially, the trail winds northward with the sculpted bedrock at the mouth of Red Canyon to the west, and Red Canyon Lake to the east. Red Canyon Lake is located on private property, so camping is not allowed in its vicinity. At 11.6 miles, the trail enters a stand of aspen and then traverses a sagebrush meadow on the side of the moraine as it continues to climb. At about 12.1 miles, the trail again enters a stand of aspen. You'll reach the **Red Canyon Trailhead** at 12.4 miles where the trail tops the moraine north of Red Canyon.

From the Red Canyon Trailhead, the trail initially follows a road. At 12.6 miles, the trail veers away from the road onto a fainter road toward the right where signs mark the direction of travel. You can find dry camping that meets U.S. Forest Service regulations and Leave No Trace guidelines along this section of the trail. At 12.9 miles, the trail separates from the faint road and bears to the right. Here three signs mark the direction of the trail and the continuation of the road as closed.

A few feet after leaving the road, you'll cross Hell Creek, and the trail enters a thick spruce-fir forest as it climbs a ridge. It'll be a challenge to find campsites that meet U.S. Forest Service regulations and Leave No Trace guidelines until you crest the ridge at 13.8 miles.

On the ridge, you'll find dry camping opportunities that meet U.S. Forest Service regulations and Leave No Trace guidelines, the last chance until you reach Lone Pine Creek valley. The trail then begins its descent into the Lone Pine valley.

At 14.7 miles, you'll reach the broad flat floor of the Lone Pine valley. For the next 0.5 miles as the trail crosses the valley, you'll discover ample campsites that meet U.S. Forest Service regulations and Leave No Trace guidelines.

At 14.9 miles, you'll reach Lone Pine Creek, which can present a swiftwater drowning hazard during spring runoff. The trail continues across the flat valley floor until you reach the **Lone Pine South Trailhead** at 15.2 miles.

At this point, the trail continues west along Forest Road 640. You can reach Lone Pine North Trailhead 0.5 miles west of Lone Pine South Trailhead, the point at which the trail leaves the road once again, turning back to the north.

Red Canyon from a spot near Grizzly Helena Trail

Lake Katherine Trail 1157

Lake Katherine Trail 1157 runs east to west beginning at its junction with Bighorn Lake Trail 1040 and ending at Lake Katherine, generally following the course of the stream that issues from Lake Katherine itself. The path switchbacks up the lip of the glacial cirque that contains Lake Katherine, climbing 440 feet in 0.9 miles.

A glacier that originated in cirques near the Continental Divide filled the Lone Pine valley with ice during the last ice age, leaving behind a receptacle for Lake Katherine. You can see the work of the glacier on the rocks from the lake and at the rim of the cirque not far from Wyoming Trail.

DIFFICULTY
Average, 440-foot climb in 0.9 miles, easy to follow

TOTAL LENGTH
0.9 miles

SCENERY
Average, with views of glacial cirque

USAGE
Moderate

ALLOWED USES
Hikers and pack stock only are allowed on this trail.

ACCESS
The trail begins near Lone Pine Trail, 1.3 miles west of Katherine Trailhead

MAPS
Trails Illustrated: #116 Hahns Peak Steamboat Lake, #117 Clark Buffalo Pass
USGS 7.5' Quadrangles: Mount Zirkel, Mount Ethel

WAYPOINTS
Lone Pine Trail 1129 marks the beginning of the trail at 0 miles
Lake Katherine marks the end of the trail at 0.9 miles

TRAIL DESCRIPTION
Lake Katherine Trail 1157 begins at its trail junction with Bighorn Lake Trail 1040 and heads west toward its terminus at Lake Katherine. The trail generally travels in spruce-fir forest, and you won't find opportunities for camping until you reach the lake.

A sign marks the trail junction of Bighorn Lake Trail 1040 and Lone Pine Trail 1129, pointing the way to the Continental Divide (you would follow Lone Pine Trail 1129 if you wanted to continue to the Divide). Here you go toward the left to begin the short walk to the origin of Lake Katherine Trail 1157. About 100 feet after you pass the junction with Lone Pine Trail 1129, Bighorn Lake Trail 1040 encounters a second trail junction where Katherine Lake Trail 1157 originates. Here a sign points left to Lake Katherine and right to Bighorn Lake. Lake Katherine Trail 1157 continues to the left toward Lake Katherine.

Just 100 feet from its origin, Lake Katherine Trail 1157 crosses Lone Pine Creek near the confluence of it and the stream that flows from Lake Katherine. This stream crossing could present a swiftwater drowning hazard during periods of high flow. After the crossing, the trail generally follows the course of the stream coming out of Lake Katherine.

The trail switchbacks as is climbs the hill that forms the lip of the glacial cirque containing Lake Katherine. Here the stream tumbles steeply down the metavolcanic bedrock. At 0.8 miles, check out the sculpted and polished rock left behind by glacial action as you crest the lip of the cirque.

At 0.9 miles, you'll see the emerald waters of Lake Katherine nestled in a beautifully sculpted cirque. The remains of a currently non-functional cement and rock dam are

ELEVATION PROFILE

located where the stream leaves the lake at its west end.

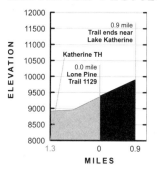

A trail leads along the north side of the lake to a few campsites meeting U.S. Forest Service regulations and Leave No Trace guidelines. If the flow of the stream leaving the east end of the lake is low enough, you can cross to search for campsites south of the lake.

Lone Pine Trail 1129

Lone Pine Trail 1129 runs east to west from the Katherine Trailhead to its terminus at Wyoming Trail 1101 and the Continental Divide. Lone Pine Trail 1129 is one of four trails connecting Wyoming Trail 1101 with Grizzly Helena Trail 1126 in the southern section of the wilderness. The other three trails are Newcomb Creek, Rainbow Lake, and Lost Ranger Trails. You can combine these trails to form various loops between the Continental Divide and the eastern base of the Park Range.

A glacier filled the Lone Pine Creek valley during the last ice age. You can witness the most strikingly beautiful work done by this glacier in the vicinity of Lake Katherine and Bighorn Lake. These lakes are located in the cirques where the glacier originated.

DIFFICULTY
Above Average, 1,900-foot climb in 4.0 miles, easy to follow along most of the way

TOTAL LENGTH
4.0 miles

SCENERY
Average, with views of North Park and Rawah Peaks in spots after about 3.5 miles

USAGE
Moderate, Light past Bighorn Lake Trail 1040

ALLOWED USES
Hikers and pack stock only are allowed on this trail.

ACCESS
This trail begins at Katherine Trailhead, see page 56.

MAPS
Trails Illustrated: #116 Hahns Peak Steamboat Lake, #117 Clark Buffalo Pass
USGS 7.5' Quadrangles: Pitchpine Mountain, Boettcher Lake, Mount Zirkel

WAYPOINTS
Katherine Trailhead marks the beginning of the trail at 0 miles
Bighorn Lake Trail 1040 — 1.3 miles
Wyoming Trail1101 and the Continental Divide mark the end of the trail at 4.0 miles

TRAIL DESCRIPTION
Lone Pine Trail 1129 begins at the Katherine Trailhead and heads west towards its terminus at the Continental Divide. The trail climbs between Lone Pine Creek and the hillside on the north side of its valley for most of the way to the Divide. Campsites that meet U.S. Forest Service regulations and Leave No Trace guidelines are difficult to find along most of this trail, with the exception of two sections noted below. The trail generally travels in a forest dominated by Englemann spruce and subalpine fir. The spruce-fir forest thins as the trail approaches the Continental Divide. Near the summit, you can take in spectacular views of the Medicine Bow and Never Summer Ranges. The trail skirts the south edge of some boulder fields along the way where you might see or hear pikas.

Shortly after leaving the trailhead, you'll encounter a split-rail fence at 0.1 miles. A narrow way is provided for foot travel, but backpackers with bulkier packs may be forced to use the stock gate located just south of the trail.

At 0.6 miles, you'll reach a sign marking the Mount Zirkel Wilderness boundary. You might have luck finding campsites that meet U.S. Forest Service regulations and Leave No Trace guidelines between the start of the hike and the wilderness boundary. From here, the climb intensifies, which makes finding a flat campsite a challenge until you reach Lone Pine Creek at 2.9 miles.

The trail reaches a boardwalk at 1.1 miles. From here you can see some of the sheer walls that head the glacial cirques at Lake Katherine and Bighorn Lake.

At 1.3 miles, the trail meets with Bighorn Lake Trail 1040. The trail junction sign indicates the direction to continue toward the Continental Divide. The Lone Pine Trail continues here to the right toward the Divide, the path to the left leads to Bighorn Lake. About 100 feet along the Bighorn Lake trail, another trail leading to Lake Katherine begins.

ELEVATION PROFILE

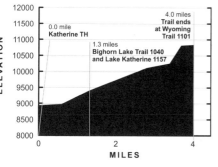

The path climbs after leaving the trail junction. At 2.6 miles, the trail becomes indistinct where it traverses a small meadow. Two posts at about 25-yard intervals lead you through this short section.

At 2.8 miles, the trail crosses Lone Pine Creek just a few feet after crossing a tributary nearly as large. The terrain flattens at this point, which makes finding a campsite meeting U.S. Forest Service regulations and Leave No Trace guidelines easier for the next 0.6 miles. At 3.1 miles, you'll cross Lone Pine Creek again.

At 3.4 miles, the trail begins the final steep ascent to the Continental Divide, climbing about 450 feet in the next 0.3 miles. The path is marked by cairns along the way and is easy to follow. Because of some exposure on this section, you should take care where the footing is loose. The view is awesome here. You can see back down the Lone Pine valley to Delaney Butte with Rawah Peaks and the Never Summer Range beyond.

At 3.7 miles, the climb eases a little as the trail reaches the shoulder of the Continental Divide, although it becomes indistinct as well. Cairns guide you to the end.

At 4.0 miles, you'll reach a sign marking the trail junction with Wyoming Trail 1101.

Lost Ranger Trail 1131

Lost Ranger Trail 1131 runs east to west from its origin where it meets Grizzly Helena Trail 1126 to its terminus at the Wyoming Trail 1101 at the Continental Divide. Lost Ranger Trail 1131 is one of four trails connecting Wyoming Trail 1101 with Grizzly Helena Trail 1126 in the southern section of the wilderness, the other three trails being Newcomb Creek, Rainbow Lakes, and Lone Pine Trails. These trails may be combined to form various loops between the Continental Divide and the eastern base of the Park Range.

A glacier filled Red Canyon during the last ice age, reaching a depth of 1,000 feet in some areas. You can see the work of the glacier in the sculpted rock and sheer walls in the canyon. These features, coupled with the rich pink-orange color of the quartz monzonite of the Mount Ethel Pluton, combine to make a canyon of extraordinary beauty. The trail consistently provides a view of the strikingly beautiful work done by the glacier along the sheer south face of the canyon. You can see this from the trail located on the opposite canyon face.

Lost Ranger Trail 1131 travels through an area heavily affected by the Burn Ridge Fire during the summer of 2002. This trail description was prepared earlier and does not depict the effects of the fire.

DIFFICULTY
Above Average, 2,200 feet climb in three miles; easy to follow most of the way

TOTAL LENGTH
5.8 miles

SCENERY
Average, with views of North Park and Medicine Bow Range and Red Canyon itself

USAGE
Light

ALLOWED USES
Hikers and pack stock only are allowed on this trail.

ACCESS
Lost Ranger Trail begins at Grizzly Helena Trail, 3.2 miles north of Pitchpine Trailhead, and 1.1 miles south of Red Canyon Trailhead.

ELEVATION PROFILE

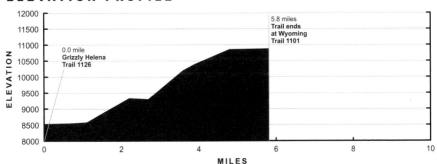

MAPS
Trails Illustrated: #117 Clark Buffalo Pass
USGS 7.5' Quadrangles: Mount Ethel, Pitchpine Mountain

WAYPOINTS
The intersection with Grizzly Helena Trail 1126 marks the beginning of the trail at 0 miles
Wyoming Trail 1101, near the Continental Divide, marks the end of the trail at 5.8 miles

TRAIL DESCRIPTION
Lost Ranger Trail 1131 begins at the mouth of Red Canyon and heads west toward its terminus at the Continental Divide. The trail climbs on the hillside on the north side of Red Canyon along most of its trek to the Divide. The trail generally travels in spruce-fir forest heavily affected by the Burn Ridge Fire during the summer of 2002. The forest thins as the trail approaches the Continental Divide.

About a tenth of a mile from your start up Red Canyon from the trail junction with Grizzly Helena Trail, you'll reach the Mount Zirkel Wilderness boundary. With the exception of two sections (near the meadow at 1.1 miles and a section of the trail near the north rim of Red Canyon) you'll have a hard time finding campsites that meet U.S. Forest Service regulations and Leave No Trace guidelines along much of the way.

At 0.7 miles, you'll cross Roaring Fork Creek. Soon after crossing the creek, you'll cross two small rivulets. The trail becomes quite difficult to follow right after you cross the second small stream. At 1.1 miles, the trail traverses a small sagebrush meadow. You'll find appropriate campsites in this area.

At about 1.7 miles, you'll begin taking in the views down the canyon toward North Park and the Medicine Bow Range beyond as the path begins to climb. Views of Red Canyon and its sheer south face also reward the hiker climbing toward the north rim of the canyon.

At 2.2 miles, the trail flattens a bit where sculpted and polished bedrock lies to the north of the trail. At 2.7 miles, you'll cross a small creek that should provide a reliable source of water. This crossing poses a swiftwater drowning hazard during periods of high flows, due to its steep gradient.

At 3.2 miles, you'll cross a small gulch that may contain a trickle of water, and the trail turns to begin a particularly steep section of the climb. At 3.6 miles, the trail switches back to the west at a spot that offers an exceptional view east down the canyon and beyond. A USGS benchmark is located about 30 yards east of this switchback in the trail.

The trail continues to climb into a thin spruce-fir forest that contains small intermittent meadows. The trail becomes indistinct for a short distance in one of these grassy sections at 3.9 miles. As the trail continues toward the Divide, the climb moderates through the thin spruce-fir forest.

Camping in accordance with U.S. Forest Service regulations and Leave No Trace guidelines becomes a possibility once again along this section of trail. At 4.3 miles, a fire ring to the north of the trail marks the location of a small spring further to the north. This spring may provide a source of water, depending on weather conditions and time of the year.

At 4.8 miles, the trail becomes indistinct where is crosses a shallow ravine. You'll see a post marking the continuation of the trail west of you about 100 yards. From this point, until the trail reaches its end at the Wyoming Trail 1101, the indistinct trail is marked with cairns or posts. Along this final one-mile section, the trail often crosses melt streams from a snowfield on a north-facing slope of Lost Ranger Peak above. You won't find opportunities for camping along this final mile of the trail.

At 5.8 miles, a sign marks the end of Lost Ranger Trail where it intersects Wyoming Trail 1101.

Red Canyon from Lost Ranger Trail (before the Burn Ridge Fire)

Luna Lake Trail 1168

Luna Lake Trail 1168 runs west to east originating from its intersection with Swamp Park Trail 1100 at the south edge of Swamp Park and reaching its terminus at Wyoming Trail 1101 above Lake Elbert. The path climbs 2,200 feet along the way to the Continental Divide from Swamp Park.

Three Island Lake and North Lake Trails also connect Wyoming and Swamp Park Trail, so you can design loops for hiking between the Continental Divide and the western base of the Park Range.

The portion of the trail east of Crags Trail also offers a way to sheltered campsites meeting U.S. Forest Service regulations and Leave No Trace guidelines. Hikers descending from Wyoming Trail to Luna Lake or Lake Elbert can combine the final segment of Luna Lake Trail with Crags Trail. This route allows travelers to descend from the Divide to sheltered camps and return without backtracking.

DIFFICULTY
Average, 2,200 feet climb in 8.4 miles

TOTAL LENGTH
8.4 miles

SCENERY
Above Average

USAGE
Light from Swamp Park Trail 1100 to Lake Margaret, Moderate from Lake Margaret to Wyoming Trail 1101

ALLOWED USES
Hikers and pack stock only are allowed on this trail.

ACCESS
Luna Lake Trail begins at Swamp Park Trail 1100 on the south edge of Swamp Park

MAPS
Trails Illustrated: # 117 Clark Buffalo Pass Colorado
USGS 7.5' Quadrangles: Mount Ethel, Floyd Peak

ELEVATION PROFILE

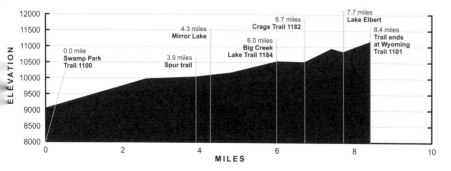

WAYPOINTS

Swamp Park Trail 1100 marks the beginning of the trail at 0 miles
Spur trail near Lake Margaret — 3.9 miles
Mirror Lake — 4.3 miles
Big Creek Lake Trail 1184 (near west end of Luna Lake) — 6.0 miles
Crags Trail 1182 (near east end of Luna Lake) — 6.7 miles
Lake Elbert — 7.7 miles
Wyoming Trail 1101 marks the end of the trail near the Continental Divide at 8.4 miles

TRAIL DESCRIPTION

Luna Lake Trail 1168 travels 8.4 miles, starting where it intersects Swamp Park Trail 1100 and concluding at Wyoming Trail and the Continental Divide. As the path climbs 2,200 feet, it traverses varied terrain ranging from aspen groves near its origin to spruce-fir forest through most of its length. You'll pass through beautiful high mountain meadows and large areas of flattened timber from the Routt Divide Blowdown. This path travels in three creek drainages along its meandering course to the Divide.

Before the Routt Divide Blowdown in 1997, Luna Lake Trail followed the North Fork of Mad Creek, stretching from a point near Lake Margaret and reaching Swamp Park. The U.S. Forest Service had considered re-routing the trail to its present path because it was drier, had nice views, and was located on the south-facing side of a ridge, which meant the snow melted off earlier. When the blowdown necessitated clearing trees from both paths, they decided to clear the present route.

The path begins where a sign marks the trail junction with Swamp Park Trail 1100. It climbs through aspen groves along the face of the glacial moraine that formed Swamp Park.

The trail continues east, climbing along the hillside on the north side of the canyon containing the Middle Fork of Mad Creek. You won't find suitable campsites along the way until you reach the North Fork of Mad Creek at 3.0 miles.

As the trail continues east, the ecosystem transitions from aspen to spruce-fir, with no more aspens after about 1.5 miles where two small trickles cross the trail in succession (from springs to the north).

At 2.5 miles, the trail passes a rock outcrop that offers beautiful views to the southwest into the Middle Fork of Mad Creek drainage. You'll see glacial sculpting and a precipitous drop off at the south edge of the outcrop. The path then turns to the northeast for the final steep climb over the divide separating the North and Middle Forks of Mad Creek drainages.

At about 2.6 miles, you'll crest the divide separating the drainages, and the path crosses an area hard hit by the Routt Divide Blowdown. The way continues east across this landscape of flattened trees, and soon you'll see the North Fork of Mad Creek.

At 3.0 miles, the trail crosses the North Fork of Mad Creek where the water meanders through a meadow. The path continues east through the meadow, and the crossing marks the beginning of camping opportunities along the trail.

At 3.2 miles, the trail enters a beautiful park and traverses toward its second crossing of the North Fork of Mad Creek.

At 3.6 miles, the path crosses back to the south side of the North Fork of Mad Creek, continuing to the south here through blown-down timber and scattered meadows.

At 3.9 miles, a sign marks Luna Lake Trail where it meets **Fish Hawk Lake Trail 1168.1A** to Margaret, Edward, Snowstorm, and Fish Hawk Lakes. The spur trail was immediately blocked by wind-thrown timber in September of 2002. This trail is to be cleared and re-opened in the future.

After passing Fish Hawk Lake Trail, Luna Lake Trail 1168 turns east again. You can catch a glimpse of Lake Margaret through the trees to the south of the trail as you travel east.

At 4.3 miles, the path passes the north edge of **Mirror Lake** before the water is obscured behind a rock outcrop south of the path. A sign marks the trail just past the east end of the lake.

At 4.8 miles, the trail enters spruce-fir forest and begins to climb a ridge. This marks the end of camping opportunities along the trail until you reach Luna Lake. The path then climbs steadily along the crest of a ridge that separates the North and South Forks of Mad Creek. The path passes two water pools along the way — one to the north, one to the south.

At 6.0 miles a sign marks the trail junction with **Big Creek Lake Trail 1184.** Big Creek Lake Trail goes off to the north here while Luna Lake Trail continues east.

At 6.1 miles, the path crosses the stream issuing from Luna Lake at the west edge of the lake. The trail continues east here along the north shore. You can find campsites that meet U.S. Forest Service regulations and Leave No Trace guidelines on the north side of the lake, and you can probably find sites more easily toward the east end of the lake.

At 6.7 miles, Luna Lake Trail meets **Crags Trail 1182** beyond the east end of the lake. Here Luna Lake Trail turns south across the meadow east of the lake toward the south wall of the cirque. Crags Trail begins here and initially travels east. Remember that campsites in the meadow east of Luna Lake do not meet Leave No Trace guidelines for staying out of sight of other campers.

Luna Lake Trail crosses the floor of the cirque before beginning a steep climb toward a saddle leading to Lake Elbert. At 7.0 miles, the path begins the very steep and treacherous climb out of the cirque.

At 7.4 miles, the path reaches the crest of the saddle and you can see **Lake Elbert** ahead. The trail continues toward the lake, crossing the stream flowing from it at 7.7 miles. You'll notice campsites that meet U.S. Forest Service regulations and Leave No Trace guidelines in clumps of trees southwest of Lake Elbert (but not near the stream leaving the lake).

The trail then climbs away from Lake Elbert toward the Continental Divide. At 8.4 miles, Luna Lake Trail ends where it intersects **Wyoming Trail 1101.** The trail junction is marked with a sign.

Newcomb Creek Trail 1132

Newcomb Creek trail runs east to west from the Newcomb Creek Trailhead to its terminus at the Wyoming Trail 1101 where it meets the Continental Divide. This trail is one of four that connect Wyoming Trail with Grizzly Helena Trail and forms a network of varied loop hiking possibilities.

A glacier filled the Newcomb Creek valley during the last ice age, leaving deposits of rocks and materials scoured from near Mouth Ethel you'll notice as you hike up the valley. Along the climb near Round Mountain, you'll see plenty of the glacier's sculpting and polishing near the trail.

DIFFICULTY
Average, 1,800 foot climb in 4.3 miles; easy to follow until the 2.0-mile mark, then becomes difficult in sections

TOTAL LENGTH
6.8 miles

SCENERY
Average, with views of North Park and Rawah peaks in spots after about 3.0 miles, and glacial features along the way to the Divide

USAGE
Light

ALLOWED USES
Hikers and pack stock only are allowed on this trail.

ACCESS
This trail begins at Newcomb Trailhead (see page 57) and ends at Wyoming Trail 2.3 miles north of Buffalo Pass Trailhead.

MAPS
Trails Illustrated: #117 Clark Buffalo Pass
USGS 7.5' Quadrangles: Buffalo Pass, Teal Lake

ELEVATION PROFILE

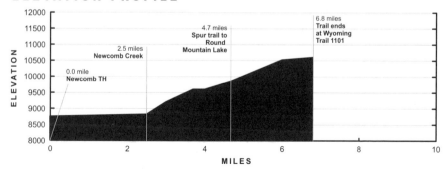

WAYPOINTS

Newcomb Trailhead marks the beginning of the trail at 0 miles

Newcomb Creek — 2.5 miles

Spur trail to Round Mountain Lake — 4.7 miles

The intersection with Wyoming Trail 1101 marks the end of the trail at 6.8 miles

TRAIL DESCRIPTION

Newcomb Creek Trail 1132 begins at the Newcomb Trailhead and heads west towards its terminus at the Continental Divide. Newcomb Creek Trail 1132 generally follows the course of Newcomb Creek for the first 2.5 miles. It climbs out of the valley near Round Mountain, heading toward the Continental Divide and meeting a spur trail to Round Mountain Lake along the way. You won't have any problem finding campsites that meet U.S. Forest Service regulations and Leave No Trace guidelines along this trail until it begins its climb toward the Divide.

The trail generally winds in and out of forest dominated by pine, subalpine fir, and numerous aspen groves along the Newcomb Creek valley. As you the climb out of the valley, you'll notice how Englemann spruce replaces pine, and the aspen groves become less common. Willow thickets line the course of Newcomb Creek, so keep your eyes open for moose. You'll traverse alpine meadows near the summit where views toward the Medicine Bow and Rabbit Ears Range are quite spectacular.

The trail crosses Whalen Creek about 0.1 miles beyond the trailhead and continues into the Newcomb Creek valley. The path winds in and out of forests dominated by pine and subalpine fir or large aspen groves as it travels up the valley. Wooded sections alternate with sagebrush meadows along the valley floor. To the south, Newcomb Creek parallels the trail, although it's often obscured by dense willow thickets. To the north, the valley wall is covered alternately with forests of pines, spruce-fir, and aspen groves.

Hikers familiar with the Wyoming Trail north of its junction with Newcomb Creek Trail will recognize boulders originally from the vicinity of Mount Ethel that rode to their present location on ancient glaciers.

The trail is easy to follow most of the way through the wide valley of Newcomb Creek. At 1.4 miles, it enters a meadow and becomes indistinct for about 150 yards. Stay on a general west-southwest heading to negotiate this section.

At 1.7 miles, Round Mountain comes into view, and for the first time, you can see where the long flat valley comes to a head at the foot of steep climbs to the west. Round Mountain has a distinct rounded silhouette that helps you navigate for the next 0.7 miles.

After you first see Round Mountain and the head of the valley, the path enters an aspen grove at the north edge of the valley at 2.0 miles. The trail then climbs through the aspens over a small ridge and descends back to the valley floor. About 150 yards from where you first enter the aspens, a distinct trail continues to the right (north). At this location, you'll notice two aspen trees, each with an axe blaze facing opposite directions of travel on the trail and each scored with several dates.

From these aspen trees, the trail continues toward Round Mountain — not along the well-worn trail to the right. For the next 0.3 miles, the trail winds along between the willow thickets to the south and the aspens and hillside to the north on a heading toward Round Mountain. In early summer, this stretch will be very muddy, so you may have to skirt it by traversing the hillside to the north.

A cairn at 2.4 miles distinguishes the trail once again from this point toward the forest lining the end of the valley. At 2.5 miles, the trail crosses Newcomb Creek soon after entering the forest, and the 1.3-mile climb out of the valley marks a stretch where it's difficult to find campsites that meet U.S. Forest Service regulations and Leave No Trace guidelines. But you can find some spots as you approach Round Mountain Lake.

You'll reach a rock outcropping with an excellent view down the Newcomb Creek valley to Rawah Peaks at 3.0 miles. The next half-mile gives you a good look at the sculpted and polished rock left behind by glaciers. Further on, you'll see more large boulders carried by glaciers from near Mount Ethel.

Newcomb Creek from Newcomb Creek Trail

At 4.7 miles, a large cairn marks the spur trail that heads 0.3 miles southwest to Round Mountain Lake, which is nestled in a glacial cirque with Round Mountain to the south and the steep headwall to the west.

Newcomb Creek Trail continues toward the Continental Divide on the path toward the west where it meets the spur trail. At 5.0 miles a cairn sits adjacent to a rock outcropping.

At 5.3 miles, you'll encounter a very steep climb with loose footing. About 100 yards before this climb, you can see the side of Round Mountain through the trees toward the south. A short hike off trail to the south here leads to a great view of Round Mountain Lake. You can also see down the Newcomb Creek valley to Rawah Peaks from here.

At 5.7 miles, you might notice a small pool to the east of the trail. As the trail nears the Continental Divide, the spruce-fir forest subsides until, at about 6.0 miles, the trail begins to traverse an alpine meadow along the shoulder of the Continental Divide where it becomes indistinct and occasionally non-existent. Using a compass, you'll generally head southwest and notice periodic cairns. There is only one instance where the path strays appreciably from the southwest heading, but this is only for a short distance.

At 6.3 miles, the path crosses a small wash marked with a small cairn on the north side of the crossing. Upon climbing the south bank of the wash, the trail turns due west, paralleling the wash for about 200 yards. The path then turns back to its southwestern heading at a cairn along the wash, continuing toward its junction with the Wyoming Trail. Cairns spaced at roughly 100-yard intervals help guide you along this final half-mile stretch. At 6.8 miles, a sign marks the junction with Wyoming Trail 1101.

North Lake Trail 1164

North Lake Trail 1164 runs west to east from its origin at North Lake Trailhead to its terminus at its junction with Wyoming Trail 1101 near the Continental Divide. North Lake Trail 1164 is part of the Continental Divide Trail (CDT) that passes through and around the wilderness. To continue north on the CDT from North Lake Trailhead, go 4.8 miles north on Forest Road 443 until it meets Forest Road 400. Then go 0.4 miles west on Forest Road 400 to Seedhouse Trailhead, where the CDT continues north on Wyoming Trail 1101.

You can reach Swamp Park Trail at the Burn Ridge Trailhead 2.8 miles west of the North Lake Trailhead on Forest Road 443. North Lake Trail 1164 and Forest Road 443 provide one of three paths connecting Wyoming Trail 1101 with Swamp Park Trail 1100 in the southern section of the wilderness.

The other two trails connecting Swamp Park Trail and Wyoming Trail are Luna Lake and Three Island Trails. These trails may be combined to form loops between the Continental Divide and the western base of the Park Range. Three Island Trailhead is 1.4 miles west of North Lake Trailhead on Forest Road 443.

Three Island and North Lake Trails can be combined with a short section of Forest Road 443 and Wyoming Trail 1101 for a 13.8-mile loop hike to the Continental Divide and back.

DIFFICULTY
Above Average, 2,300 feet climb in 5.4 miles; easy to follow

TOTAL LENGTH
5.4 miles

SCENERY
Below Average, nice views of Lost Ranger Peak and The Dome near Continental Divide

USAGE
Heavy

ALLOWED USES
Hikers and pack stock only are allowed on this trail.

ACCESS
This trail begins at North Lake Trailhead, see page 58.

ELEVATION PROFILE

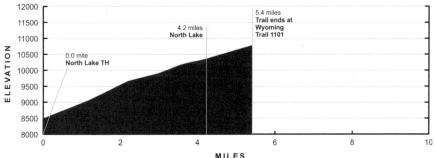

MAPS

Trails Illustrated: #116 Hahns Peak Steamboat Lake, #117 Clark Buffalo Pass
USGS 7.5' Quadrangles: Mount Zirkel, Mount Ethel

WAYPOINTS

North Lake Trailhead marks the beginning of the trail at 0 miles
North Lake — 4.2 miles
Wyoming Trail 1101 marks the end of the trail at 5.4 miles

TRAIL DESCRIPTION

North Lake Trail 1164 begins at North Lake Trailhead and heads east toward its terminus
at Wyoming Trail 1101 and the Continental Divide. You can find campsites that meet
U.S. Forest Service regulations and Leave No Trace guidelines along two sections of the
trail, which are noted below. The trail generally travels in spruce-fir forest.

You'll reach a sign marking the Mount Zirkel Wilderness boundary at 0.2 miles, and cross a
creek soon after. Then the trail begins a steep climb through a series of switchbacks to the
south of this small creek, climbing 1,100 feet in its first two miles. The path approaches
the creek at 0.4 miles before turning away to continue climbing. At 1.2 miles, the path
approaches the creek a second and final time before turning away toward a ridge.

At this point, the trail begins a ridge hike, although the rate of the climb remains quick.
At about 2.2 miles, the climb eases and it becomes possible to find dry campsites that meet
U.S. Forest Service regulations and Leave No Trace guidelines along the ridge. Camping
remains a possibility along this dry ridge for about a mile. The ridge hike persists until
the path begins to climb once again before reaching a small stream. At 3.6 miles, you'll
cross the small stream, and the trail continues to rise beyond the stream.

You'll cross a dry gulch at 3.9 miles, and you'll quickly encounter a small meadow to the south
of the trail. This marks the beginning of a section of the trail where you can find campsites
that meet U.S. Forest Service regulations and Leave No Trace guidelines nearby.

You'll reach North Lake at 4.2 miles where you'll notice how the Burn Ridge Fire burned
some trees on the south side of the lake during the summer of 2002. The path continues
to rise, following the stream that feeds North Lake. At about 4.7 miles, it becomes difficult
to find campsites that meet U.S. Forest Service regulations and Leave No Trace guidelines
near the trail. Campsites remain difficult to find until you reach the trail's end.

At 5.1 miles, the climb eases as you approach the Divide. You'll pass a large pool that marks
the beginning of the stream feeding North Lake at 5.3 miles. Marked with a sign, the trail
ends at its junction with Wyoming Trail 1101 at 5.4 miles. The Burn Ridge Fire crossed the
Continental Divide just south of North Lake Trail during the summer of 2002.

Rainbow Lake Trail 1130

Rainbow Lake Trail 1130 runs east to west from the Rainbow Trailhead to its terminus at the Wyoming Trail 1101 at the Continental Divide. The trail parallels Norris Creek along most of its trek.

Rainbow Lake Trail 1130 is one of four trails connecting Wyoming Trail 1101 with Grizzly Helena Trail 1126 in the southern section of the wilderness. The other three trails are Newcomb Creek, Lost Ranger, and Lone Pine Trails. You can combine these trails to form various loops between the Continental Divide and the eastern base of the Park Range.

The landscape above Rainbow Lake is dominated by glacially sculpted and polished bedrock. The glacier that filled the Norris Creek valley during the last ice age carved the valley floor in stair-step fashion, leaving five lake beds along its path.

DIFFICULTY
Average, 2,600 feet climb in 8.7 miles, easy to follow

TOTAL LENGTH
8.7 miles

SCENERY
Average, with views of Mount Ethel, heavily glaciated landscape above Rainbow Lake, and panoramic views near the Continental Divide

USAGE
Heavy, this trail is the most heavily used on the east side of the Continental Divide. Usage is slightly less beyond Rainbow Lake. This trail is a poor choice if you're seeking solitude and a true wilderness experience.

ALLOWED USES
Hikers and pack stock are allowed all along the trail. Single-track motorized vehicles and mountain bikes are allowed from Rainbow Trailhead as far west (0.6 miles) as Grizzly Helena Trail 1126.

ACCESS
This trail begins at Rainbow Trailhead, see page 58.

MAPS
Trails Illustrated: #117 Clark Buffalo Pass
USGS 7.5' Quadrangles: Pitchpine Mountain, Mount Ethel

ELEVATION PROFILE

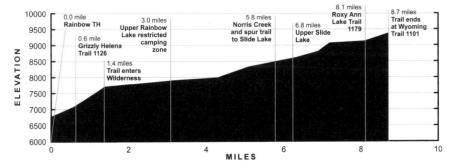

WAYPOINTS

Rainbow Trailhead marks the beginning of the trail at 0 miles
Grizzly Helena Trail 1126 — 0.6 miles
Mount Zirkel Wilderness boundary — 1.4 miles
Restricted camping zone near Upper Rainbow Lake — 3.0 miles
Norris Creek and spur trail to Slide Lake — 5.8 miles
Upper Slide Lake — 6.8 miles
Roxy Ann Lake Trail 1179 — 8.1 miles
Wyoming Trail 1101 near the Continental Divide marks the end of the trail at 8.7 miles

TRAIL DESCRIPTION

Rainbow Lake Trail 1130 begins at the Rainbow Trailhead and heads west towards its terminus at the Continental Divide. It won't be easy finding campsites that meet U.S. Forest Service regulations and Leave No Trace guidelines along most of this trail, with the exception of the areas surrounding the lakes and a few other sections. The path generally travels in spruce-fir forest.

Rainbow Lake Trail travels near five subalpine lakes that are very popular camping and fishing destinations. Upper, Middle, and Lower Rainbow Lakes see the heaviest usage. The large size of Rainbow Lake allows it to accommodate more users than the other smaller lakes, helping to offset the heavy usage. Camping is prohibited in a zone between Rainbow Lakes and the trail. Wilderness rangers strictly enforce the no-camping zone without exceptions. If you camp in the no-camping zone near Rainbow Lake, you will be ticketed and compelled to move. The trail sees less traffic above Rainbow Lake than the lower sections of the trail.

Upon leaving the Rainbow Trailhead, the path begins climbing along the lateral moraine left by Norris Creek's glacier. As the path rises along the ridgeline, you'll see large rounded boulders. You can camp according to U.S. Forest Service regulations and Leave No Trace guidelines along the trail for the first 0.8 miles.

At 0.6 miles, you'll reach the trail junction with Grizzly Helena Trail. Rainbow Trail continues to ascend the ridge through an aspen grove, revealing views of Rabbit Ears Peak and the Rabbit Ears Range to the south.

At the Mount Zirkel Wilderness boundary sign, you'll be 1.4 miles into your journey. The path leaves the ridgeline here and begins to descend into the Norris Creek Valley. You'll cross a small stream at 2.6 miles.

When you reach the sign marking the beginning of camping restrictions near Rainbow Lake you're at 3.0 miles. From this point, camping is forbidden between Rainbow Lakes and the trail. You'll reach a small cascade between Upper and Middle Rainbow Lakes at 3.2 miles. The trail travels along the south shore of Rainbow Lake as it continues west.

At 4.3 miles, the path crosses Norris Creek at the base of a cascade, an area of concern for swiftwater drowning hazards during periods of high flow. The trail passes west of Rainbow Lake, and a spur trail leads to the north side of the lake shortly after the crossing.

Not long after you cross Norris Creek, Rainbow Lake Trail turns to the west and begins to ascend toward Slide Lake. The trail initially rises along the north side of Norris Creek, which cascades over a sculpted bedrock lip left by the glacier. From this point westward, sculpted and polished bedrock dominates the landscape as the trail continues to climb. With close examination, you can see striations in the bedrock that indicate the direction ice traveled over the rock. The trail continues west with Norris Creek to the south.

At 5.8 miles, the trail crosses Norris Creek where it cascades down a bedrock shelf from the north. Rainbow Lake Trail continues west to follow another stream, which may appear larger than Norris Creek.

After crossing Norris Creek, you can reach Slide Lake by going off-trail and following Norris Creek north, preferably along the west side of the creek as it cascades down the bedrock slope. Slide Lake is 0.3 miles north of Rainbow Lake Trail. The south and east shores of the lake have suitable campsites for meeting U.S. Forest Service regulations and Leave No Trace guidelines.

After crossing Norris Creek, Rainbow Lake Trail climbs as it continues westward. At 6.3 miles, the climb eases and you'll find more campsites that meet U.S. Forest Service regulations and Leave No Trace guidelines for the next 0.5 miles.

At 6.8 miles, Upper Slide Lake comes into view. The trail continues west of the lake, and at 6.9 miles, you'll cross Norris Creek again. The path then rises until, at 7.2 miles, the ascent eases once again where the trail nears timberline.

As the trail continues, it primarily leads through meadows with scattered clumps of trees and small pools. The path remains easy to follow.

At 8.1 miles, Roxy Ann Lake Trail 1179 intersects the trail, a trail junction marked with a post only. From here, Roxy Ann Lake is 1.7 miles east and about 1,000 feet lower along a steep trail. See the trail description for Roxy Ann Lake Trail 1179.

Rainbow Lake Trail continues northwest toward the Continental Divide after the junction with Roxy Ann Lake Trail. As you near the Divide, you can see Roxy Ann Lake to the east.

At 8.7 miles, the trail ends at its junction with Wyoming Trail 1101. Water is available near the trail about 150 yards from its terminus.

Red Dirt Trail 1171

Red Dirt Trail 1171 runs south to north from the Red Dirt Trailhead to Swamp Park Trail. This trail provides alternate access to Swamp Park Trail and Ditch Creek Trail, both of which lead to Swamp Park and points north and east.

For those who don't like to backtrack, Red Dirt Trail 1171, Swamp Park Trail, and Routt County Road 129 can be combined for a 15-mile loop hike with about 2,800 feet of elevation gain and loss. You can also combine Saddle Trail with Red Dirt Trail and Swamp Park Trail for a 5.7-mile loop hike with only 800 feet of elevation gain and loss.

DIFFICULTY
Average, relatively small elevation gains, easy to follow

TOTAL LENGTH
6.7 miles

SCENERY
Above Average, nice views of Elk River valley and Mad Creek canyon

USAGE
Light to Moderate past Saddle Trail, Moderate to Heavy near the trailhead. The Swamp Park Trail / Saddle Trail / Red Dirt Trail loop is very popular with mountain bikers.

ALLOWED USES
Hikers and pack stock are allowed along the length of the trail. Mountain bikes are allowed from the trailhead to the wilderness boundary, but motorized use is not allowed on this trail.

ACCESS
This trail begins at Red Dirt Trailhead, see page 59.

MAPS
Trails Illustrated: #117 Clark Buffalo Pass
USGS 7.5' Quadrangles: Floyd Peak, Rocky Peak, Mad Creek

WAYPOINTS
Red Dirt Trailhead marks the beginning of the trail at 0 miles
Saddle Trail 1140 — 1.8 miles
Mount Zirkel Wilderness boundary — 5.3 miles
Ditch Creek Trail 1099 — 6.4 miles
Swamp Park Trail 1100 marks the end of the trail at 6.7 miles

ELEVATION PROFILE

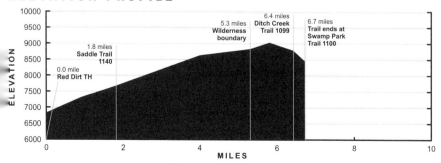

TRAIL DESCRIPTION

Red Dirt Trail 1171 takes the high road to Swamp Park Trail, offering a challenging 2,800 feet of elevation gain and loss on its way. The path travels through a variety of ecosystems including mountain shrublands dominated by gambel oaks, aspen groves with bracken fern groundcover, and cool, moist fir forests. The first 5.3 miles of this trail lies outside the wilderness, so mountain bikes are allowed as far as the wilderness boundary. You can find dry campsites meeting U.S. Forest Service regulations and Leave No Trace guidelines on a single section of this trail. You won't find water along this trail, but Mad Creek is a short distance from its terminus.

The trail leaves the Red Dirt Trailhead and begins to climb immediately. Sign the register soon after leaving the trailhead. The path cuts into the hillside east of Elk River and traverses upward out of the valley. As the path climbs steadily through a series of switchbacks away from Elk River, the views up the river continue to improve.

At 0.9 miles, the path goes under a set of power lines that mark the eastern rim of the Elk River Valley. The trail continues east here.

As the path heads toward its junction with Swamp Park Trail, it passes through varied forests and shrublands. You'll see mountain shrublands dominated by gambel oaks along some of the drier, more exposed sections. Aspen forests thrive through here, and sometimes the ground is carpeted with bracken fern below. Perhaps the most surprising features along this trail are the frequent groves of firs. Douglas fir dominates many of these damp and shady stands.

At 1.4 miles, a user trail coming from the southeast meets Red Dirt Trail in a clearing. Be careful not to confuse this trail with Saddle Trail, which meets the path further ahead. Two other user trails branch off to the northwest in this area, and another user trail intersects the path here also. Continue forward to stay on Red Dirt Trail in this section.

At 1.8 miles, the trail meets a sign marking the Saddle Trail 1140 junction. This 1.1-mile trail provides access to Swamp Park Trail to the south.

Red Dirt Trail continues northeast after leaving the Saddle Trail junction. The path soon travels through mountain shrublands near the north rim of Mad Creek Canyon at 2.1 miles.

At 2.4 miles, the path passes a stock-watering trough to the north. When I passed this trough in September 2002, it was dry. In fact, you won't find any reliable water sources along this trail.

At 3.2 miles, the path traverses a ridge with views of the Elk River valley to the west.

At 3.5 miles, you'll pass a second stock-watering tank, again to the north of the trail. The path continues to climb toward a ridge, which it eventually crests at 4.0 miles. The trail begins a moderate descent here.

At about 4.3 miles, the path enters a section where dry campsites meeting U.S. Forest Service regulations and Leave No Trace guidelines may be found. The trail continues its moderate descent and enters a fir forest.

At 4.7 miles, the path begins to climb again. This marks the end of camping opportunities along the trail. The path continues to climb and quickly enters a stand of aspen.

The Mount Zirkel Wilderness boundary sign near the edge of Mad Creek's canyon marks the 5.3-mile point. Follow the path on the west rim of the canyon where you can catch nice views into the drainage. You can see Elk Park Trail descending the opposite side of the canyon, if you know where to look.

The path continues a gentle ascent near the rim of the canyon before finally beginning to descend into the drainage at 5.8 miles. At 6.4 miles, the trail meets Ditch Creek Trail 1099. Red Dirt Trail 1171 continues to descend toward the floor of the Mad Creek drainage.

At 6.7 miles, Red Dirt Trail ends where it intersects Swamp Park Trail 1100. Water is available a short distance to the east here in Mad Creek. Campsites meeting U.S. Forest Service regulations and Leave No Trace guidelines are

Elk River Valley from Red Dirt Trail

available along Swamp Park Trail not far to the north and south of the trail junction. Cattle graze here in summer, making this area less than optimal for overnight stays.

Roaring Fork Trail 1166

Roaring Fork Trail 1166 runs west to east from the Roaring Fork Trailhead to Swamp Park Trail. This trail provides access from Forest Road 471.1B in the Big Creek drainage to Swamp Park Trail 1100.

Roaring Fork Trail can be combined with Swamp Park Trail 1100, Chilton Trail 1170, and Forest Roads 471 and 471.1B to make a 11.4-mile loop hike with about 1,400 feet of elevation gain and loss.

The trail ends near Swamp Park, the marshy zone located south of the trail junction with Swamp Park Trail. This park holds water within the remnants of a glacial moraine left over from the last ice age.

DIFFICULTY
Above Average, 1,400-foot climb in 2.6 miles

TOTAL LENGTH
3.3 miles

SCENERY
Below Average, travels through spruce-fir forest

USAGE
Light

ALLOWED USES
Hikers and pack stock only are allowed on this trail.

ACCESS
15 This trail begins at Roaring Fork Trailhead, see page 59.

MAPS
Trails Illustrated: #117 Clark Buffalo Pass
USGS 7.5' Quadrangle: Floyd Peak

WAYPOINTS
Roaring Fork Trailhead marks the beginning of the trail at 0 miles
User trail that follows Roaring Fork Creek meets trail — 0.9 miles
Mount Zirkel Wilderness boundary — 2.9 miles
The intersection with Swamp Park 1100 marks the end of the trail at 3.3 miles

TRAIL DESCRIPTION
Roaring Fork Trail 1166 climbs around the shoulder of an unnamed mountain through spruce-fir forest on its way to Swamp Park. The path follows Roaring Fork Creek about a mile before traversing ridges that surround the mountain's peak. The path then drops into a meadow adjacent to Swamp Park where it intersects Swamp Park Trail. You won't be able to find campsites that meet U.S. Forest Service regulations and Leave No Trace guidelines along this trail until it nears Swamp Park.

Roaring Fork Trail begins to climb immediately from the trailhead. At 0.2 miles, the path reaches Roaring Fork Creek and begins to follow its course. The climb is steep and rocky along this section of the trail.

At 0.9 miles, the path crosses a small tributary to the creek, and a user trail branches east. A sign marks the continuation of Roaring Fork Trail, which maintains its course following the main flow of the creek.

The user trail that branches off to the east here travels up the north side of Roaring Fork Creek through a 2.3-mile trek to Swamp Park Trail. This trail was in good shape

ELEVATION PROFILE

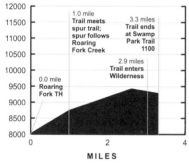

MILES

when I traveled it in 2002. There were a few downed trees across the path, but the route was distinct and marked with axe blazes throughout. Since this is only a user trail (which means it's not maintained by the U.S. Forest Service), this could change with the passing of a single storm. So use this trail with caution and at your own discretion.

Roaring Fork Trail crosses Roaring Fork Creek at 1.0 miles. It then follows upstream for about 100 yards before turning to follow a tributary of the creek. The path crosses this tributary at 1.2 miles and begins to traverse a ridge, steadily climbing. As the trail continues, the climb becomes more moderate when it traverses a series of ridges. You'll discover some relatively level sections along this portion of the trail, as well as more climbing.

The path reaches its greatest elevation at about 2.6 miles and begins to descend toward Swamp Park.

A sign marks the Mount Zirkel Wilderness boundary at 2.9 miles. The path continues through spruce-fir forest and scattered boulders here.

At 3.1 miles, a large meadow comes into view ahead and to the right of the trail. The path travels around the north edge of this meadow about 200 yards before entering it. At the 3.3-mile mark, a sign in the middle of this meadow marks the junction with Swamp Park Trail 1100.

Roxy Ann Lake Trail 1179

Roxy Ann Lake Trail 1179 runs west to east from its junction with Rainbow Lake Trail to its terminus at the Roxy Ann Lake. Descending 1,000 feet along the way to the lake, this trail sees light use. But it offers a one-way trip to a very beautiful, secluded mountain lake.

The landscape along the trek to Roxy Ann Lake is dominated by glacially sculpted and polished bedrock left over from when the glacier filled Red Canyon during the last ice age. The glacier carved the valley floor in stair-step fashion, leaving Roxy Ann Lake along its path.

DIFFICULTY
Above Average, 1,000 foot descent in 1.7 miles, trail indistinct in sections

TOTAL LENGTH
1.7 miles

SCENERY
Average, with beautiful lake and heavily glaciated landscape

USAGE
Light

ALLOWED USES
Hikers and pack stock only are allowed on this trail. The U.S. Forest Service does not recommend this trail for horses, due to its steep and treacherous nature.

ACCESS
Roxy Ann Lake Trail begins at Rainbow Lake Trail, 8.1 miles west of Rainbow Trailhead.

MAPS
Trails Illustrated: #117 Clark Buffalo Pass
USGS 7.5' Quadrangles: Pitchpine Mountain, Mount Ethel

WAYPOINTS
The intersection with Rainbow Lake Trail 1130 marks the beginning of the trail at 0 miles
Roxy Ann Lake marks the end of the trail at 1.7 miles

TRAIL DESCRIPTION
Roxy Ann Lake Trail 1179 begins where it intersects Rainbow Lake Trail and heads east toward its terminus at Roxy Ann Lake. You'll have a hard time finding campsites that meet U.S. Forest Service regulations and Leave No Trace guidelines along most of this trail.

The upper sections of the trail travel through subalpine meadow where it may be very muddy in certain areas during early summer. The lower sections of this trail are reminiscent of slickrock desert hikes where you descend valleys along seams in the bedrock. But unlike sandstone, this trail travels on quartz monzonite bedrock of the Mount Ethel Pluton. The bedrock crumbles easier than sandstone, leaving loose rocky footing along this difficult descent.

When the trail begins to descend into Red Canyon, it becomes indistinct in sections, but cairns help guide the way. At 0.5 miles, a post marks the path where you cross a small trickle of a stream.

At 0.8 miles, you can see Roxy Ann Lake for the first time. The trail then descends steeply over loose rocky footing. At 0.9 miles, you'll cross a stream below a waterfall. At about 1.1 miles, you'll notice a small pool south of the trail. Look to the west to see the sculpted bedrock step.

ELEVATION PROFILE

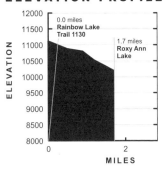

Two-tenths of a mile above the lake itself, you'll cross the stream that feeds Roxy Ann Lake at 1.5 miles.

Roxy Ann Lake

Saddle Trail 1140

Saddle Trail 1140 runs south to north from Swamp Park Trail to Red Dirt Trail. This trail provides loop mountain biking or hiking options with Red Dirt Trail, Swamp Park Trail, and Routt County Road 129. You can combine Red Dirt Trail, Swamp Park Trail, Saddle Trail, and Routt County Road 129 for a 5.7-mile loop hike with about 800 feet of elevation gain and loss, or you can combine Saddle Trail 1140 with Red Dirt Trail and Swamp Park Trail for longer loops up Mad Creek and back without using Routt County Road 129.

DIFFICULTY
Average, relatively small elevation gains

TOTAL LENGTH
1.1 miles

SCENERY
Average

USAGE
Moderate to Heavy

ALLOWED USES
Hikers, pack stock, and mountain bikes are allowed on the trail, but motorized use is not.

ACCESS
Saddle Trail begins at Swamp Park Trail 1100, 1.6 miles west of the Mad Creek Trailhead and ends at Red Dirt Trail 1171, 1.8 miles west of Red Dirt Trailhead.

MAPS
Trails Illustrated: #117 Clark Buffalo Pass
USGS 7.5' Quadrangles: Rocky Peak, Mad Creek

WAYPOINTS
Swamp Park Trail 1100 marks the beginning of the trail at 0 miles
Red Dirt Trail 1171 marks the end of the trail at 1.1 miles

TRAIL DESCRIPTION
Saddle Trail 1140 connects Swamp Park and Red Dirt Trails. The path travels through mountain shrublands dominated by gambel oaks and aspen groves. Mountain bikes are allowed on this trail along with hikers and horseback riders. However, this trail has neither water sources nor campsites.

Saddle Trail 1140 begins at Swamp Park Trail and goes north to its terminus at Red Dirt Trail. Both trail junctions are marked with signs. The trail leaves Swamp Park Trail and begins to climb immediately through thin aspen groves.

ELEVATION PROFILE

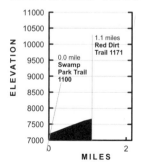

At 0.8 miles, the trail passes the first of three posts that mark it, but several user trails and old roads in this area might confuse you.

Soon after you pass the last post marking the trail, you'll reach the trail's high point at 0.9 miles.

At 1.1 miles, Red Dirt Trail 1171 intersects Saddle Trail, and a sign marks the end of the trail.

South Fork Trail 1100.3A

South Fork Trail runs west to east from the South Fork Trailhead to Swamp Park Trail. This trail provides access from Hinman Park via the South Fork of the Elk River to Swamp Park Trail 1100.

You can combine South Fork Trail with Swamp Park Trail 1100 and Forest Roads 400, 443, and 440 to make an 11.1-mile loop hike or mountain bike trek — with a difficult river crossing.

This trail crosses the South Fork of the Elk River, which has substantial flow all year. Your feet will get wet on this crossing, in your boots or out of them. You may want to bring along sandals for this trail.

DIFFICULTY
Below Average, relatively flat and easy to follow

TOTAL LENGTH
3.0 miles

SCENERY
Average, travels up the South Fork of the Elk River valley

USAGE
Moderate

ALLOWED USES
Hikers, pack stock, and mountain bikes are allowed along the entire length of this trail. Motorized use is not allowed on this trail.

ACCESS
 This trail begins at South Fork Trailhead, see page 60.

MAPS
Trails Illustrated: #117 Clark Buffalo Pass
USGS 7.5' Quadrangle: Floyd Peak

WAYPOINTS
South Fork Trailhead marks the beginning of the trail at 0 miles
South Fork of the Elk River — 1.4 miles
Swamp Park Trail 1100 marks the end of the trail — 3.0 miles

TRAIL DESCRIPTION
South Fork Trail 1100.3A travels on both sides of the South Fork of Elk River on its way to intersecting Swamp Park Trail 1100. The path initially travels over glacial till deposited south of Hinman Park from the glaciers that filled both forks of the Elk River. The path next crosses — then follows — the South Fork of the Elk River atop a bluff along its north bank. You can find campsites that meet U.S. Forest Service regulations and Leave No Trace guidelines on this bluff, as the trail travels through lodgepole pine forest and sage meadows.

The path begins by crossing meadows near the trailhead. You'll pass the trailhead register at 0.1 miles, and the trail continues southeast toward the hills to the south. You'll cross a small stream flowing under the trail in a culvert at 0.3 miles. The path soon reaches what appears to be a hillside south of the trailhead, but it is actually a deposit of glacial till. The trail enters this hummock-pocked terrain first in aspen, then spruce-fir.

At 1.0 miles, the trail passes through an opening in a fenceline. The path continues toward the southwest along a distinct tread.

At 1.4 miles, the trail crosses the South Fork of the Elk River. Your feet will get wet on this crossing, whether they are in your boots, in sandals, or barefoot. Plan on it. This stream constitutes a swiftwater drowning hazard during periods of high flow.

After crossing the South Fork of the Elk, the path follows along the north edge of its valley, skirting north of willow thickets. At 1.5 miles, the trail crosses a trickle of a stream where a distinct user trail follows the west side of the small stream. The South Fork Trail crosses the stream here, and it immediately begins a steep, rocky climb up the east side of the small stream toward a bluff north of the South Fork.

ELEVATION PROFILE

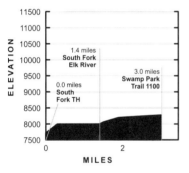

At 1.9 miles, you can find campsites that meet U.S. Forest Service regulations and Leave No Trace guidelines in the lodgepole pine forest south of the trail on the bluff. The path continues to follow well north of the river, occasionally entering the lodgepole pine forest, occasionally traveling through small sage meadows.

At 2.8 miles, the path enters a boulder field. This appears to be glacial till that was deposited in the lee of a ridge visible just ahead. At least 20 feet in diameter, a single boulder of what appears to be quartz monzonite from the Mount Ethel Pluton sits very near the trail here.

At 2.9 miles, the trail passes through an opening in a fence line where it comes along the side of the South Fork of the Elk River. The trail continues to follow the river upstream.

At 3.0 miles, a sign marks the end of the trail where it intersects Swamp Park Trail 1100 in a lodgepole pine forest. Swamp Park Trail 1100 continues eastward straight ahead or makes a 90-degree turn to the south here, soon crossing the South Fork of the Elk River.

Swamp Park Trail 1100

Swamp Park Trail 1100 runs south to north from the Mad Creek Trailhead to the Burn Ridge Trailhead. This trail provides access from points on the west side of the wilderness to the system of trails in the southern portion of the wilderness via Luna Lake Trail 1168.

Swamp Park Trail only intersects Luna Lake Trail, so it does not provide loop hiking options using trails only. However, you can form loop hikes via Crags Trail and Wyoming Trail if you use Forest Road 443 to connect Swamp Park Trail with either the North Lake or Three Island Lake Trails.

You can access the trail systems in the central and northern sections of the wilderness from the northern terminus of the Swamp Park Trail, at Burn Ridge Trailhead, via Forest Road 443 and Forest Road 400 (Seedhouse Road), following these roads to reach the Slavonia Trailhead or Wyoming Trail 1101 — northern section.

Swamp Park Trail gets its name from the marshy park located along the path. This park holds water because of glacial moraine remnants from the last ice age.

DIFFICULTY

Average, the length of this trail (and the variety of terrain it crosses) makes it average overall with more difficult sections and easier sections

TOTAL LENGTH

21.3 miles

SCENERY

Average, the length of this trail (and the variety of terrain it crosses) makes it average overall

USAGE

Light to Moderate, heavy near Mad Creek and Burn Ridge Trailheads

ALLOWED USES

Hikers and pack stock are allowed along the entire length of the trail. Mountain bikes are allowed from Mad Creek Trailhead north to the Mount Zirkel Wilderness boundary. Mountain bikes are also allowed from Burn Ridge Trailhead south to South Fork Trail 1100.3A. No motorized use is allowed on this trail.

ACCESS

 This trail begins at Mad Creek Trailhead (page 57) and ends at Burn Ridge Trailhead (page 54).

ELEVATION PROFILE

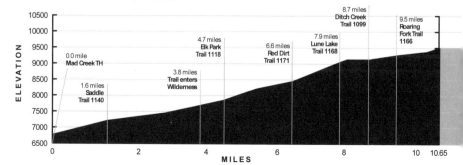

MAPS

Trails Illustrated: #117 Clark Buffalo Pass, #116 Hahns Peak Steamboat Lake
USGS 7.5' Quadrangles: Farwell Mountain, Floyd Peak, Rocky Peak, Mad Creek

WAYPOINTS

Mad Creek Trailhead marks the beginning of the trail at 0 miles
Saddle Trail 1140 — 1.6 miles
Mount Zirkel Wilderness boundary — 3.8 miles
Elk Park Trail 1118 — 4.7 miles
Red Dirt Trail 1171 — 6.6 miles
Luna Lake Trail 1168 — 7.9 miles
Ditch Creek Trail 1099 — 8.7 miles
Roaring Fork Trail 1166 — 9.5 miles
Roaring Fork Creek — 11.7 miles
Chilton Trail 1170 — 13.7 miles
Burn Ridge — 15.8 miles
South Fork Trail 1100.3A — 19.2 miles
Burn Ridge Trailhead marks the end of the trail at 21.3 miles

TRAIL DESCRIPTION

Swamp Park Trail 1100 travels along the west side of the Park Range over a wide variety
of terrain as it works north, passing through every ecosystem found in and around the
wilderness. Your journey begins in mountain shrublands, climbs through aspen groves
and lodgepole pine forests, and finally reaches spruce-fir forest south of Swamp Park.
The trail follows the course of Mad Creek initially, so it passes through various types
of mountain wetlands as well. You can find campsites that meet U.S. Forest Service
regulations and Leave No Trace guidelines in various locations along the trail.

The trail begins by following above the west side of Mad Creek. At 1.2 miles, you'll find a
large rounded boulder along the trail that appears to be quartz monzonite. This boulder
probably came from somewhere on the Mount Ethel Pluton, possibly near Margaret
Lake, and the glacier that filled Mad Creek transported it here. This is the first of many
glacial remnants you'll witness along the trail.

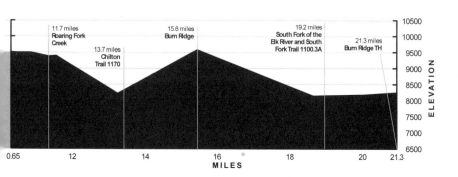

At 1.5 miles, the path reaches a gate marking the beginning of a wood fence. You'll see a couple buildings ahead, and the course of the trail becomes confusing here. The trail continues through (or over or around) the gate along the west side of the fence. Avoid using the well-worn path that cuts through the pasture east of the fence, traveling closer to the creek. Remember to respect property and livelihood, avoid the pasture and let the cows get fat in peace.

The well-worn path continues west of the wooden fence. At 1.6 miles, a sign marks the trail junction with **Saddle Trail 1140**. The Swamp Park Trail continues north here, passing by the buildings and entering a meadow to the northwest.

A sign marks the trail as it enters the meadow, and it soon begins to follow the fence line that is alternately wood or barbed wire. At 2.3 miles, the path reaches the end of the fence line and continues across an open meadow. You'll discover campsites meeting U.S. Forest Service regulations and Leave No Trace guidelines starting at this point and continuing for the next 0.8 miles.

As the trail continues along the valley floor, you'll see large quartz monzonite boulders courtesy of the frontal moraine of the glacier that carved Mad Creek valley. Notice the boulders do not match the exposed bedrock on the sides of the valley.

The path continues through the valley, entering and then leaving a small aspen grove. At 3.1 miles, the trail enters a large grove of aspen on the west side of the valley and begins climbing through a thick undergrowth of gambel oak and bracken fern. As the trail continues for the next 1.6 miles, the terrain is too steep and overgrown to allow camping.

At 3.8 miles a sign marks the **Mount Zirkel Wilderness boundary.** The path begins a rocky climb past the wilderness boundary sign, occasionally switching back as it climbs about 400 feet over the next 0.9 miles through dense underbrush and aspen.

The path finally levels out, and you cross Mad Creek at 4.7 miles. A few feet after crossing the creek, you'll reach a sign marking the trail junction with **Elk Park Trail 1118.**

Swamp Park Trail 1100 continues a short distance up the east bank of Mad Creek. At 4.9 miles, the path crosses Mad Creek again and turns north to climb the west bank of the creek.

After following the creek, the path turns to the west, climbing the west side of the valley. The views back down the valley are quite nice along this climb. The glacial sculpting in the valley is particularly evident on this section of the trail. The path switches back toward the east and the climb soon moderates and turns north. Remember it is illegal to shortcut switchbacks on National Forest land.

At 5.6 miles, the path reaches a relatively level section. You can find campsites that meet U.S. Forest Service regulations and Leave No Trace guidelines in various locations along the trail for about the next half-mile.

Upon reaching this section of the trail, you'll notice how the gambel oaks and aspen groves that were abundant below this elevation become scarce as the ecosystem transitions to spruce-fir forest. The path continues north through a subalpine meadow.

After leaving the meadow, you'll run out of opportunities for camping on the west side of the creek because it comes too close to the trail on the east side of the path (and the wall of the valley is too close on the west side).

At 6.6 miles, a sign marks the trail junction with **Red Dirt Trail 1171.** Another sign a few feet north indicates you are leaving the wilderness if you travel north.

The path moves north past the Red Dirt Trail junction through aspen groves and scattered boulders. You can find campsites that meet U.S. Forest Service regulations and Leave No Trace guidelines in various locations as you continue north, until you cross Mad Creek again. Cattle graze here in summer, making this area less than optimal for overnight stays.

At 7.2 miles, the trail crosses Mad Creek not far after passing a wilderness boundary marker that indicates you are re-entering the wilderness. Another sign on the east side of the creek points the way to Swamp Park.

Soon after crossing Mad Creek, the trail begins to climb the massive moraine left by the glacier that carved the North Fork of Mad Creek. This marks the end of camping opportunities until the climb moderates.

The moraine you climb here is the resting-place for the material excavated by the glacier that made Luna Lake and its basin. The path climbs through large rounded boulders and scattered aspens. You'll appreciate the views down Mad Creek valley as the trail traverses the moraine, climbing toward Swamp Park.

At 7.9 miles, the trail meets **Luna Lake Trail 1168** (and a sign marks the junction). Swamp Park Trail 1100 switches back to the northwest, and the climb soon moderates as you approach Swamp Park.

Swamp Park was formed by material impounded by the moraine left by the Mad Creek glacier. Mad Creek meanders slowly across this nearly level plateau. You can easily find campsites that meet U.S. Forest Service regulations and Leave No Trace guidelines as the trail heads north across Swamp Park.

After completing the climb to the Swamp Park plateau, the path travels through spruce-fir forest for a short distance. At 8.4 miles, the trail crosses the North Fork of Mad Creek.

Not far after crossing the North Fork of Mad Creek, a post marks Swamp Park Trail. The trail enters a small meadow as it continues north and becomes indistinct. Another post marks the path at the north end of this meadow, about 200 yards away from the first post on an approximate heading of northwest.

At 8.6 miles, the path enters and crosses the south edge the largest meadow of Swamp Park. You can see blowdown burned in the 2001 Mad Creek Fire to the northeast. A sign marks the old trail junction with Luna Lake Trail and indicates the trail is now 0.75 miles south of this point. Luna Lake Trail was re-routed in 2001 after the Routt Divide Blowdown.

Swamp Park Trail turns westward in this meadow and crosses Mad Creek heading toward another sign marking the Ditch Creek Trail junction. At 8.7 miles, a sign marks the trail junction with **Ditch Creek Trail 1099**. Swamp Park Trail continues north of here through spruce-fir forest.

At 9.5 miles, the trail enters a meadow where a sign marks the trail junction with **Roaring Fork Trail 1166**. The path continues north here, angling toward the west edge of the meadow. This meadow may be wet and marshy, and the tread may be faint or non-existent in sections. Be prepared to use your map and compass.

As the path continues northeast, it begins to follow the course of a small stream in the upstream direction. At 10.3 miles, the trail parallels the stream and begins to follow it closely, bending to the northeast. This marks the end of camping opportunities until you get close to Roaring Fork Creek.

As the path continues northesat, you can see a large area of blown-down and burned trees on the opposite bank.

At 10.6 miles, the trail leaves the side of the creek and turns north. The path skirts the west edge of burned wind-thrown timber and climbs a hill. The tread on the trail becomes indistinct where it crosses open meadow here, and you won't notice footprints again for about a half-mile. Some map and compass work may be necessary to stay on track through this section.

At 10.9 miles, you'll top the hill and take in beautiful views of the Sawtooth Range and Mount Zirkel to the northeast. A post marks the trail at the crest of the hill, and three more posts mark the trail toward Big Agnes Mountain.

At 11.2 miles, the path enters the forest and begins descending toward Roaring Fork Creek. The trail emerges from the forest at 11.7 miles into a meadow adjacent to Roaring Fork Creek. You can find campsites that meet U.S. Forest Service regulations and Leave No Trace guidelines in the vicinity of the creek.

At 11.7 miles, the trail crosses **Roaring Fork Creek** and passes a user trail that travels down the north side of the creek through its 2.3-mile trek to Roaring Fork Trail.

The user trail on the north side of Roaring Fork Creek was in good shape when I traveled it in 2002. I noticed a few downed trees across the trail, but the route was distinct and marked with axe blazes throughout. This is only a user trail, and it is not maintained by the U.S. Forest Service, so this could change with the passing of a single storm. If you choose to use this trail, do so with caution, exercising your own discretion.

The path climbs away from Roaring Fork Creek and continues north toward Big Creek. At 11.9 miles, you'll reach the edge of Big Creek's valley and begin a descent toward the creek.

The trail initially descends for about a half mile through scattered fir trees among mostly blown-down spruce trees near the summit. The path continues to descend more steeply toward Big Creek through a series of switchback turns across wind-thrown trees that cover the south hillside of the valley.

At 13.3 miles, the path emerges from the blowdown onto a small windblown shelf above Big Creek. The shelf is mostly covered in grasses and is marked with small cairns along the way.

At 13.6 miles, the trail crosses Big Creek. This crossing presents a swiftwater drowning hazard during periods of high flows because the water is deep and the gradient steep.

At 13.7 miles, **Chilton Trail 1170** intersects the trail. Marked with a sign, the trail junction is in a small clearing surrounded by spruce-fir forest, except for aspens toward the north. Near the trail junction, you can find campsites that meet U.S. Forest Service regulations and Leave No Trace guidelines.

The path continues from the north edge of the clearing, soon turning toward the northwest to begin a traverse up the north side of the Big Creek canyon. The views of the canyon are quite nice during the beginning of the climb.

The trail initially climbs through sage and gambel oaks along the lower reaches of the canyon. Then it jogs a short distance through two switchbacks before reaching the North Fork of Big Creek.

At 14.2 miles, the path crosses the North Fork of Big Creek. This crossing could prove deadly during periods of high flow because the stream descends toward Big Creek quite precipitously. The path continues to climb the north wall of Big Creek's canyon, traversing toward the northwest at this point.

Next you'll climb through a series of five switchback turns before beginning to traverse the north wall of the canyon heading northeast. The trail enters a light and airy aspen grove about halfway through the set of switchbacks, and it continues to climb through the aspens.

At about 15.0 miles, some spruce and fir trees begin to infiltrate the aspen stand as the trail continues to traverse toward the northeast.

At 15.3 miles, the path jogs slightly through two more switchback turns spaced about 40 yards apart before resuming its course northeast toward Burn Ridge.

At 15.5 miles, the trail reaches the area affected by the Burn Ridge Fire in 2002 and continues toward the crest of Burn Ridge.

At 15.8 miles, the trail tops **Burn Ridge** just after crossing the area affected by the fire. The path then begins to follow west of Burn Creek on a north heading.

Burn Ridge got its name from a wildfire that struck here in 1910, and 92 years later it was proved conclusively that lightning can indeed strike the same place twice. The Burn Ridge fire originated only about a quarter mile west of here in 2002 before burning a path that affected about nine miles and 16,000 acres of burned forest east of the ridge. Burned timber creates a mosaic pattern east of the ridge as far as the eye can see.

After cresting Burn Ridge, the path continues north, following the course of Burn Creek on the west side of the ridge along the creek. For the next 2.5 miles, the path travels along the ridge, mostly through spruce-fir forest. You'll cross occasional aspen groves along the way, and the voids from blown-down timber provide nice views in spots.

At 18.3 miles, the path crosses Burn Creek. The trail turns and continues to follow the creek for a short distance before entering a section of blown-down timber. Here the path turns to descend to the South Fork of the Elk River.

At 18.9 miles, the path passes through a fence line near a fallen tree. The trail soon reaches the floor of the South Fork of the Elk River valley after crossing the fence. You can find campsites that meet U.S. Forest Service regulations and Leave No Trace guidelines easily from this point until the path leaves the floor of the valley to ascend to Burn Ridge Trailhead.

At 19.2 miles, the path crosses the **South Fork of the Elk River.** This crossing is a swiftwater drowning hazard during periods of high flow. Even at low flows, it's not possible to get across the river in all but the highest hiking boots without getting your socks wet. Sandals could prove quite useful when trying to ford this river.

About 40 yards after crossing the South Fork of the Elk River, South Fork Trail 1100.3A intersects Swamp Park Trail. This trail junction is easy to miss if you are traveling north to south. The sign marking the trail junction is tucked away inconspicuously in the patch of forest where the trails connect.

When approaching the trail junction from the north, the well-worn straight ahead is South Fork Trail while the less-used path to the south that forms a T-intersection is the continuation of Swamp Park Trail. When traveling from the north, you'll find the trail junction in a patch of lodgepole pines the first time the path approaches within 50 yards of the South Fork of the Elk River. If you reach a boulder field and a fence line, you've passed the trail junction.

After the junction with South Fork Trail, the path travels up the South Fork of the Elk River valley. This is a beautiful walk through sage meadows with nice views of Mount Zirkel to the southeast. The trail enters a good-sized aspen grove on the valley floor at 19.7 miles, continuing up the valley after leaving the grove.

At 20.4 miles, the trail begins to climb out of the river valley. This marks the end of camping opportunities along the trail. The path rises through spruce-fir forest toward Burn Ridge Trailhead. The climb soon moderates, and the path continues north into an aspen grove. As it approaches the trailhead, the trail crosses a small regenerating clearcut.

After leaving the meadow, the path passes the trailhead register and ultimately ends at 21.3 miles at **Burn Ridge Trailhead.**

Three Island Trail 1163

Three Island Trail 1163 runs west to east from its origin at Three Island Trailhead to its terminus where it intersects Wyoming Trail 1101 at the Continental Divide. Three Island Trail is one of three trails connecting Wyoming Trail 1101 with Swamp Park Trail 1100 in the southern section of the wilderness. You can reach Swamp Park Trail at the Burn Ridge Trailhead 1.4 miles west of the Three Island Trailhead on Forest Road 443. The other two trails are Luna Lake and North Lake Trails, all of which can be combined to form various loops between the Continental Divide and the western base of the Park Range.

North Lake Trailhead is 1.4 miles east of Three Island Trailhead on Forest Road 443. You can combine Three Island Lake and North Lake Trails with a short section of Forest Road 443 and Wyoming Trail 1101 for a 13.8-mile loop hike to the Continental Divide and back with about 2,600 feet of elevation gain and loss.

DIFFICULTY
Average, 2,300-foot climb in 6.2 miles, easy to follow

TOTAL LENGTH
6.2 miles

SCENERY
Below Average, nice views of Red Canyon, Lost Ranger Peak, and The Dome near the Continental Divide

USAGE
Heavy, this trail sees almost as much use as the Gold Creek / Gilpin Creek loop leaving the Slavonia Trailhead (a poor choice for solitude and a true wilderness experience)

ALLOWED USES
Hikers and pack stock only are allowed on this trail.

ACCESS
This trail begins at Three Island Trailhead, see page 60.

MAPS
Trails Illustrated: #116 Hahns Peak Steamboat Lake, #117 Clark Buffalo Pass
USGS 7.5' Quadrangles: Mount Zirkel, Mount Ethel

ELEVATION PROFILE

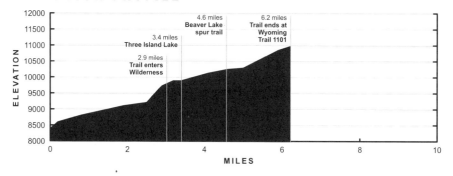

WAYPOINTS
Three Island Trailhead marks the beginning of the trail at 0 miles
Mount Zirkel Wilderness boundary — 2.9 miles
Three Island Lake — 3.4 miles
Spur trail to Beaver Lake — 4.6 miles
Wyoming Trail 1101 near the Continental Divide — 6.2 miles

TRAIL DESCRIPTION
Three Island Trail 1163 begins at Three Island Trailhead and heads east toward its terminus at Wyoming Trail 1101 and the Continental Divide. The trail treks along Three Island Creek through most of its length. You'll have difficulty finding campsites that meet U.S. Forest Service regulations and Leave No Trace guidelines along most of this trail, with some exceptions noted below. The trail generally travels through spruce-fir forest, and you'll pass through areas affected by the Routt Divide Blowdown along the way. However, wind-thrown trees have been removed from the path.

The trail begins its trek to the Divide by climbing a short distance from the trailhead to where Three Island Trail meets Trail 1163.1A, which comes from the west. You'll reach the trail junction at 0.2 miles, where there's a nice view of The Dome up the South Fork of the Elk River. The Three Island Trail continues to rise to the east through a spruce-fir forest.

At 1.0 miles, you'll cross a small stream after you enter a stand of aspen. The path crosses an open ridge for about a half-mile, beginning at the 1.3-mile mark from the trailhead. After leaving the open ridge, the trail soon comes within sight of Three Island Creek. For about the next half-mile, the path closely follows the course of Three Island Creek cascading down its channel. At 2.3 miles, the trail leaves the creek to climb through the forest.

At 2.9 miles, you'll reach the Mount Zirkel Wilderness boundary sign not far beyond the point where the trail rejoins Three Island Creek.

You'll notice a sign marking the beginning of camping restrictions in the Three Island Creek area, 3.2 miles from the start of your hike. Camping is not allowed within a quarter-mile of Three Island Lake. Wilderness rangers strictly enforce this restricted camping zone with no exceptions. If you camp within the restricted camping zone, you will be ticketed and forced to move.

The path then skirts the southern edge of a meadow before reaching the crystal-clear waters of Three Island Lake at about 3.4 miles. The trail works around the lake before beginning to ascend through spruce-fir forest.

You'll reach the sign that marks the end of the camping restrictions to the east of the lake at 3.9 miles. At 4.1 miles, the trail crosses Three Island Creek and proceeds through subalpine meadows from which you can witness glacial sculpting on the valley walls.

At 4.6 miles, the path crosses the stream that issues from Beaver Lake, which is about 0.2 miles to the southwest from this point. You can follow the stream to a few campsites that meet U.S. Forest Service regulations and Leave No Trace guidelines near Beaver Lake. This also marks the beginning of a section of the Three Island Lake Trail where you can find acceptable campsites.

At 5.0 miles, you'll cross Three Island Creek again. The path continues to parallel the creek as it rises. If you're looking for a spot, you'll find acceptable campsites in a small meadow to the north of the trail at 5.4 miles. But this marks the end of camping opportunities along this trail.

At 5.9 miles, the trail reaches treeline and you can see the sign marking the trail's end on the ridgeline ahead. You'll cross a stream that provides a reliable water source at 6.0 miles, the last opportunity for water along the trail.

A sign marks the end of the Three Island Trail at the junction with the Wyoming Trail 1101 at 6.2 miles on the windswept ridge of the Continental Divide.

Wyoming Trail 1101— Southern Section

Wyoming Trail 1101 runs south to north from the Buffalo Pass Trailhead to its terminus where it meets with Gold Creek Trail near Gold Creek Lake. From Buffalo Pass Trailhead to where it meets North Lake Trail 1164, Wyoming Trail 1101 is the southernmost segment of the Continental Divide Trail (CDT) described in this book. The trail follows the Continental Divide along most of its course, essentially dissecting the southern section of the wilderness along its north-south axis. Along the way, eight trails intersect Wyoming Trail 1101, four on each side of the Divide.

On the east side of the Divide, Newcomb Creek, Rainbow Lake, Lost Ranger, and Lone Pine Trails connect Wyoming Trail 1101 with Grizzly Helena Trail like rungs on a ladder, allowing various options for loop hiking. Likewise on the west side of the divide, Luna Lake, Crags, North Lake and Three Island Lake Trails provide access to Swamp Park Trail 1100, also allowing loop hiking options.

DIFFICULTY
Below Average, moderate elevation gains, easy to follow

TOTAL LENGTH
20.3 miles

SCENERY
Above Average, views of North Park and Rawah peaks in spots after about 3.0 miles, also views of the Flat Tops Mountains, Rabbit Ears Range, and the Elkhead Mountains

USAGE
Very Heavy near Buffalo Pass, moderate use north of Luna Lake Trail

ALLOWED USES
Hikers and pack stock only are allowed on this trail.

ACCESS
This trail section begins at Buffalo Pass Trailhead (see page 54) and ends at Gold Creek Trail 3.4 miles east of Slavonia Trailhead.

MAPS
Trails Illustrated: #116 Hahns Peak Steamboat Lake, #117 Clark Buffalo Pass
USGS 7.5' Quadrangles: Buffalo Pass, Mount Ethel, Mount Zirkel

ELEVATION PROFILE

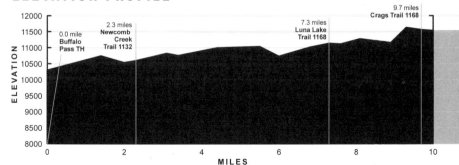

WAYPOINTS
Buffalo Pass Trailhead marks the beginning of the trail at 0 miles
Newcomb Creek Trail 1132 — 2.3 miles
Luna Lake Trail 1168 (near Lake Elbert) — 7.3 miles
Crags Trail 1182 — 9.7 miles
Rainbow Lake Trail 1130 — 11.0 miles
Lost Ranger Peak summit plateau — 12.6 miles
Lost Ranger Trail 1130 — 14.2 miles
North Lake Trail 1164 — 15.4 miles
Three Island Lake Trail 1163 — 16.2 miles
Lone Pine Trail 1129 — 18.1 miles
Gold Creek Lake Trail 1150 marks the end of the trail at 20.3 miles

TRAIL DESCRIPTION
Wyoming Trail 1101 begins in thin stands of spruce-fir forest at the Buffalo Pass Trailhead and heads north toward its terminus near Gold Creek Lake. Wyoming Trail travels primarily in alpine meadows near treeline through scattered forest and krummholz, generally following the course of the Continental Divide until it drops into the Gold Creek drainage on the west side of the Divide.

It is unwise to attempt camping along high mountain ridges due to the ever-present danger of high winds and lightning. Since this trail stays mainly on or near the Continental Divide, it's best to descend to find shelter.

The trail crosses the Buffalo Pass Road near the trailhead. You'll find the Mount Zirkel Wilderness boundary sign at 0.3 miles into your journey. The trail continues north on a gentle climb through thin stands of Englemann spruce and subalpine fir.

At 1.0 miles, the trail enters alpine meadows that open up to reveal pleasing views to the east and west. Also at about this point, the trail passes by a banded slate outcropping to the west. The outcrop shows glacial sculpting over its top, revealing that a glacial cap covered this section of the Continental Divide during previous ice ages.

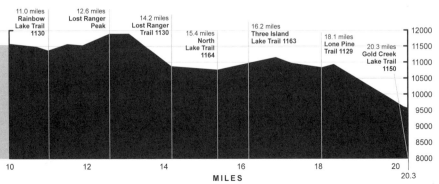

The trail continues its gentle climb until, at about 1.4 mile point, you crest the first hill and catch a glimpse of Mount Ethel to the north. You can see the course of the trail for some distance ahead from this point.

The path then begins a gentle descent that flattens at 2.0 miles at the base of the first depression it crosses. You'll see pools of water to the west of the trail. The path then climbs north once again.

At 2.3 miles, Wyoming Trail 1101 meets with **Newcomb Creek Trail 1132.** From the trail junction sign, the Wyoming Trail continues north.

At 3.4 miles, the trail passes west of a small pond and climbs gently, eventually reaching a broad, flat ridgetop at about 3.6 miles.

At this point, the path enters a section where the ridgetop ends abruptly to the east at the edge of a cirque above the Newcomb Creek basin. You can see the cirque itself at the 3.8-mile mark where you come within a few feet of the edge of the precipice. The trail then moves away from the edge of the cirque, continuing to parallel it for about 0.3 miles before finally turning away. The views into the Newcomb Creek basin and beyond are quite spectacular from the edge of the cirque along this section of trail.

As the path continues, it begins traveling across bedrock of the Mount Ethel Pluton. This area is marked with outcroppings of grey-to-pink quartz monzonite. Since this rock solidified (or crystallized) deep within the earth's crust, you can see the crystals that formed within the rock during this relatively slow cooling process.

These large crystals tend to flake off as the rock weathers, leading to a coarse granular trail tread. The trail travels over this type of bedrock until it nears Lost Ranger Peak more than 7 miles to the north. In fact, the pluton is one solid rock of immense size formed during a single event within the earth's crust about 1.8 billion years ago. So you will be walking over a single rock for seven miles, traversing it at a relatively narrow point. The exposed surface of this rock is 18 miles across at its widest point.

At 5.5 miles, the trail reaches the southern edge of a deep valley that marks the upper reaches of the Newcomb Creek drainage. At this point, you can see Mount Ethel to the north, as well as the unique and beautiful effect of glaciers on the mountain.

As you look to the north, you will notice that the broad valley that marks the upper reaches of Newcomb Creek is quite dry. Its walls are sculpted and polished smooth, and the valley exhibits the U-shape that gives clues that it was carved by ice, not the erosive effects of water. You'll learn answers to the mystery of the origin of the large boulders found along the Newcomb Creek Trail here as well. The bedrock in this area should look familiar to Newcomb Creek Trail hikers who noticed the large rounded boulders along that particular trail.

A look to the northern side of the valley and beyond gives a glimpse of the terrain that will dominate the landscape for the next several miles. You'll see beautifully sculpted and polished bedrock, smooth clumps of grasses clinging to the thin veneer of soil that covers portions of the bedrock, and scattered spruce and fir trees that lend the landscape some coarse texture.

At 6.0 miles, the trail bottoms out in the dry gulch marking the upper reaches of Newcomb Creek. The trail then begins its climb up the north side of the valley. The views back into the Newcomb Creek basin and beyond are quite spectacular along the climb. You'll discover a pool of water to the east not far from the trail at 6.5 miles.

At 7.3 miles, the trail meets with **Luna Lake Trail 1168.** The well-beaten path continues toward Luna Lake here, while the Wyoming Trail 1101 continues on the fainter path to the north. The old jeep road that the Wyoming Trail often follows continues toward Luna Lake here.

The section of the trail from the Luna Lake Trail junction to the Crags Trail junction does not see as much traffic as other sections of the Wyoming Trail. Many hikers traveling through this area divert to Luna Lake, Lake Elbert, or Lake of the Crags where they can find campsites that meet U.S. Forest Service regulations and Leave No Trace guidelines. Wyoming Trail is sometimes hard to follow through this section, but rock cairns mark most indistinct sections.

The trail initially descends into a shallow gulch that leads to Lake Elbert, then climbs from this depression to a ridge where the gulch above Luna Lake lies ahead. From this ridge, you can see Lake of the Crags resting at the foot of an unnamed mountain to the northwest.

The trail then descends into the gulch above Luna Lake. Views toward Luna Lake below are quite nice as the trail treks north. At 8.9 miles, the trail passes a spring before climbing out of the depression above Luna Lake. The trail reaches a beautiful vista where The Dome and Lost Ranger Peak come into view at 9.3 miles.

At 9.7 miles, the trail meets with **Crags Trail 1182.** As you continue north of the Crags Trail junction, you cross a windswept plain to the northwest of Mount Ethel. You can find a series of pools to the east of the trail beginning at 10.0 miles and ending at 10.2 miles. The trail also travels through scattered krummholz along this section, until you reach a ridge where another depression lies ahead at 10.7 miles.

At 11.0 miles, **Rainbow Lake Trail 1130** intersects Wyoming Trail 1101. You'll find water about 150 yards to the east of the trail junction near the Rainbow Lakes Trail. Wyoming Trail 1101 continues north along a gentle climb through scattered krummholz.

You'll encounter a broad shallow basin at the base of Lost Ranger Peak next. Near the low point of this basin, at 12.0 miles, the bedrock transitions from quartz monzonite to the metamorphic volcanic rock that dominates the trail to the north. The trail is indistinct in sections here, but rock cairns mark the course through the basin.

The trail soon reaches the base of Lost Ranger Peak and begins to climb toward the plateau above. At 12.6 miles, you'll reach the southern edge of the plateau adjacent to **Lost Ranger Peak** and then cross the plateau to the east of the peak.

It's worth the hike to the edge of the plateau toward the east so you can take a look at Red Canyon. A rock outcropping along the eastern edge of the plateau marks a good vantage point. At 13.1 miles, the trail reaches the northern edge of the plateau and begins to descend from the peak.

At 14.2 miles, the trail meets with **Lost Ranger Trail 1131**. A few feet after the trail junction sign, Wyoming Trail 1101 crosses a small seasonal stream and then you'll continue north across a broad nearly flat meadow where the trail is easy to follow.

At 15.4 miles, a sign marks the intersection with **North Lake Trail 1164**. Another sign on the post indicates that the Continental Divide Trail continues north along the North Lake Trail. You won't find reliable water sources between the trail junctions with Lost Ranger and North Lake Trails.

The trail continues north from the North Lake Trail junction across alpine meadows before beginning a gentle climb toward a ridge along the divide.

At 16.2 miles, a sign marks the intersection with **Three Island Trail 1163**. As with the previous section, you won't find reliable water sources between the trail junctions with North Lake and Three Island Lake Trails. The trail is easy to follow along this section.

As the climb progresses north of Three Island Lake Trail, the views south to Lost Ranger Peak, The Dome, and the south face of Red Canyon continue to improve. At the Three Island Lake Trail junction, remarkable vistas begin to materialize to the north of Mount Zirkel and the Sawtooth Range.

The trail continues the gentle climb to the ridge ahead across thick grasses before becoming so indistinct you have to rely on posts and cairns across the meadows.

At 16.9 miles, the path crests the ridge at a very beautiful spot. To the north you'll see Mount Zirkel, Flattop Mountain, and the Sawtooth Range. To the south, equally nice vistas of Lost Ranger Peak, The Dome, and the south face of Red Canyon catch your attention. The views into the cirques containing Lake Katherine and Bighorn Lake are quite spectacular from the chasm rims east of the trail.

The trail continues north along a gentle descent into a shallow valley. It remains indistinct along this section, but it's marked by posts. At 17.3 miles, the trail reaches the bottom of the shallow valley where a spring provides a reliable source of water.

The trail continues its northward trek along the west side of a north-south trending ridge. The crest of the ridge marks the Continental Divide in this area.

The trail continues along the west side of the ridge before descending to the saddle above Lone Pine Creek. At 18.1 miles, you'll see a sign indicating an intersection with **Lone Pine Trail 1129.**

Wymong Trail 1101 continues north, climbing to another high meadow where, at 18.5 miles, you'll see pools of water to the west of the trail.

About 100 yards beyond the pools, the trail reaches the edge of the Gold Creek valley where Mount Zirkel, Flattop Mountain, and the Sawtooth range offer beautiful views to the north. The path begins its descent into the Gold Creek drainage.

At 19.0 miles, you'll reach a small meadow where you can find campsites that meet U.S. Forest Service regulations and Leave No Trace guidelines. The trail continues to descend until it crosses Gold Creek at 19.5 miles.

At 20.2 miles, the path reaches the valley floor where you can find campsites that meet U.S. Forest Service regulations and Leave No Trace guidelines until this section of the trail ends at its junction with **Gold Creek Trail 1150** at 20.3 miles. The trail junction is marked with a sign.

Luna Lake from Wyoming Trail 1101 southern section

MILES

0   1   2   3

- - - Trail
——— Secondary highway
——— Forest Service Road
- - - High-clearance road
······· Four wheel drive road
-·-·- Continental Divide

Lake / River
Trailhead
Campground
Restrooms
Water
Trailhead

Central Wilderness Overview

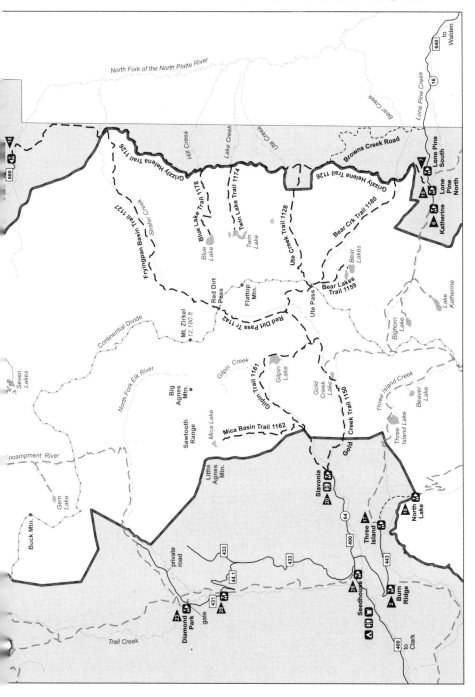

North Fork of the North Platte River

to Walden

Lone Pine Creek

Bear Creek

Ute Creek

Hill Creek

Lake Creek

Grizzly Helena Trail 1126

Browns Creek Road

Grizzly Helena Trail 1126

Lone Pine South

Lone Pine North

Katherine

Blue Lake Trail 1178

Twin Lake Trail 1174

Ute Creek Trail 1128

Bear Crk Trail 1180

Shafer Creek

Fryingpan Basin Trail 1127

Blue Lake

Twin Lake

Bear Lakes

Red Dirt Pass

Flattop Mtn.

Ute Pass

Bear Lakes Trail 1159

Continental Divide

Mt. Zirkel
12,180 ft

Red Dirt Pass Tr 1142

Lake Katherine

Bighorn Lake

Seven Lakes

North Fork Elk River

Big Agnes Mtn.

Gilpin Creek

Gilpin Trail 1161

Gilpin Lake

Gold Creek Lake

Gold Creek Trail 1150

Three Island Creek

Beaver Lake

Mica Lake

Sawtooth Range

Mica Basin Trail 1162

Three Island Lake

Encampment River

Little Agnes Mtn.

Gold Creek

Slavonia

20

64

Three Island

North Lake

Buck Mtn.

Gem Lake

private road

433

44.1

433

400

443

Seedhouse

Burn Ridge

Diamond Park

gate

431

28

Trail Creek

400

to Clark

Central Wilderness Trails At-a-Glance

Name	USGS Quads (Colorado)	National Geographic Trails Illustrated Maps (Colorado)
Bear Creek Trail 1180	Boettcher Lake, Mount Zirkel	#116 Hahns Peak Steamboat Lake
Bear Lakes Trail 1159	Mount Zirkel	#116 Hahns Peak Steamboat Lake
Blue Lake Trail 1178	Boettcher Lake	#116 Hahns Peak Steamboat Lake
Fryingpan Basin Trail 1127	Mount Zirkel	#116 Hahns Peak Steamboat Lake
Gilpin Trail 1161	Mount Zirkel	#116 Hahns Peak Steamboat Lake
Gold Creek Trail 1150	Mount Zirkel	#116 Hahns Peak Steamboat Lake
Grizzly Helena 1126 — Northern Section	Pitchpine Mountain, Boettcher Lake, Pearl	#116 Hahns Peak Steamboat Lake, #117 Clark Buffalo Pass
Mica Basin Trail 1162	Mount Zirkel	#116 Hahns Peak Steamboat Lake
Red Dirt Pass Trail 1142	Mount Zirkel	#116 Hahns Peak Steamboat Lake
Twin Lake Trail 1174	Boettcher Lake	#116 Hahns Peak Steamboat Lake
Ute Creek Trail 1128	Mount Zirkel, Boettcher Lake	#116 Hahns Peak Steamboat Lake

Difficulty	Scenery	Usage	Total Length (miles)	Page Number
Average	Above Average	Light to Moderate	4.0	132
Average	Average	Light	1.0	134
Below Average	Below Average	Light	2.0	136
Above Average	Below Average	Light	6.9	138
Average	Above Average	Heavy	6.2	140
Average	Above Average	Heavy	7.4	142
Below Average	Average	Moderate to Heavy	15.2	145
Average	Above Average	Heavy	2.9	150
Above Average	Above Average	Heavy	2.3	152
Below Average	Below Average	Light	1.8	154
Above Average	Average	Light	3.7	156

Central Wilderness Trailheads

Helena Trailhead (37.6 miles from the start)

18 **Starting at Walden,** drive 9.3 miles north on Colorado State Highway 14/125 to Cowdrey.

Turn west onto Jackson County Road 6W (CR 6W) at Cowdrey and drive 18.6 miles until meeting CR 6A at Pearl. *Note:* Winter maintenance on CR 6W ends 11.5 miles west of the turnoff from Colorado State Highway 14/125.

Turn south onto CR 6A at Pearl (toward where signs indicate the direction to Big Creek Lakes) and drive 5.6 miles until you reach FR 660 at Big Creek Lakes. *Note:* CR 6A becomes FR 600 at the National Forest boundary.

Turn left (east) onto FR 660 at Big Creek Lakes and follow it 4.1 miles southeast to the Helena Trailhead. *Notes:* Although it's possible to access Helena Trailhead via an alternate route of FR 609, it is not recommended because this route is much harder to follow and is blocked by a deep stream that must be forded just east of the trailhead. You'll find plentiful parking for vehicles and trailers at Helena Trailhead.

Lone Pine North Trailhead (19.3 miles from the start)

19 **Starting at Walden,** drive 0.6 miles west on Colorado State Highway 14/125 to the intersection with Jackson County Road 12W (CR 12W).

Turn west onto Jackson County Road (CR) 12W and drive 5.1 miles on CR 12W to where it meets CR 18.

Turn north where CR 18 meets CR 12W and continue 6.8 miles (north, then west) on CR 12W until it meets CR 16 between Sheep Mountain and Delaney Butte. *Notes:* CR 12W meets CR 18 at a T intersection where CR 12W turns to the north and CR 18 continues straight ahead.

Turn left onto the gravel CR 16 and drive 6.8 miles west on CR 16 to the Lone Pine North Trailhead. *Notes:* Winter road maintenance ends at Lone Pine Ranch, 2.2 miles west of the intersection of CR 12W and CR 16. CR 16 becomes FR 640 at the U.S Forest Service boundary, 5.1 miles west of the intersection of CR 12W and CR 16 (where you'll find a fence and parking area). If you're towing a trailer, you may want to leave it here to scout turnaround and parking opportunities further along FR 640, especially during holiday weekends. Lone Pine North Trailhead has parking for only three or four vehicles and no room for vehicles towing trailers. Lone Pine South Trailhead offers similar opportunities to park 0.5 miles east of Lone Pine North Trailhead and Katherine Trailhead provides parking for about six vehicles as well as room for a couple vehicles with trailers, 1.0 miles west of Lone Pine North Trailhead on FR 640.

Slavonia Trailhead (29.4 miles from the start)

20 Starting at the stoplight on US 40 just west of the Steamboat Springs city limits (US 40 and Elk River Road), turn north onto Routt County Road CR 129 (CR 129 or Elk River Road) and drive 17.5 miles to the intersection with FR 400 (Seedhouse Road). *Note:* Seedhouse Road intersects CR 129 past the Clark Store at Glen Eden, just after crossing the Elk River.

Turn east onto FR 400 and drive 11.9 miles to its end and the Slavonia Trailhead. *Note:* Winter maintenance on FR 400 ends about 5.5 miles east of CR 129, just past where FR 440 intersects it. Slavonia Trailhead provides parking for about 18 vehicles, but the parking area fills quickly, especially on weekends and holidays.

Bear Creek Trail 1180

Bear Creek Trail 1180 runs east to west from where it intersects Grizzly Helena Trail 1126 until it reaches Ute Pass and the Continental Divide. Along the way to the Divide, Bear Creek Trail 1180 meets Bear Lakes Trail 1159, which takes you to Bear Lakes.

At Ute Pass, Bear Creek Trail 1180 meets Ute Creek Trail and Gold Creek Trail. This junction offers options of hiking into the Gold Creek valley or back to Grizzly Helena Trail via Ute Creek Trail. Once you descend into the Gold Creek valley, you can access the Grizzly Helena Trail via Red Dirt Pass and Fryingpan Basin or Wyoming Trail and one of the other trails dropping off the east side of the Park Range from Wyoming Trail.

As you hike up the valley, you'll see significant deposits of rocks and materials scoured from the mountains above, remnants from glacial activity in the Bear Creek valley during the last ice age. You'll also see an abandoned mining cabin not far from the origin of the trail.

DIFFICULTY
Average, 1,900 foot climb in 4.0 miles, easy to follow

TOTAL LENGTH
4.0 miles

SCENERY
Above Average, spectacular views of North Park and Parkview Mountain in spots after about 1.7 miles, glacial features of the Divide

USAGE
Light to Moderate

ALLOWED USES
Hiking and pack stock only are allowed on this trail.

ACCESS
Bear Creek Trail 1180 begins where it intersects Grizzly Helena Trail, 1.6 miles north of the Lone Pine North Trailhead and 13.6 miles south of the Helena Trailhead.

MAPS
Trails Illustrated: #116 Hahns Peak Steamboat Lake
USGS 7.5' Quadrangles: Boettcher Lake, Mount Zirkel

WAYPOINTS
Grizzly Helena Trail marks the beginning of the trail at 0 miles
Pass an old miner's cabin — 0.4 miles
Bear Lakes Trail — 3.6 miles
Ute Pass marks the end of the trail at 4.0 miles

TRAIL DESCRIPTION
Bear Creek Trail 1180 begins at the trail junction with the Grizzly Helena Trail and heads west towards the Continental Divide. The trail follows the Bear Creek valley throughout its course, climbing between Bear Creek and Bear Mountain on the north side of the valley. Campsites meeting U.S. Forest Service regulations and Leave No Trace guidelines are never far away when hiking this trail. The path generally travels in

a forest of mostly lodgepole pine, Englemann spruce, and subalpine fir along its lower section. After the first mile, the lodgepole pines become less common.

The Englemann spruce and subalpine fir forest thins as the trail climbs to the Continental Divide, revealing nice views back down the valley. You'll traverse subalpine meadows near the summit where views toward Parkview Mountain and the Rabbit Ears Range are

ELEVATION PROFILE

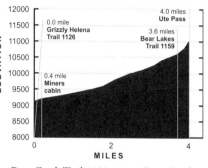

quite spectacular. Horse forage is adequate along Bear Creek, but it's scarce along the rest of the trail.

Two signs mark the origin of Bear Creek Trail 1180 at the Grizzly Helena Trail, and the Mount Zirkel Wilderness boundary sign sits about 100 feet west of the trail junction.

At 0.4 miles, the trail drops along Bear Creek near the ruins of an old mining cabin. According to the (Trails Illustrated) map, Bear Creek Trail 1180 crosses Bear Creek in the vicinity of the abandoned cabin. But I have searched for the location of the creek crossing (twice) and have found no visible tread leading across the creek. This trail description refers to the visible tread north of Bear Creek and west of the cabin, a route that leads to the continuation of the trail marked on the maps.

About 100 yards west of the cabin, tailings mark old mine activity on the slope to the north of the trail. From the mining cabin, the trail becomes narrow and rocky, sandwiched between the rocky hillside to the north and Bear Creek to the south.

At 0.6 miles, the condition of the trail improves as it continues to climb along the north side of the creek and follows the route marked on the maps once again.

At 1.7 miles, the trail enters an open meadow on the hillside. For the next 0.6 miles, you'll find yourself walking primarily through meadow rather than the wooded areas that have predominated to this point. Take in the views back to North Park and the Rabbit Ears Range beyond as you pass through this section of trail.

At about 3.0 miles, the trail crosses a large tributary to Bear Creek. The climb intensifies from this point as the trail continues toward the trail junction with Bear Lakes Trail 1159.

At 3.6 miles, only two small rock cairns mark the trail junction with Bear Lakes Trail (which goes southeast).

From here, Bear Creek Trail 1180 turns toward the northwest and scales a steep slope via a series of switchbacks. Not far west of the trail junction, Bear Creek Trail 1180 reaches a bench where you can camp. A depression on this bench may hold water through mid-summer.

The path then continues its climb to Ute Pass through a series of switchbacks. Only a cairn marks the trail junction on Ute Pass at 4.0 miles.

Bear Lakes Trail 1159

Bear Lakes Trail 1159 runs north to south from its junction with the Bear Creek Trail 1180 to its terminus east of Bear Lakes. The trail traverses relatively flat terrain for the first 0.7 miles before you face a steep descent and climb.

A glacier filled the Bear Creek valley during the last ice age, originating in cirques in the area of Bear Lakes. The quarrying action of the glacier is visible today on the headwall adjacent to the Continental Divide to the west.

DIFFICULTY
Average, trail is indistinct in two sections

TOTAL LENGTH
1.0 miles

SCENERY
Average, with views of glacial features near the Divide

USAGE
Light

ALLOWED USES
Hiking and pack stock only are allowed on this trail.

ACCESS
Bear Lakes Trail 1159 begins where it intersects Bear Creek Trail, 3.6 miles west of Bear Creek Trail's origin at Grizzly Helena Trail.

MAPS
Trails Illustrated: #116 Hahns Peak Steamboat Lake
USGS 7.5' Quadrangle: Mount Zirkel

WAYPOINTS
Bear Creek Trail marks the beginning of the trail at 0 miles
Bear Lakes mark the end of the trail at 1.0 miles

TRAIL DESCRIPTION
Bear Lakes Trail 1159 begins at its trail junction with Bear Creek Trail 1180 and heads south-southeast to its terminus east of Bear Lakes. Campsites meeting U.S. Forest Service regulations and Leave No Trace guidelines are never far away when you're hiking along this trail. The trail generally travels in subalpine meadows and patches of forest dominated by Englemann spruce and subalpine fir.

ELEVATION PROFILE

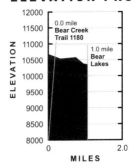

Two small cairns mark the trail junction with the Bear Creek Trail. From here, Bear Creek Trail turns northwest and scales a steep slope through a series of switchbacks. The trail to Bear Lakes goes toward the southeast.

At 0.1 miles, the trail becomes indistinct, although you can see a small cairn to the east from here. Toward the south-southwest, you'll be able to see a couple of small streams with a false trail on the other side. Bear Lakes Trail 1159 goes east toward the cairn. From the cairn you should be able to spot tree blazes that mark the trail ahead. At 0.2 miles, the trail crosses Bear Creek.

At 0.3 miles, the trail becomes indistinct again where it crosses a small meadow. You may be able to see where the trail re-enters the forest toward the southeast. You'll hike in a semicircle through the meadow, bowing toward the southwest around the muddy area in the center. A cairn along the path helps guide you. At 0.4 miles, the trail is distinct once again.

At 0.7 miles, the trail descends steeply for about the next 0.2 miles. At 0.9 miles, a steep climb returns you to the elevation of the lakes. Finally at 1.0 miles, you'll cross a significant stream where Bear Lakes Trail 1159 ends. From here, side trails lead to campsites meeting U.S. Forest Service regulations and Leave No Trace guidelines between the lakes and to the east of the larger lake.

Blue Lake Trail 1178

Blue Lake Trail 1178 runs east to west from its origin where it intersects Grizzly Helena Trail to its terminus at Blue Lake.

A glacier descended the side of Flattop Mountain and flowed toward the valley of the North Fork of the North Platte River during the last ice age. This glacier left its mark by excavating the basin for Blue Lake (which is 132 feet deep). The work of the glacier is also evident in the glacial sculpting along the climb and near the lake.

DIFFICULTY
Below Average, with a 700-foot climb in 2.0 miles, easy to follow

TOTAL LENGTH
2.0 miles

SCENERY
Below Average, but the trail ends at Blue Lake in a beautifully sculpted cirque on the side of Flattop Mountain

USAGE
Light

ALLOWED USES
Hikers and pack stock only are allowed on this trail.

ACCESS
Blue Lake Trail 1178 begins where it intersects Grizzly Helena Trail, 8.2 miles north of Lone Pine North Trail and 7.0 miles south of the Helena Trailhead.

MAPS
Trails Illustrated: #116 Hahns Peak Steamboat Lake
USGS 7.5' Quadrangle: Boettcher Lake

WAYPOINTS
Grizzly Helena Trail marks the beginning of the trail at 0 miles
Blue Lake marks the end of the trail at 2.0 miles

TRAIL DESCRIPTION
Blue Lake Trail 1178 begins at its junction with Grizzly Helena Trail 1126 and heads west toward its conclusion at Blue Lake. Primarily passing through spruce-fir forest, the trail treks along Hill Creek most of the way.

ELEVATION PROFILE

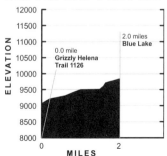

After you leave Grizzly Helena Trail, Blue Lake Trail begins climbing. At 0.4 miles, you'll cross a log boardwalk that marks the beginning of a trail section where you can find campsites meeting U.S. Forest Service regulations and Leave No Trace guidelines. At 0.6 miles, the path begins to parallel Hill Creek. Acceptable campsites become difficult to find starting at this point.

At 1.2 miles, the trail travels between a boulder field to the west and a large pool of water to the east. After the trail clears the north edge of the pool, you can find campsites that meet U.S. Forest Service regulations and Leave No Trace guidelines (for about the next 0.4 miles).

At 1.5 miles, the path crosses two streams in succession. Soon after you cross the streams, the trail turns and begins its final steep climb to Blue Lake.

At 2.0 miles, you'll catch your first glimpse of Blue Lake. The trail passes by a few campsites meeting U.S. Forest Service regulations and Leave No Trace guidelines as you approach the lake, but it's hard to find acceptable campsites within view of the lake.

Blue Lake

Fryingpan Basin Trail 1127

Fryingpan Basin Trail 1127 runs east to west from its origin where it intersects Grizzly Helena Trail 1126 to its terminus at Red Dirt Pass. This trail offers one of only three direct access routes to the headwaters of the Elk River from Grizzly Helena Trail on the east side of the Continental Divide.

This trail is extremely hard to follow from the 3-mile mark through a dense spruce-fir forest (where it's difficult to make compass sightings). Also, several downed trees along the path make travel extremely difficult, so only those with expert map and compass skills should attempt navigating this trail.

A glacier filled Fryingpan Basin between Flattop Mountain and Mount Zirkel during the last ice age and excavated the area. You'll notice an active rock glacier today in the basin below Mount Zirkel.

DIFFICULTY
Above Average, with 2,800 foot climb in 6.9 miles. No tread, ax blazes, or cairns along the final four miles of trail

TOTAL LENGTH
6.9 miles

SCENERY
Below Average, trail travels through forest until it reaches Fryingpan Basin

USAGE
Light

ALLOWED USES
Hikers and pack stock only are allowed on this trail. The climb to Red Dirt Pass is not suitable for pack stock.

ACCESS
Fryingpan Basin Trail 1127 begins where it intersects Grizzly Helena Trail, 11.3 miles north of the Lone Pine North Trailhead and 3.9 miles south of the Helena Trailhead.

MAPS
Trails Illustrated: #116 Hahns Peak Steamboat Lake
USGS 7.5' Quadrangle: Mount Zirkel

ELEVATION PROFILE

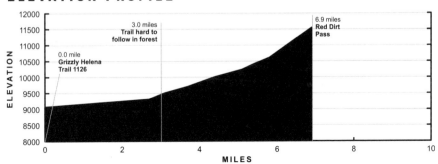

WAYPOINTS

Grizzly Helena Trail (just south of Shafer Creek) marks the beginning of the trail at 0 miles
Fryingpan Basin Trail becomes indistinct in thick spruce-fir forest — 3.0 miles
Red Dirt Pass and the junction with Red Dirt Pass Trail marks the end of the trail at 6.9 miles

TRAIL DESCRIPTION

Fryingpan Basin Trail 1127 begins at its junction with Grizzly Helena Trail 1126 and heads west toward its terminus at Red Dirt Pass, generally traveling in spruce-fir forest until you enter alpine tundra near Red Dirt Pass. For the first three miles of trail, you won't have a hard time finding campsites that meet U.S. Forest Service regulations and Leave No Trace guidelines.

The trail initially travels through a section with several downed trees. At 1.6 miles, the trail begins to parallel Shafer Creek for the first time. At 2.4 miles, you'll reach a sign marking the trail shortly before crossing a small stream. At 2.7 miles, you'll cross Shafter Creek, which could possibly present a swiftwater drowning hazard during peak spring runoff.

After crossing Shafer Creek, you'll find it harder to follow the tread. At about three miles from the Grizzly Helena Trail, Fryingpan Basin Trail 1127 dissolves into a labyrinth of game trails through a dense spruce-fir forest. You won't find tread, ax blazes, or cairns to guide you, but for the most part you'll continue along Shafer Creek until you near Fryingpan Basin.

After the tread disappears, you'll be forced to rely on map and compass skills to negotiate the remainder of the way to Red Dirt Pass. To complicate matters, traveling through a dense spruce-fir forest that obscures local landmarks makes map and compass navigation more difficult. And negotiating around numerous downed trees further complicates your quest. Do not attempt this trek to Red Dirt Pass unless you have rock-solid map and compass and backcountry survival skills.

At about 5 miles from the Grizzly Helena Trail, the trail shifts bearings toward Red Dirt Pass and emerges from the forest into Fryingpan Basin. The path then picks its way through the boulder fields in Fryingpan Basin along the final two miles to Red Dirt Pass. You need to negotiate these boulder fields with caution. The boulders can easily shift, potentially trapping or crushing you in the boulder field.

You can access the Mount Zirkel summit from Red Dirt Pass. See the Red Dirt Pass Trail description for details about reaching the summit from the pass.

Gilpin Trail 1161

Gilpin Trail 1161 runs west to east from its origin at Slavonia Trailhead to its terminus where it meets Gold Creek Trail 1150 for the second time. Since this trail meets Gold Creek Trail twice, you have the option to hike a loop through Gold and Gilpin Creek valleys. Mica Basin Trail (which allows access to Mica Lake) also intersects Gilpin Trail.

A glacier filled the Gilpin Creek valley to a depth of 1,500 feet in some areas during the last ice age. The cirque at the head of the Gilpin Creek valley is one the catchment basins that contributed to this glacier. The sculpted, polished, and striated bedrock you'll notice along the climb to the lake, and other glacial features surrounding the lake itself, show the work done by the glacier. The Hinman Fire affected some sections of Gilpin Trail during the summer of 2002.

DIFFICULTY
Average, 2,400 foot climb in 5.2 miles, easy to follow

TOTAL LENGTH
6.2 miles

SCENERY
Above Average, with views of Mount Zirkel, Lost Ranger Peak, and The Dome from the divide separating Gilpin Creek from Gold Creek

USAGE
Heavy, the Gold Creek / Gilpin Creek Loop sees the heaviest use in the wilderness. This trail is a poor choice for those seeking solitude and a true wilderness experience.

ALLOWED USES
Hikers and pack stock only are allowed on this trail. The U.S. Forest Service discourages horse use on all trails leaving Slavonia Trailhead because there is insufficient parking and the trails are so crowded in the area that stock use creates safety hazards for hikers sharing the trail. There are no suitable campsites for stock parties east of Slavonia Trailhead.

ACCESS
 This trail begins at Slavonia Trailhead, see page 131.

MAPS
Trails Illustrated: #116 Hahns Peak Steamboat Lake
USGS 7.5' Quadrangle: Mount Zirkel

ELEVATION PROFILE

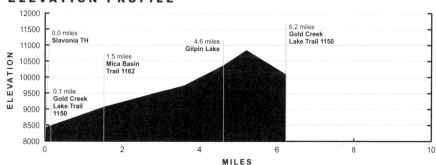

WAYPOINTS

Slavonia Trailhead marks the beginning of the trail at 0 miles

First intersection with Gold Creek Trail — 0.1 miles

Mica Basin Trail — 1.5 miles

Gilpin Lake — 4.6 miles

Gilpin Trail 1161 meets Gold Creek Trail for the second time, marking the end of the trail at 6.2 miles

TRAIL DESCRIPTION

Gilpin Trail 1161 begins at Slavonia Trailhead and heads east toward its terminus at Gold Creek Trail 1150. The trail climbs along Gilpin Creek until reaching the glacial cirque containing Gilpin Lake. You'll continue climbing past Gilpin Lake before descending into the Gold Creek valley to the trail's end at the Gold Creek Trail. You'll have a hard time finding campsites that meet U.S. Forest Service regulations and Leave No Trace guidelines along the length of the path. The trail generally travels in a spruce-fir forest, including areas affected by the Routt Divide Blowdown (although wind-thrown trees have been removed from the path).

The trail leaves Slavonia Trailhead and very soon reaches its first junction with Gold Creek Trail 1150 at 0.1 miles. This is the origin of Gold Creek Trail, which is marked with signs and a trailhead register. Gilpin Trail 1161 continues to the northeast here and begins to climb toward Gilpin Lake. You'll spot evidence of the Routt Divide Blowdown along the first two miles of the trail.

At 1.1 miles, you'll reach the Mount Zirkel Wilderness boundary sign. The trail meets with Mica Basin Trail 1162 at 1.5 miles. The trail junction sign indicates that Mica Basin Trail goes toward the north, but you'll stay on Gilpin Trail 1161 and cross Mica Creek at 1.8 miles.

As Gilpin Trail 1161continues toward Gilpin Creek, sculpted and polished bedrock along the path (with striations in some cases) show the work of glacial activity. At 2.5 miles, you'll first glimpse a meadow south of Gilpin Creek. At about 3.5 miles, the views down Gilpin Creek valley are quite nice, and you'll cross Gilpin Creek at 3.6 miles.

At 4.0 miles, a sign proclaims "No Camping Within 1/4 mile of Gilpin Lake." Wilderness rangers strictly enforce this restricted camping zone with no exceptions, so you will be ticketed and forced to move if you disregard the notice. The trail continues its climb past the sign until you reach Gilpin Lake at 4.6 miles.

The path then circles around the east side of the lake before climbing the headwall of the cirque containing the lake. At 5.2 miles, you'll top the divide separating Gilpin Creek from Gold Creek. Another sign reading "No Camping Within 1/4 mile of Gilpin Lake" marks the southern boundary of the restricted camping zone surrounding Gilpin Lake. From this point, you'll be able to see Lost Ranger Peak and The Dome to the south. The trail then begins a steep descent into the Gold Creek drainage.

A meadow comes into view to the west of the trail at 5.5 miles. Finally at 6.2 miles, the trail ends at its second junction with Gold Creek Trail 1150.

Gold Creek Trail 1150

Gold Creek Trail 1150 runs west to east for from its origin at its first junction with Gilpin Trail to its terminus at Ute Pass. This trail meets Gilpin Trail twice, allowing the option of a loop hike through Gold and Gilpin Creek valleys.

On the way to Ute Pass, Gold Creek Trail 1150 also meets with Wyoming Trail, which connects the network of trails in the central portion of the wilderness with the trail network in the southern portion of the wilderness. You can orchestrate loop hikes toward the south by returning to Slavonia Trailhead via Three Island Lake Trail or North Lake Trail and Forest Roads 443 and 400.

Red Dirt Pass Trail also intersects Gold Creek Trail 1150 on its way to Ute Pass. Since both Red Dirt Pass and Ute Pass offer access to the east side of the Continental Divide, you can complete loop hikes across the Divide via these passes and Fryingpan Basin, Grizzly Helena, and either Ute Creek or Bear Creek Trails.

During previous ice ages, a glacier filled the Gold Creek valley to a depth of 1,500 feet in some areas. You'll see the work of the glacier in the sculpted, polished, and striated bedrock along the climb to the pass. The Hinman Fire also affected the forest along the western end of the trail during the summer of 2002.

Ute Pass was so named because early explorers who entered the area noted how tree markings indicated this was the route used by Native Americans of the Ute Tribe traveling from the Elk River Basin to North Park.

DIFFICULTY
Average, 2,600 foot climb in 7.4 miles, easy to follow

TOTAL LENGTH
7.4 miles

SCENERY
Above Average, nice views back down Gold Creek valley near Ute Pass

USAGE
Heavy, the Gold Creek / Gilpin Creek Loop sees the heaviest use in the wilderness. This trail is a poor choice for those seeking solitude and a true wilderness experience.

ELEVATION PROFILE

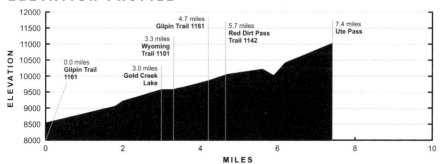

ALLOWED USES

Hikers and pack stock only are allowed on this trail. The U.S. Forest Service discourages horse use on all trails leaving Slavonia Trailhead because there is insufficient parking and the trails are so crowded in the area that stock use creates safety hazards for hikers sharing the trail. You won't find suitable campsites for stock parties east of Slavonia Trailhead.

ACCESS

Gold Creek Trail 1150 begins where it intersects Gilpin Trail, 0.1 miles east of the Slavonia Trailhead.

MAPS

Trails Illustrated: #116 Hahns Peak Steamboat Lake

USGS 7.5' Quadrangle: Mount Zirkel

WAYPOINTS

The point where Gold Creek Trail 1150 meets Gilpin Trail 1161 for the first time marks the beginning of the trek at 0 miles

Gold Creek Lake — 3.0 miles

Wyoming Trail 1101 — 3.3 miles

Trail meets Gilpin Trail 1161 the second time — 4.7 miles

Red Dirt Pass Trail 1142 — 5.6 miles

Ute Pass marks the end of the trail at 7.4 miles

TRAIL DESCRIPTION

Gold Creek Trail 1150 begins at its first junction with Gilpin Trail 1161 and heads east toward its terminus at Ute Pass. The first junction with Gilpin Trail is located 0.1 miles east of the Slavonia Trailhead. The trail treks along Gold Creek, and then along an unnamed tributary of the creek, before crossing the Park Mountain Range at Ute Pass. The path generally travels in spruce-fir forest, and you'll travel through some areas affected by the Routt Divide Blowdown. However, windthrown trees have been removed from the path.

The trail begins its climb following the Middle Fork of the Elk River. You'll use a bridge to cross Gilpin Creek at 0.2 miles where the trail begins to follow Gold Creek. At 1.0 miles, you'll come to a sign marking the wilderness boundary. The path continues to climb along the creek until you cross it at 1.8 miles. At 2.0 miles, the trail crosses Gold Creek a second time as it continues climbing toward Gold Creek Lake. These crossings are swiftwater drowning hazards during spring runoff. In fact, the trail above the crossing is likely blocked by snowfall during the spring runoff.

You'll reach the first of two signs that read "No Camping Within 1/4 Mile Of Gold Creek Lake" at 2.8 miles. Wilderness rangers enforce the restricted camping zone around Gold Creek Lake with no exceptions. If you disregard the restricted camping zone, you will be ticketed and forced to move.

At 3.0 miles, you'll reach Gold Creek Lake. The trail continues around the north side of the lake and then meets with Wyoming Trail 1101 at 3.3 miles where the trail junction sign shares its post with a second sign reading "No Camping Within 1/4 Mile Of Gold

Creek Lake." This marks the location where the path enters the restricted camping area around Gold Creek Lake when going west (and leaves it when going east). At this point, Wyoming Trail actually follows Gold Creek toward the Continental Divide to the south. Gold Creek Trail follows an unnamed tributary of the creek toward Ute Pass to the east here.

The Wyoming Trail junction also marks the beginning of camping possibilities within U.S. Forest Service regulations and Leave No Trace guidelines, but you'll pass beyond this area at about 3.5 miles when the trail resumes its climb toward Ute Pass.

At 3.7 miles, you'll enter a small meadow where you can find acceptable campsites in the vicinity. The trail continues to climb through spruce-fir forest after leaving the small meadow until you reach a second, much larger meadow at 4.2 miles. At this point you'll be able to see Ute Pass. The trail skirts the north edge of the meadow and travels along the hillside to the north of the valley floor.

At 4.7 miles, the trail meets with Gilpin Trail 1161 for the second time. This trail junction marks the end of the Gilpin Trail. Gold Creek Trail 1150 continues toward Ute Pass along the hillside to the north of the valley floor.

Gold Creek Trail 1150 is intersected by Red Dirt Pass Trail 1142 at 5.6 miles. This trail junction marks the origin of Red Dirt Pass Trail, which continues to follow the unnamed tributary of Gold Creek toward the Continental Divide and the pass for which it was named. Gold Creek Trail 1150 descends into the valley here to cross the unnamed tributary and climb the opposite wall of the valley toward Ute Pass.

At 5.9 miles, the path reaches the creek at the base of the valley and crosses the small stream to begin its climb to Ute Pass. The trail ascends through a series of switchbacks until at 6.6 miles, the path begins to skirt the base of a large boulder field (followed by a series of smaller ones).

At 7.4 miles, you'll reach the Ute Pass summit where the trail junction with Ute Creek and Bear Creek Trails is marked with only a cairn.

Grizzly Helena Trail 1126 —
North of Lone Pine North Trailhead

The northern section of the Grizzly Helena Trail 1126 runs south to north from the Lone Pine North Trailhead to the Helena Trailhead. The southern section of the Grizzly Helena Trail ends at the Lone Pine South Trailhead, 0.5 miles east of the Lone Pine North Trailhead on Forest Road 640. Lone Pine Trail 1129 begins at the Katherine Trailhead, 1.0 mile west of the Lone Pine North Trailhead on Forest Road 640.

Along the way north from Lone Pine North Trailhead, Grizzly Helena Trail 1126 intersects Bear Creek Trail 1180 and Ute Creek Trail 1128, two trails that provide access to the Gold Creek valley west of Flattop Mountain via Ute Pass. Fryingpan Basin Trail 1127 also provides access to the Gold Creek valley from Grizzly Helena Trail 1126 via Red Dirt Pass. These trails may be combined for hikes across the Continental Divide and back. Twin Lake Trail 1174 and Blue Lake Trail 1178 also intersect the northern section of Grizzly Helena Trail 1126, both permitting one-way access to scenic lakes on the eastern face of Flattop Mountain.

DIFFICULTY
Below Average, relatively small elevation gains, easy to follow

TOTAL LENGTH
15.2 miles

SCENERY
Average, nice views of North Park and Rawah Peaks

USAGE
Moderate to Heavy

ALLOWED USES
Hikers, pack stock, mountain bikes, and single-track motorized vehicles are allowed all along the trail. Double-track motorized vehicles are allowed north of Browns Creek Road (which meets the trail 3.9 miles north of Lone Pine North Trailhead) only. Browns Creek Road allows motorized access from Lone Pine Road (FR 640) north to Grizzly Helena Trail.

ACCESS
This trail begins at Lone Pine North Trailhead (see page 130) and ends at Helena Trailhead (see page 130).

MAPS
Trails Illustrated: #116 Hahns Peak Steamboat Lake, #117 Clark Buffalo Pass
USGS 7.5' Quadrangles: Pitchpine Mountain, Boettcher Lake, Pearl

WAYPOINTS
Lone Pine Road marks the beginning of the trail at 0 miles
Bear Creek Trail 1080 — 1.6 miles
Browns Creek Road — 3.9 miles
Ute Creek Trail 1128 — 4.8 miles
Twin Lake Trail 1148 — 7.3 miles
Blue Lake Trail 1178 — 8.2 miles
Fryingpan Basin Trail 1127 — 11.3 miles
Helena Trailhead marks the end of the trail at 15.2 miles

TRAIL DESCRIPTION

Grizzly Helena Trail 1126 winds along the foot of the Park Range between the mountain range and the North Fork of the North Platte River. The trail is relatively flat and easy to follow. As it continues along the base of the mountains, the path travels through a variety of terrains ranging from forests to sagebrush meadows to willow thickets. On this trail, you will often encounter forests of aspen, lodgepole pine, Englemann spruce, and mixed fir. These forests are separated by subalpine meadows or willow thickets on the valley floors adjacent to streams.

This trail lies outside of the wilderness boundary, so motorized vehicles and mountain bikes are allowed on it. Multi-track (four-wheel) off road vehicle (ORV) usage is not allowed from Lone Pine North Trailhead to where it meets Browns Creek Road. Multi-track ORVs may use Browns Creek Road to bypass this section of trail. Horse forage areas are scattered but adequate.

From the Lone Pine North Trailhead, the Grizzly Helena Trail 1126 climbs about 350 feet to the crest of the ridge south of Bear Creek. The path winds through an aspen forest on its climb to the ridge. At 0.2 miles, the trail passes rock outcroppings where you can catch nice views toward North Park and the Medicine Bow Range beyond. The trail then climbs toward the crest of the ridge separating Lone Pine Creek from Bear Creek, through the aspen forest. At 0.8 miles, as it nears the crest of the ridge, the trail enters a stand of lodgepole pine. At 0.9 miles, the trail crests the ridge where a seven-foot stump marks the start of a descent into the Bear Creek drainage.

At 1.5 miles, the trail crosses Bear Creek. This stream could present a swiftwater drowning hazard if you try to cross during peak spring runoff. Refer to the section on safer swiftwater crossing strategies.

At 1.6 miles, two signs mark the trail junction with **Bear Creek Trail 1080**. Bear Creek Trail tracks west from here, while Grizzly Helena Trail continues north.

After the trail junction with Bear Creek Trail, you'll climb through a series of switchbacks up a hill that's actually the moraine left by a glacier that flowed down the Bear Creek valley during the last ice age. The ridge is composed of glacial till, rocks and debris excavated by the glacier from Bear Creek Canyon and deposited where it reached its maximum

ELEVATION PROFILE

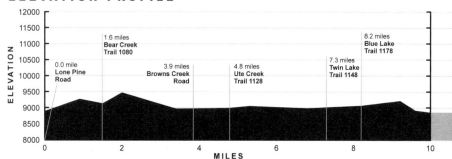

extent. At 2.0 miles, you'll top the ridge and travel a short distance over the flat crest before descending the other side.

As the path continues north, dropping toward Browns Creek, it passes through two clearings where views toward Rawah Peaks and the Rabbit Ears range are quite beautiful. At 3.4 miles, you will see a pond to the east of the path. You'll find plenty of campsites that meet U.S. Forest Service regulations and Leave No Trace guidelines from this point until after you cross Ute Creek to the north.

At 3.9 miles, you will cross a stream that meanders through willow thickets that make good moose habitat. The trail meets **Browns Creek Road** about 200 feet north of the stream. Although the trail junction is not marked, other signs here indicate the direction of travel of the Grizzly Helena Trail. You'll reach Browns Creek at 4.4 miles.

At 4.8 miles, a sign marks the point where the trail meets with **Ute Creek Trail 1128.** About 200 yards past the trail junction with Ute Creek Trail, you'll cross Lookout Ditch. You'll reach Ute Creek itself at 5.3 miles, where campsites meeting U.S. Forest Service regulations and Leave No Trace guidelines become difficult to find as you continue north (although you'll begin to find opportunities again near the junction with Twin Lake Trail).

At 6.2 miles, you can see a small marsh covered in willow pads to the east of the trail. A much larger marsh, also covered in willow pads, sits east of the trail at 6.8 miles.

At 7.3 miles, **Twin Lake Trail 1148** intersects the trail. Although it is possible to find campsites that meet U.S. Forest Service regulations and Leave No Trace guidelines near the Twin Lake Trail junction, choices decline between the Twin Lake and Blue Lake Trail junctions.

At 8.2 miles, **Blue Lake Trail 1178** intersects the trail. You'll find campsites meeting U.S. Forest Service regulations and Leave No Trace guidelines near this trail junction until about 0.3 miles north of the Blue Lake Trail junction where nice views of the North Platte valley await. At 8.5 miles, a section of trail begins where the path travels along a hillside, marking the start of campsite scarcity.

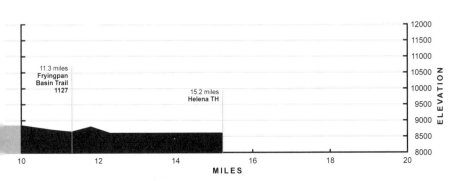

The path continues along the hillside until, at 9.2 miles, the trail begins a long descent. This descent ends near the elevation of the North Fork of the North Platte valley floor, at 9.6 miles. Here, an old road joins the trail from the east. This location marks the beginning of a half-mile section of trail where you can find campsites that meet U.S. Forest Service regulations and Leave No Trace guidelines.

At 10.1 miles, a sign viewed from the south marks the direction of the trail, and an old road branches toward the west. This location marks the end of the section where acceptable campsites may be found.

Grizzly Helena Trail northern section

At 10.8 miles, soon after entering a stand of aspens, you'll pass a well-used campsite near a large pond covered with lily pads to the west. Campsites meeting U.S. Forest Service regulations and Leave No Trace guidelines are abundant from this point until the Helena Trailhead is reached.

At 11.3 miles, the trail meets with **Fryingpan Basin Trail 1127** and continues north through the lodgepole forest (while Fryingpan Basin Trail goes to the west).

At 11.8 miles, be careful when you cross Shafer Creek, especially during peak spring runoff when it poses a swiftwater drowning hazard. Again, refer to the section on safer swiftwater crossing strategies.

The trail finally exits the lodgepole forest at 13.1 miles. From this point, the terrain alternates between forest and sagebrush meadows until it reaches the Helena Trailhead.

After exiting the lodgepole forest, the path soon leads you to the first of several irrigation ditch crossings, as you follow the ditch for 0.3 miles. The path travels through willow thickets and meadows before leaving the ditch, and then the trail continues across a sagebrush meadow for a short distance.

Soon after entering forest once again, the trail crosses Goose Creek at 13.9 miles. You'll cross Forester Creek at 14.3 miles, soon after re-entering the forest. The trail continues through lodgepole pine and aspen before entering willow thickets adjacent to the North Fork of the North Platte River, which you eventually cross at 14.8 miles.

At 14.9 miles, the trail joins FR 660 and heads northwest toward the **Helena Trailhead,** which you reach at 15.2 miles.

Mica Basin Trail 1162

Mica Basin Trail 1162 runs south to north from where it begins at its intersection with Gilpin Trail 1161 to its terminus at Mica Lake. This trail offers the only opportunity to venture into the heart of the Sawtooth Range on trail in the wilderness.

A glacier filled the Elk River valley during the last ice age to a depth of 1,500 feet in some areas, and Mica Basin is one of the catchment basins that contributed to this glacier. You'll see the work of the glacier in the sculpted, polished, and striated bedrock along the climb to the basin.

DIFFICULTY
Average, 1,400 foot climb in 2.9 miles, easy to follow

TOTAL LENGTH
2.9 miles

SCENERY
Above Average, with beautiful glacial markings in the valley and views to the south of Lost Ranger Peak, Mount Ethel, and The Dome near Mica Lake

USAGE
Heavy, this trail is a poor choice for those seeking solitude and a true wilderness experience.

ALLOWED USES
Hikers and pack stock only are allowed on this trail. The U.S. Forest Service discourages horse use on all trails leaving Slavonia Trailhead because there is insufficient parking and the trails are so crowded in the area that stock use creates safety hazards for hikers sharing the trail. Also, you won't find suitable campsites for stock parties east of Slavonia Trailhead.

ACCESS
Mica Basin Trail begins where it intersects Gilpin Trail, 1.5 miles east of the Slavonia Trailhead.

MAPS
Trails Illustrated: #116 Hahns Peak Steamboat Lake
USGS 7.5' Quadrangle: Mount Zirkel

WAYPOINTS
The intersection of Mica Basin Trail 1162 and Gilpin Trail 1161 marks the beginning of the trail at 0 miles
Mica Lake marks the end of the trail at 2.9 miles

TRAIL DESCRIPTION
Nowhere in the Mount Zirkel Wilderness is the work of glaciers so pronounced and striking than on the jagged peaks of the Sawtooth Range. Ice originated in two large cirques west of Mount Zirkel and flowed westward on each side of the Sawtooth Range, down the valleys where Gilpin Creek and the North Fork of the Elk River now flow. Mica Basin is the largest bowl where ice collected in the Sawtooth Range and eventually fed into the larger flows on each side of the range. The ice flowing from Mica Basin formed a hanging valley marked at its southern edge by a waterfall you can spot along the trail.

Mica Basin Trail 1162 begins where it intersects Gilpin Trail 1161 and heads north toward its terminus at Mica Lake. The trail follows Mica Creek along the way, generally in a forest dominated by Englemann spruce and subalpine fir with occasional meadows and willow thickets. You'll also hike through areas affected by the Routt Divide Blowdown, but the wind-thrown trees have been removed from the path. If you're looking for campsites that meet U.S. Forest Service regulations and Leave No Trace guidelines, your search will be limited to the area around Mica Lake.

When you leave the intersection with Gilpin Trail, the Mica Basin Trail almost immediately travels near Mica Creek. At 0.9 miles, the trail reaches a waterfall and switches away from the creek. You'll cross Mica Creek at 1.9 miles where the trail enters a meadow primarily covered in willows. The path continues toward Mica Lake, traveling along the west edge of the meadow.

The Hinman Fire burned through Mica Basin during the summer of 2002 and left several standing burned tree snags. Remember to keep an eye on these trees when traveling through the area, especially during windy periods.

You'll enter a second smaller meadow at 1.9 miles and get a good look at some very nice glacial sculpting along the west wall of the valley. Look for the areas where blown-down (and burned) trees have exposed the bedrock surface. The trail continues to rise, passing by polished, striated rock at 2.1 miles. At 2.3 miles, you'll skirt the east side of another small meadow. The trail begins its final climb to Mica Lake after passing this meadow.

You'll finally reach Mica Lake in a beautiful glacial cirque at 2.9 miles. Big and Little Agnes Peaks form part of the bowl surrounding the lake, where you can see Lost Ranger Peak and The Dome to the south. This is also one of the few spots where Mount Ethel offers a view from the north (it's usually obscured by Lost Ranger Peak in this part of the wilderness).

ELEVATION PROFILE

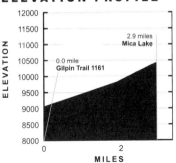

Red Dirt Pass Trail 1142

Red Dirt Pass Trail 1142 runs south to north from its origin where it intersects Gold Creek Trail to its terminus at Red Dirt Pass at the Continental Divide. The trail climbs 1,300 feet over 2.3 miles along its way to the pass. Red Dirt Pass Trail offers access to the Mount Zirkel summit from the pass, as well as access to trails on the east side of the Continental Divide via Fryingpan Basin Trail. Hiking into Fryingpan Basin gives you the options of loop hikes across the Divide via Grizzly Helena Trail and either Ute Creek or Bear Creek Trails.

A glacier filled the Gold Creek valley to a depth of 1,500 feet in some areas during the last ice age. The valley below Red Dirt Pass is one of several basins that contributed to this glacier, the work of which is evident in the sculpted, polished, and striated bedrock along the climb to the pass.

DIFFICULTY
Above Average, 1,300-foot climb in 2.3 miles, easy to follow

TOTAL LENGTH
2.3 miles

SCENERY
Above Average, nice views back down Gold Creek Valley and into Fryingpan Basin near Red Dirt Pass

USAGE
Heavy

ALLOWED USES
Hikers and pack stock only are allowed on this trail. The U.S. Forest Service discourages horse use on all trails leaving Slavonia Trailhead because there is insufficient parking, and the trails are so crowded in the area that stock use creates safety hazards for hikers sharing the trail. You won't find suitable campsites for stock parties east of Slavonia Trailhead.

ACCESS
Red Dirt Pass Trail 1142 begins where it intersects Gold Creek Lake Trail, 5.7 miles east of the Slavonia Trailhead.

MAPS
Trails Illustrated: #116 Hahns Peak Steamboat Lake
USGS 7.5' Quadrangle: Mount Zirkel

WAYPOINTS
The intersection with Gold Creek Lake Trail 1150 marks the beginning of the trail at 0 miles
Slavonia mining camp — 0.5 miles
Red Dirt Pass marks the end of the trail at 2.3 miles

TRAIL DESCRIPTION
Red Dirt Pass Trail 1142 begins at its intersection with Gold Creek Lake Trail 1150 and heads east toward its terminus at Red Dirt Pass. With the exception of the area around the old Slavonia Mine works, you'll have a hard time finding campsites that meet U.S. Forest Service regulations and Leave No Trace guidelines along this trail.

After leaving the trail junction with Gold Creek Lake Trail, Red Dirt Pass Trail 1142 climbs steadily toward the Slavonia Mine site. At 0.5 miles, the path travels by the ruins of some cabins that mark the location of the mine. Remember that it is illegal to disturb archeological sites on National Forest land. Soon after passing the cabins, the trail crosses a small stream, which marks the end of the camping area.

The path then climbs steadily along the hillside to the west of the creek leading to the pass, soon rising above treeline. At 1.5 miles, the trail crosses the creek and begins the final climb through a series of switchbacks toward Red Dirt Pass.

The views back down the canyon continue to improve along the final climb until the path crests the summit at 2.3 miles. Here, views into Fryingpan Basin mark the end of Red Dirt Pass Trail.

Red Dirt Pass offers access to the Mount Zirkel summit a little more than a mile toward the northwest. You'll climb a ridge adjacent to the pass before you reach the summit.

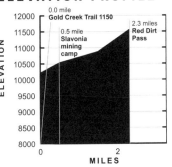

ELEVATION PROFILE

When you top this first ridge at about 0.3 miles, the route to the summit is obvious across a broad plateau. Remember that the Leave No Trace guideline for traveling on durable surfaces is especially important on the fragile tundra above treeline. These areas recover extremely slowly from damage, if at all, so it is very important to tread lightly here. If you are in a group, do not travel in single file.

The views into the cirques at the base of Mount Zirkel are truly spectacular along the way across the plateau. At 1.0 miles from the pass, you'll reach the base of the summit and face a final 150-yard boulder scramble to the summit. The summit of Mount Zirkel is the third rocky knob along this final ridge.

Twin Lake Trail 1174

Twin Lake Trail 1174 runs east to west from its intersection with Grizzly Helena Trail 1126 to its terminus at Twin Lakes.

During the last ice age, a glacier formed on the east side of Flattop Mountain and flowed toward the valley of the North Fork of the North Platte River below. This glacier excavated the basin for Twin Lakes and left sculpted rock outcrops west of the lakes.

DIFFICULTY
Below Average, with a 900-foot climb in 1.8 miles, easy to follow

TOTAL LENGTH
1.8 miles

SCENERY
Below Average, but you'll find a beautifully sculpted cirque at Twin Lakes on the side of Flat Top Mountain

USAGE
Light

ALLOWED USES
Hikers and pack stock only are allowed on this trail.

ACCESS
Twin Lake Trail 1174 begins where it intersects Grizzly Helena Trail, 7.3 miles north of the Lone Pine North Trailhead and 7.9 miles south of Helena Trailhead.

MAPS
Trails Illustrated: #116 Hahns Peak Steamboat Lake
USGS 7.5' Quadrangle: Boettcher Lake

WAYPOINTS
Grizzly Helena Trail 1126 marks the beginning of the trail at 0 miles
Twin Lakes mark the end of the trail at 1.8 miles

TRAIL DESCRIPTION
Twin Lake Trail 1174 begins where it meets Grizzly Helena Trail 1126, heads west, and ends at Twin Lakes. The trail treks along Lake Creek most of the way to the lake, generally through a forest dominated by Englemann spruce and subalpine fir. Forage is scarce, so the U.S. Forest Service does not recommend this trail for horse use.

ELEVATION PROFILE

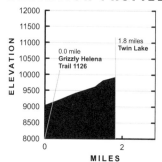

You'll find campsites meeting U.S. Forest Service regulations and Leave No Trace guidelines along the first 0.2 miles of the trail. Twin Lake Trail 1174 begins to parallel Lake Creek at about 0.5 miles, but at 0.8 miles, the trail moves away from the creek to travel in spruce-fir forest.

At 1.4 miles, the path reaches the first of three streams that it crosses in quick succession. The trail reaches Twin Lakes at 1.8 miles between a large and impressive boulder field to the south and a rocky ridge to the north. You'll find a few campsites that meet U.S. Forest Service regulations and Leave No Trace guidelines near the end of the trail.

Twin Lake

Ute Creek Trail 1128

Ute Creek Trail 1128 runs east to west from its origin where it intersects Grizzly Helena Trail to its terminus at Ute Pass.

At Ute Pass, Ute Creek Trail meets Bear Creek Trail and Gold Creek Trail. This trail junction at the Continental Divide gives you options for hiking into the Gold Creek valley or back to Grizzly Helena Trail via Bear Creek Trail. Once you get into the Gold Creek valley, you can access Grizzly Helena Trail via Red Dirt Pass and Fryingpan Basin Trails or Wyoming Trail and one of the trails descending the east side of the Park Range from Wyoming Trail.

Ute Creek and Ute Pass were so named because when early white explorers entered the area, tree markings indicated this was the route used by Ute Indians traveling from the Elk River Basin to North Park.

DIFFICULTY
Above Average, 2,200 foot climb in 3.4 miles, easy to follow

TOTAL LENGTH
3.7 miles

SCENERY
Average, beautiful views of North Park and Bear Creek Canyon from near Ute Pass

USAGE
Light

ALLOWED USES
Hikers and pack stock only are allowed on this trail.

ACCESS
Ute Creek Trail 1128 begins where it intersects Grizzly Helena Trail, 4.8 miles north of the Lone Pine North Trailhead and 10.4 miles south of the Helena Trailhead.

MAPS
Trails Illustrated #116 Hahns Peak Steamboat Lake
USGS 7.5' Quadrangles: Mount Zirkel, Boettcher Lake

WAYPOINTS
Grizzly Helena Trail 1126 marks the beginning of the trail at 0 miles
The intersection of Bear Creek Trail and Gold Creek Lake Trail on Ute Pass marks the end of the trail at 3.7 miles

TRAIL DESCRIPTION
Ute Creek Trail 1128 begins at its junction with Grizzly Helena Trail 1126 and heads west toward its terminus at Ute Pass. The trail treks along Ute Creek much of the way to the Continental Divide. Campsites meeting U.S. Forest Service regulations and Leave No Trace guidelines along this trail are limited to an area within about 1.4 miles of its origin. The trail generally courses through spruce-fir forest until it begins to travel above treeline at about 2.8 miles.

After you leave Grizzly Helena Trail, Ute Creek Trail quickly reaches the sign marking the Mount Zirkel Wilderness boundary. You'll reach a device for measuring precipitation at 0.6 miles.

From 0.7 miles to 1.4 miles, it becomes easier to find campsites that meet U.S. Forest Service regulations and Leave No Trace guidelines. You'll cross Ute Creek at 1.2 miles, and the trail continues to follow the course of the creek as it climbs.

At 2.0 miles, you'll cross Ute Creek a second time. The trail departs from the course of the creek after its second crossing.

At about 2.8 miles, the trail climbs above treeline. Views into the Bear Creek drainage are quite nice when you crest the divide between Bear and Ute Creeks on Bear Mountain at 3.2 miles.

The trail continues over the southern shoulder of Flattop Mountain, reaching its highest elevation at the 3.4-mile mark. The path then descends until you reach Ute Pass at 3.7 miles where nothing more than a cairn marks this trail junction.

ELEVATION PROFILE

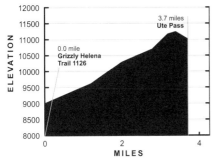

Northern Wilderness Overview

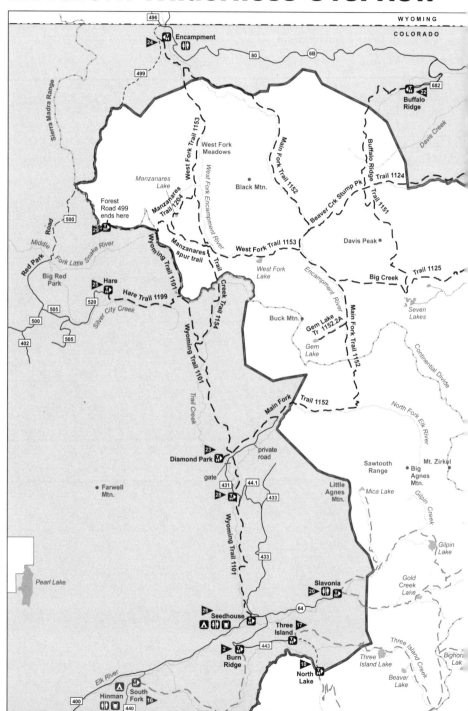

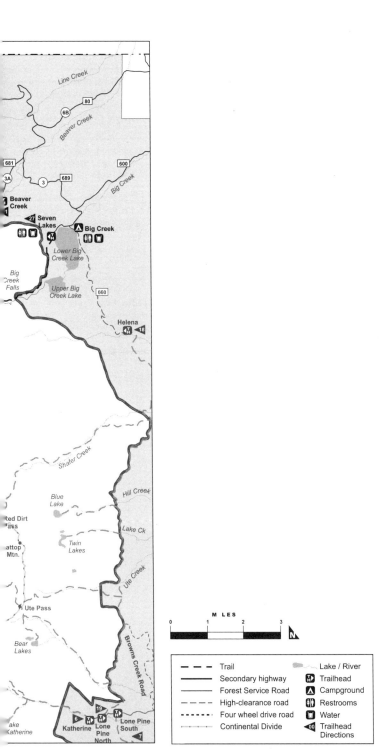

Line Creek

80
6B

Beaver Creek

681

600

3A
3
689

Big Creek

Beaver Creek

27 Seven Lakes

Big Creek

Lower Big Creek Lake

Big Creek Falls

Upper Big Creek Lake

660

Helena
18

Shafer Creek

Blue Lake

Hill Creek

Red Dirt Pass

Lake Ck

attop Mtn.

Twin Lakes

Ute Creek

Ute Pass

Bear Lakes

Browns Creek Road

Lake Katherine

19

6

Katherine

Lone Pine North

Lone Pine South

7

MILES

0   1   2   3

N

Trail
Secondary highway
Forest Service Road
High-clearance road
Four wheel drive road
Continental Divide

Lake / River
Trailhead
Campground
Restrooms
Water
Trailhead Directions

Northern Wilderness Trails At-a-Glance

Name	USGS Quads (Colorado)	National Geographic Trails Illustrated Maps (Colorado)
Beaver Creek Stump Park Trail 1124	Davis Peak	#116 Hahns Peak Steamboat Lake
Big Creek Trail 1125	Davis Peak, Pearl	#116 Hahns Peak Steamboat Lake
Buffalo Ridge Trail 1151	Davis Peak	#116 Hahns Peak Steamboat Lake
Gem Lake Trail 1152.2A	Davis Peak	#116 Hahns Peak Steamboat Lake
Hare Trail 1199	West Fork Lake	#116 Hahns Peak Steamboat Lake
Main Fork Trail 1152	Farwell Mountain, Mount Zirkel, Davis Peak, West Fork Lake	#116 Hahns Peak Steamboat Lake
Manzaneres Trail 1204	West Fork Lake	#116 Hahns Peak Steamboat Lake
Trail Creek Trail 1154	West Fork Lake	#116 Hahns Peak Steamboat Lake
West Fork Trail 1153	Davis Peak, West Fork Lake	#116 Hahns Peak Steamboat Lake
Wyoming Trail 1101 — Northern Section	Farwell Mountain, West Fork Lake	#116 Hahns Peak Steamboat Lake

Difficulty	Scenery	Usage	Total Length (miles)	Page Number
Below Average	Below Average	Light	5.4	166
Average	Above Average	Moderate	8.4	168
Average	Above Average	Light	8.1	171
Below Average	Below Average	Light	1.1	176
Average	Below Average	Light	2.5	178
Below Average	Below Average	Moderate	18.3	180
Above Average	Average	Light	2.1	185
Average	Below Average	Light	3.8	188
Below Average	Below Average	Moderate to Heavy	8.7	190
Below Average	Above Average	Moderate to Heavy	13.5	193

Northern Wilderness Trailheads

Beaver Creek Trailhead (37.2 miles from the start)

Starting at Walden, drive 9.3 miles north on Colorado State Highway (SH) 14/125 to Cowdrey.

Turn west onto Jackson County Road 6W (CR 6W) at Cowdrey and drive 18.6 miles until you meet CR 6A at Pearl. *Note:* Winter maintenance on CR 6W ends 11.5 miles west of SH 125.

Turn south onto CR 6A at Pearl (toward where signs indicate the direction to Big Creek Lakes) and drive 4.9 miles until it meets FR 689. *Note:* CR 6A becomes FR 600 at the National Forest boundary.

Turn right onto CR 3 / FR 689 and follow it 2.7 miles until you meet CR 3A / FR 681.

Take a hard left onto CR 3A / FR 681 and drive 1.7 miles to Beaver Creek Trailhead. *Note:* You'll find ample parking for vehicles and trailers at Beaver Creek Trailhead.

Buffalo Ridge Trailhead (40.3 miles from the start)

Starting at Walden, drive 9.3 miles north on Colorado State Highway (SH) 14/125 to Cowdrey.

Turn west onto Jackson County Road 6W (CR 6W) at Cowdrey and drive 20.3 miles until you meet CR 6B. *Note:* Winter maintenance on CR 6W ends 11.5 miles west of SH 125. You'll pass Pearl (where CR 6W meets CR 6A) 1.7 miles before reaching CR 6B.

Turn left (southwest) onto CR 6B and drive 8.1 miles west until it meets FR 682. *Note:* CR 6B becomes FR 80 when it enters National Forest land.

Turn left (south) onto FR 682 and drive 2.6 miles to the Buffalo Ridge Trailhead. *Note:* You'll find parking for about six vehicles and a couple towing trailers at the Buffalo Ridge Trailhead.

Diamond Park or North Fork Trailhead (34.2 miles from the start)

Important note: A high-clearance four-wheel drive vehicle is required to reach Diamond Park or North Fork Trailhead.

Starting at the stoplight on US 40 just west of the Steamboat Springs city limits (US 40 and Elk River Road), turn north onto Routt County Road 129 (CR 129 or Elk River Road) and drive 17.5 miles to the intersection with FR 400 (Seedhouse Road). *Note:* Seedhouse Road intersects CR 129 past the Clark Store at Glen Eden, just after crossing the Elk River.

Turn right (east) onto FR 400 and follow it 9.2 miles to the intersection with FR 433 (Lost Dog Road). *Note:* Winter maintenance on FR 400 ends about 5.5 miles east of CR 129, just past where FR 440 intersects it.

Turn left (north) onto FR 433 and drive 3.9 miles to the intersection with FR 44.1 (Stiletto Road).

Turn left (west) onto FR 44.1 (Stiletto Road) and drive about 2.1 miles, descending to a bridge that crosses the North Fork of the Elk River and FR 431 (on the west bank).

Continue north on FR 431 about 1.5 miles to the North Fork or Diamond Park Trailhead. *Note:* A high-clearance four-wheel drive vehicle is required north of FR 44.1. A gate on the road into Diamond Park marks the beginning of a private road. Avoid trespassing on private property in Diamond Park by only traveling on the trails in the park. Do not drive or walk on the road east of the gate near the trailhead. You'll find room to park about four vehicles (none with trailers) at the trailhead.

Encampment Trailhead from Walden (about 49 miles from the start)

Starting at Walden, drive 9.3 miles north on Colorado State Highway (SH) 14/125 to Cowdrey.

Turn west onto Jackson County Road 6W (CR 6W) at Cowdrey and drive 20.3 miles until you meet CR 6B. *Note:* Winter maintenance on CR 6W ends 11.5 miles west of SH 125. You'll pass Pearl (where CR 6W meets CR 6A) 1.7 miles before reaching CR 6B.

Turn left (southwest) onto CR 6B and drive about 19 miles until meeting FR 496 near the Encampment River. *Note:* CR 6B becomes FR 80 when it enters National Forest land.

Continue straight (west) onto FR 496 about 0.2 miles to the spur road to Encampment Trailhead. *Note:* You'll cross the Encampment River on a bridge immediately after meeting FR 496.

Turn left (south) onto the spur road to the Encampment Trailhead and drive about 0.2 miles to the trailhead. *Note:* You'll pass FR 499 along the way to the trailhead. You'll find ample parking for vehicles and vehicles towing trailers at the trailhead, located south of FR 496 just west of the Encampment River.

Encampment Trailhead from Steamboat Springs (57.3 miles from the start)

Starting at the stoplight on US 40 just west of the Steamboat Springs city limits (US 40 and Elk River Road), turn north onto Routt County Road 129 (CR 129 or Elk River Road) and drive 29.5 miles until it meets FR 550. *Note:* You'll pass through Clark, Glen Eden, and Hahns Peak Village along the way to the intersection, just north of Columbine, Colorado. Winter road maintenance ends at FR 550.

Turn right (northeast) onto FR 550 and travel 23.6 miles to where it intersects FR 496. *Notes:* You'll pass FR 500 near Little Red Park (at 3.6 miles along the way), and then you'll pass through Whiskey Park and into Wyoming before finally reaching FR 496.

Turn right (south) onto FR 496 and travel about 4 miles to a spur road to the Encampment Trailhead. *Note:* You'll reach the trailhead just before crossing the Encampment River on a bridge.

Turn right (south) onto the spur road to the Encampment Trailhead and drive about 0.2 miles to the trailhead. *Note:* You'll pass FR 499 along the way to the trailhead. You'll find ample parking for vehicles and vehicles towing trailers at the trailhead, located south of FR 496 just west of the Encampment River.

Hare Trailhead (38.5 miles from the start)

25 **Starting at the stoplight on US 40** just west of the Steamboat Springs city limits (US 40 and Elk River Road), turn north onto Routt County Road 129 (CR 129 or Elk River Road) and drive 29.5 miles until it meets FR 550. *Note:* You'll pass through Clark, Glen Eden, and Hahns Peak Village along the way to the intersection, just north of Columbine, Colorado. Winter road maintenance ends at FR 550.

Turn right (northeast) onto FR 550 and drive 3.6 miles until it meets FR 500 near Little Red Park.

Turn right (east) onto FR 500 and drive 2.6 miles until it meets FR 505.

Turn right (south) onto FR 505 and follow it 0.8 miles until it meets FR 520. *Note:* FR 505 meets FR 520 at a T intersection where FR 505 turns to the west and FR 520 continues straight ahead.

Continue straight (south) onto FR 520 and drive 2.0 miles to the Hare Trailhead. *Note:* You'll find room for about four vehicles and one or two vehicles with trailers near Hare Trailhead.

Seedhouse Trailhead (26.5 miles from the start)

26 **Starting at the stoplight on US 40** just west of the Steamboat Springs city limits (US 40 and Elk River Road), turn north onto Routt County Road 129 (CR 129 or Elk River Road) and drive 17.5 miles to the intersection with FR 400 (Seedhouse Road). *Note:* Seedhouse Road intersects CR 129 past the Clark Store at Glen Eden, just after crossing the Elk River.

Turn right (east) onto FR 400 and follow it 9.0 miles to the Seedhouse Trailhead. *Note:* Winter maintenance on FR 400 ends about 5.5 miles east of CR 129, just past where FR 440 intersects it. You'll find the trailhead on the south side of FR 400 near the Seedhouse Campground, and you'll also find ample parking for vehicles and trailers at the trailhead.

Seven Lakes Trailhead (34.2 miles from the start)

27 **Starting at Walden,** drive 9.3 miles north on Colorado State Highway (SH) 14/125 to Cowdrey.

Turn west onto Jackson County Road 6W (CR 6W) at Cowdrey and drive 18.6 miles until meeting CR 6A at Pearl. *Note:* Winter maintenance on CR 6W ends 11.5 miles west of SH 125.

Turn south onto CR 6A at Pearl (toward where signs indicate the direction to Big Creek Lakes) and drive 5.6 miles until you reach Big Creek Lakes. *Note:* CR 6A becomes FR 600 at the National Forest boundary.

Bear right at Big Creek Lakes and follow the signs 0.7 miles to Seven Lakes Trailhead. *Notes:* You'll find parking for about 10 vehicles and a couple vehicles with trailers at the trailhead. You'll also find running (drinking) water there.

Wyoming Trail 1101 at Stiletto Road (south of Diamond Park)
(32.7 miles from the start)

28 **Starting at the stoplight on US 40** just west of the Steamboat Springs city limits (US 40 and Elk River Road), turn north onto Routt County Road 129 (CR 129 or Elk River Road) and drive 17.5 miles to the intersection with FR 400 (Seedhouse Road). *Note:* Seedhouse Road intersects CR 129 past the Clark Store at Glen Eden, just after crossing the Elk River.

Turn right (east) onto FR 400 and follow it 9.2 miles to the intersection with FR 433 (Lost Dog Road). *Note:* Winter maintenance on FR 400 ends about 5.5 miles east of CR 129, just past where FR 440 intersects it.

Turn left (north) onto FR 433 and drive 3.9 miles to the intersection with FR 44.1 (Stiletto Road).

Turn left (west) onto FR 44.1 (Stiletto Road) and drive about 2.1 miles, descending to the North Fork of the Elk River, where Wyoming Trail 1101 intersects FR 44.1 just east of the bridge. *Note:* You'll find room to park a few vehicles on the west side of the bridge.

Wyoming Trail 1101 at Forest Road 499
(42.8 miles from the start)

9 *Important note:* A high-clearance four-wheel drive vehicle is required to reach the end of FR 499.

Starting at the stoplight on US 40 just west of the Steamboat Springs city limits (US 40 and Elk River Road), turn north onto Routt County Road 129 (CR 129 or Elk River Road) and drive 29.5 miles until it meets FR 550. *Note:* You'll pass through Clark, Glen Eden, and Hahns Peak Village along the way to the intersection, just north of Columbine, Colorado. Winter road maintenance ends at FR 550.

Turn right (northeast) onto FR 550 and drive 3.6 miles until it meets FR 500 near Little Red Park.

Turn right (east) onto FR 500 and drive 7.6 miles until it meets FR 499 at the Continental Divide (on the Sierra Madre Range). *Notes:* You'll need a high-clearance four-wheel drive vehicle after FR 500 leaves Big Red Park and begins to climb toward the Divide, about 5.8 miles along the way.

Turn right (south) onto FR 499 and drive 2.1 miles to where the road ends and Wyoming Trail 1101 continues. *Notes:* FR 499 is also Wyoming Trail 1101 as it follows the Fireline Trail south along the Continental Divide. The end of FR 499 is marked with a post. You'll discover parking for a few vehicles at the end of FR 499.

Beaver Creek Stump Park Trail 1124

Beaver Creek Stump Park Trail 1124 runs east to west from the Beaver Creek Trailhead to its terminus at the Main Fork Trail 1152 near the Encampment River. Along the way, it intersects Buffalo Ridge Trail 1151, which opens up possibilities for open-ended hikes (requiring shuttle) to Seven Lakes Trailhead via Buffalo Ridge Trail 1151 and Big Creek Trail 1125. Hiking to the Buffalo Ridge Trailhead via Buffalo Ridge Trail 1151 is another choice. The path ends at the Main Fork Trail, which provides access to the system of trails in the Encampment River drainage as well as the northern reaches of the Elk River drainage.

A glacier filled the Beaver Creek valley during the most recent ice age. This glacier left behind rocks and materials scoured from the valley above (such as the large boulders near the trailhead) as it retreated during the warming cycle following this period.

DIFFICULTY
Below Average, with a 1,000-foot climb in 3.3 miles, trail is easy to follow.

TOTAL LENGTH
5.4 miles

SCENERY
Below Average, with views of surrounding peaks near Stump Park

USAGE
Light

ALLOWED USES
Hikers and pack stock only are allowed on this trail.

ACCESS
◄21 The trail begins at Beaver Creek Trailhead, see page 162.

MAPS
Trails Illustrated: #116 Hahns Peak Steamboat Lake
USGS 7.5' Quadrangle: Davis Peak

WAYPOINTS
Beaver Creek Trailhead marks the beginning of the trail at 0 miles
Buffalo Ridge Trail near Stump Park — 3.3 miles
The trail ends near Encampment River about 5.4 miles from its start

TRAIL DESCRIPTION
Beaver Creek Stump Park Trail 1124 begins at the Beaver Creek Trailhead, heads west, and finally reaches the Encampment River. Campsites meeting U.S. Forest Service regulations and Leave No Trace guidelines are never far away when hiking along this trail, with the exception of three sections noted below. The trail generally winds through a forest dominated by Englemann spruce and subalpine fir along its entire length. Subalpine meadows or willow thickets along the course of Beaver Creek occasionally break up the forested areas.

The trail follows the course of the Beaver Creek valley for the first 3.3 miles before dropping into the Encampment River drainage. You'll climb about 1,000 feet to the divide that separates the Big Creek drainage from the Encampment River valley.

The first 0.7 miles winds along a hill strewn with boulders left by past glaciers on what is now the north side of Beaver Creek.

At about 1.4 miles, the path crosses an intermittent stream and begins to track along the hillside that flanks the north side of the Beaver Creek. From this point, you won't easily find campsites that meet U.S. Forest Service regulations and Leave No Trace guidelines along the trail until about 2.0 miles from the trailhead. As the path travels along the hillside, the trail is about 200 feet above the creek at its highest divergence. You'll come to the Mount Zirkel Wilderness boundary sign at 1.8 miles.

At 2.0 miles, the terrain near the trail flattens and provides camping options for the next half-mile.

ELEVATION PROFILE

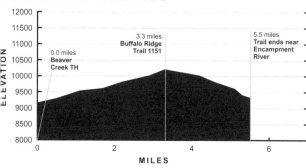

You'll reach the last reliable water source along Beaver Creek at about the 2.8-mile point. The next reliable water source along this trail is about 2 miles west.

At 3.3 miles, the trail intersects Buffalo Ridge Trail 1151 in a grassy area marked by a post. Beaver Creek Stump Park Trail 1124 continues west from the trail junction where it traverses the divide near Stump Park and begins to descend into the Encampment River drainage. Camping in accordance with U.S. Forest Service regulations and Leave No Trace guidelines becomes a possibility from near the trail junction until the descent to the Encampment River begins at 4.4 miles.

You'll see Stump Park to the north, and the trail crosses the park near its southwestern edge at 3.6 miles before returning to the forest. The trail becomes a bit indistinct where it crosses Stump Park, but a post marks it at about the midpoint of the crossing.

The descent into the Encampment River valley begins at about 4.4 miles, and campsites meeting U.S. Forest Service regulations and Leave No Trace guidelines become difficult to find from this point until about 4.8 miles, near where the trail crosses a small stream providing a reliable water source.

At 5.4 miles, the trail crosses the Encampment River. This ford presents a swiftwater drowning hazard during periods of high flow. Refer to the swiftwater crossing section in this book for safer river crossing strategies, and the links on www.mountzirkelwilderness.com access real-time reports of the Encampment River flow.

At 5.5 miles, only an uprooted tree marks the end of Beaver Creek Stump Park Trail 1124 where it intersects Main Fork Trail 1152.

Big Creek Trail 1125

Big Creek Trail 1125 runs east to west from Seven Lakes Trailhead to Main Fork Trail 1152 at the Encampment River. Along the way, Buffalo Ridge Trail 1151 intersects the path and provides options for open-ended hikes (requiring shuttle) to Beaver Creek Trailhead via Beaver Creek Stump Park Trail 1124. You can also enjoy open-ended hiking to Buffalo Ridge Trailhead via Buffalo Ridge Trail 1151. The trail ends at the Main Fork Trail, from which you can access the system of trails in the Encampment River drainage as well as the northern reaches of the Elk River drainage.

A glacier filled the Big Creek valley during the last ice age, sculpting and polishing the rock lining it. Material scoured from the valley above was deposited as moraine to form a natural dam impounding Big Creek Lakes. You'll see evidence of this in the Big Creek valley above the lakes and in the area near Big Creek falls, where the creek drops about 40 feet.

DIFFICULTY
Average, with a 1,600-foot climb in 6 miles (1,000 feet in 1.2 miles), narrow rocky trail is easy to follow

TOTAL LENGTH
8.4 miles

SCENERY
Above Average, with views of Big Creek falls and glaciated valley to help offset the tough climb

USAGE
Moderate

ALLOWED USES
Hikers and pack stock only are allowed on this trail.

ACCESS
 Big Creek Trail 1125 begins at Seven Lakes Trailhead, see page 164

MAPS
Trails Illustrated: #116 Hahns Peak Steamboat Lake
USGS 7.5' Quadrangles: Davis Peak, Pearl

ELEVATION PROFILE

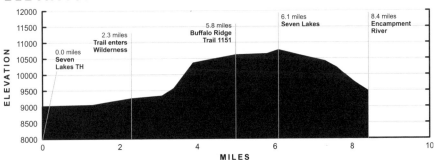

WAYPOINTS

Seven Lakes Trailhead marks the beginning of the trail at 0 miles
Wilderness boundary near Big Creek Falls — 2.3 miles
Buffalo Ridge Trail 1151 — 5.8 miles
Seven Lakes — 6.1 miles
Encampment River marks the end of the trail at 8.4 miles

TRAIL DESCRIPTION

Big Creek Trail 1125 begins at the Seven Lakes Trailhead and heads west toward its end at the Encampment River. The trail generally follows the course of the Big Creek valley for about the first six miles before dropping into the Encampment River drainage. The climb to the divide that separates the Big Creek drainage from the Encampment River valley is about 1,600 feet. The trail generally travels through spruce-fir forest along its entire length.

Big Creek Trail 1125 begins at the Seven Lakes Trailhead on the west side of the Big Creek Lakes. The first 0.6 miles travels along the hill that flanks the west side of the lake. You won't find opportunities to camp through this section. From 0.6 miles to 1.6 miles, the terrain flattens out a bit and camping opportunities become more plentiful.

Soon after you see the Mount Zirkel Wilderness boundary sign at 2.3 miles, you'll reach Big Creek Falls. You'll notice the glacial sculpting on the bedrock near the trail as you continue west of the falls.

Above the Big Creek Falls, the valley becomes flatter and you can find campsites that meet U.S. Forest Service regulations and Leave No Trace guidelines until you begin the climb out of the valley at 3.1 miles. Over the next 1.2 miles, the trail climbs 1,000 feet along the north side of Big Creek valley.

At 3.4 miles, the path crosses a small stream as it climbs, and you can search to the northwest of the trail here to find suitable campsites.

The path continues to rise past the small stream. The views of the Big Creek valley and of North Park and its sand dunes beyond are excellent near the end of the 1,000-foot climb that ends at 4.3 miles.

The trail continues to rise another 200 feet until you reach some scattered subalpine meadows at 5.0 miles. The path skirts these meadows as it continues west, revealing camping opportunities (in accordance with U.S. Forest Service regulations and Leave No Trace guidelines) from this point until just beyond the junction with the spur trail to the Seven Lakes area at 6.1 miles.

At 5.8 miles, a sign marks the point where the trail meets with Buffalo Ridge Trail 1151. Big Creek Trail 1125 continues toward the Seven Lakes area. At 6.1 miles, another sign marks the trail junction with a spur trail leading to the Seven Lakes area.

Located a short hike south on the spur trail, the Seven Lakes area is a beautiful expanse of mostly subalpine meadow with several shallow depressions filled with water. This area is far enough below the surrounding ridges for camping, and it offers plenty of camping opportunities in accordance with U.S. Forest Service regulations and Leave No Trace guidelines.

As Big Creek Trail 1125 continues toward the Encampment River, it becomes difficult to find campsites until you get close to the river.

The trail begins a long gradual descent toward the Encampment River, traveling along a hillside on the south side of the valley of a tributary of the Encampment.

You'll reach a short section where the tread is supported by logs on either side at 7.7 miles. At about this point, the descent becomes considerably steeper.

At 8.4 miles, Big Creek Trail 1125 ends where a sign marks its junction with Main Fork Trail 1152. The last half-mile of Big Creek Trail 1125 is steep and rocky.

Early-summer meadow along Big Creek Trail

Buffalo Ridge Trail 1151

Buffalo Ridge Trail 1151 runs north to south from the Buffalo Ridge Trailhead to the Seven Lakes area near the headwaters of Big Creek. Along the way, it intersects Beaver Creek Stump Park Trail 1124, which provides the possibility for open-ended hikes (requiring shuttle) to Beaver Creek Trailhead. Big Creek Trail 1125 also provides the possibility for open-ended hikes to Seven Lakes Trailhead. Both Beaver Creek Stump Park Trail and Big Creek Trail provide access to Main Fork Trail further to the west. Main Fork Trail provides access to the system of trails in the Encampment River drainage as well as the northern reaches of the Elk River drainage.

DIFFICULTY
Average, with 1,900 foot elevation gain in 3.8 miles (two separate climbs), but the trail is indistinct and difficult to follow in several locations

TOTAL LENGTH
8.1 miles

SCENERY
Above Average, with views from ridges along the east side of the Park Range toward North Park, the Medicine Bows, and the Snowy Range

USAGE
Light

ALLOWED USES
Hikers and pack stock only are allowed on this trail.

ACCESS
Buffalo Ridge Trail 1151 begins at Buffalo Ridge Trailhead, see page 162

MAPS
Trails Illustrated: #116 Hahns Peak Steamboat Lake
USGS 7.5' Quadrangle: Davis Peak

WAYPOINTS
Buffalo Ridge Trailhead marks the beginning of the trail at 0 miles
Buffalo Ridge summit — 2.1 miles
Beaver Creek Stump Park Trail — 4.0 miles
Davis Peak is neared — 6.2 miles
Big Creek Trail marks the end of the trail at 8.1 miles

ELEVATION PROFILE

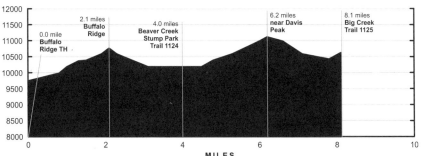

TRAIL DESCRIPTION

Buffalo Ridge Trail 1151 begins at the Buffalo Ridge Trailhead, and winds its way through a recently logged area for the first 0.8 miles before entering an older spruce-fir forest. From this point, the trail alternates between the forest and subalpine meadows where it becomes hard to follow in spots. Higher up, the trail travels through the alpine tundra at the base of Davis Peak before returning to forest and meadows on its way to Seven Lakes. You can find numerous camping opportunities that meet U.S. Forest Service regulations and Leave No Trace guidelines along the trail.

The first 0.3 miles of the trail winds along the west side of Line Creek. The path leaves Line Creek at 0.3 miles, and the next reliable water source is Davis Creek at 3.3 miles. From 0.3 miles to 0.8 miles, the trail follows some switchbacks along an old logging road through a recently logged area.

At 0.8 miles, the trail leaves the logging road and becomes single-track where a sign indicates the direction of travel. At 1.0 miles, the path tops a ridge with excellent vistas to the east and north.

You'll find dry camping opportunities meeting U.S. Forest Service regulations and Leave No Trace guidelines from this ridge until the steep climb adjacent to Buffalo Ridge begins at about 1.6 miles.

View south from Buffalo Ridge

You'll see the sign marking the Mount Zirkel Wilderness boundary at 1.5 miles. The path continues to climb toward Buffalo Ridge past the sign.

The climb tops out at **Buffalo Ridge** 2.1 miles from the trailhead. It is worth the 150-yard walk off the trail (to the east) to enjoy the vista from Buffalo Ridge. At this point, you'll not only see north into Wyoming and east to the Medicine Bow range. The views to the south open up toward Davis Peak and Buck Mountain further to the southwest as well.

The trail becomes indistinct as it crests Buffalo Ridge, but cairns make the route easy to follow. Along the descent of the south side of Buffalo Ridge, cairns mark the path to the base of the hill.

From the vantage point of the last cairn on the hillside, a cairn in the meadow at the base of the hillside and two posts roughly in a line mark the course of the trail across a long grassy meadow.

This meadow is relatively easy to negotiate from the north, but from south to north, it can be difficult to spot the trail on the hillside. The lowest cairn on the hillside is roughly in line with the cairn in the meadow at the base of the hill and the two posts in the meadow.

Beginning at the base of the hillside adjacent to Buffalo Ridge, campsites that meet U.S. Forest Service regulations and Leave No Trace guidelines are plentiful along the trail until it begins to climb toward Davis Peak at 4.5 miles.

Buffalo Ridge Trail 1151 works its way south across several subalpine meadows separated by patches of forest as it continues toward Stump Park.

At 2.7 miles, the trail disappears when it enters a small meadow, but cairns mark the path. The bearing of the trail changes midway through this meadow, possibly making some map and compass work necessary here.

You'll ford Davis Creek at 3.3 miles. Cairns mark the path across the meadow to the west-southwest of the creek, and a blown-over tree marks where the trail re-enters the forest on the north side of the Davis Creek trail crossing.

The path skirts Stump Park at 3.8 miles where it becomes double-track. Marked with a post at 4.0 miles, the trail intersects **Beaver Creek Stump Park Trail.**

The trail continues south, soon skirting the western edge of two small meadows. Two posts mark the way across the second meadow.

As the trail enters the forest past this second meadow, it begins its climb toward Davis Peak (at about 4.5 miles). This marks the end of camping possibilities along the trail until you reach another meadow at 7.8 miles.

The trail soon begins working its way upward along a hillside as it continues south. As you approach Davis Peak, you'll hear the sound of a small stream. At 5.4 miles, the trail comes within a few feet of the stream. The path soon reaches treeline where you can see Davis Peak to the south-southwest.

At 5.7 miles, the trail becomes indistinct in the alpine meadow adjacent to Davis Peak. In fact, you won't see the tread again until the trail re-enters the forest on the north side of Davis Peak at 7.1 miles. Through this section, posts and cairns let you know you are on course, but you may need to employ some map and compass work initially to identify local landmarks and the general direction of the trail.

The trail continues toward a ridge extending east from Davis Peak. You'll cross another small stream (this one flowing to the east) at the base of the ridge at about 5.8 miles. The trail then climbs to the ridge adjacent to Davis Peak.

The path crests the ridge next to **Davis Peak** at 6.2 miles and reveals nice views of Mount Zirkel, the cirque northwest of the peak, and the Sawtooth Range toward the south.

You'll witness even better panoramic views from the top of Davis Peak. The 0.3-mile route to the summit is obvious from the crest of the ridge. If you choose to investigate Davis Peak, do so while observing the peak bagging ethics in the introductory section of this book, and use extra care negotiating the large boulders near the peak (that may shift and crush or trap you).

Buffalo Ridge Trail 1151 now begins its descent from the ridge near Davis Peak, following a bearing toward Mount Zirkel. As the path descends, its heading changes twice and gently curves toward the west.

When you can no longer see posts or cairns on the heading toward Mount Zirkel, look toward the Sawtooth Range for the next bearing. Finally, after heading toward the Sawtooths, the bearing shifts west once more where the trail bears toward Buck Mountain.

As you near treeline at 6.9 miles, the trail switches back toward the east. You'll enter the forest at a second switchback at 7.1 miles. The tread becomes easy to follow again at this point. The trail descends further through another switchback before continuing south along a hillside.

At 7.8 miles, you'll cross a small stream at the north edge of a small meadow, an area where you will find campsites that meet U.S. Forest Service regulations and Leave No Trace guidelines in the vicinity.

The trail then climbs south on the east side of another stream to the west of the meadow. At 8.1 miles, the trail ends where it intersects **Big Creek Trail 1125**. The trail junction is marked with a sign indicating the direction to Davis Peak and Big Creek Lakes.

Stump Park

Gem Lake Trail 1152.2A

Gem Lake Trail 1152.2A runs east to west from its junction with Main Fork Trail 1152 to its conclusion at Gem Lake. The trail treks along the stream issuing from the lake at the headwaters of the Encampment River.

DIFFICULTY
Below Average, 600-foot climb in 1.1 miles, easy to follow

TOTAL LENGTH
1.1 miles

SCENERY
Below Average, but you'll enjoy the view of crystal-clear Gem Lake in a cirque on Buck Mountain

USAGE
Light

ALLOWED USES
Hikers and pack stock only are allowed on this trail.

ACCESS
This trail begins at Main Fork Trail 1152, 8.0 miles north of Diamond Park Trailhead.

MAPS
Trails Illustrated: #116 Hahns Peak Steamboat Lake
USGS 7.5' Quadrangle: Davis Peak

WAYPOINTS
Main Fork Trail 1152 in Encampment Meadows marks the beginning of the trail at 0 miles
Gem Lake marks the end of the trail at 1.1 miles

TRAIL DESCRIPTION
Gem Lake Trail 1152.2A begins at its junction with Main Fork Trail 1152 and heads west to its terminus at Gem Lake. You'll find campsites meeting U.S. Forest Service regulations and Leave No Trace guidelines after a subalpine meadow on the way to the lake. The path generally travels in spruce-fir forest.

ELEVATION PROFILE No signs mark the start of the hike where Gem Lake Trail 1152.2A intersects Main Fork Trail. Gem Lake Trail 1152.2A treks to the west toward Gem Lake, and the tread is clearly visible where it meets the tread of Main Fork Trail 1152. The path initially climbs through spruce-fir forest following the stream leaving the lake. The trail makes its way through some blown-down timber, but the trees have been removed from the trail.

Elevation profile chart:
- Y-axis: ELEVATION (8000 to 12000)
- X-axis: MILES (0)
- 0.0 mile Main Fork Trail 1152
- 1.1 miles Trail ends near Gem Lake

At 0.6 miles, the path enters a subalpine meadow where you can see Gem Lake's cirque to the west. Campsites meeting U.S. Forest Service regulations and Leave No Trace guidelines become easier to find from this point until you reach the lake.

After traveling through the meadow, the trail makes its final climb to Gem Lake, which you'll reach at 1.1 miles. The lake earned its name for the crystal-clear waters that give it the appearance of a Gem adorning the east slope of Buck Mountain.

Hare Trail 1199

Hare Trail 1199 runs west to east from its origin at the end of Forest Road 520 to its terminus at the Wyoming Trail 1101 on the Continental Divide. Hare Trail 1199 provides access to Wyoming Trail 1101, which you can combine with other trails in and around the northern section of the wilderness for medium or long distance hikes. But because it is outside the Mount Zirkel Wilderness, Hare Trail is open to single- or double-track motorized use, as is Wyoming Trail 1101 in this area. The trail shows more wear than you would expect on most foot or horse paths, but the damage is relatively moderate for an ATV trail.

DIFFICULTY
Average, 1,000-foot climb in 2.5 miles, easy to follow

TOTAL LENGTH
2.5 miles

SCENERY
Below Average

USAGE
Light

ALLOWED USES
Hikers, pack stock, mountain bikes, and single- and double-track motorized vehicles are allowed on this trail.

ACCESS
 This trail begins at Hare Trailhead, see page 164.

MAPS
Trails Illustrated: #116 Hahns Peak Steamboat Lake
USGS 7.5' Quadrangle: West Fork Lake

WAYPOINTS
Hare Trailhead marks the beginning of the trail at 0 miles
Wyoming Trail 1101 at the Continental Divide marks the end of the trail at 2.5 miles

TRAIL DESCRIPTION
Hare Trail 1199 begins at the Hare Trailhead and heads east toward its terminus at the Continental Divide. The trail climbs along a tributary of Silver City Creek along most of its trek to the Divide. You'll be able to find campsites near the trail after the path enters a meadow 1.4 miles from the trailhead. The trail generally travels in spruce-fir forest, although it traverses a meadow with willow thickets lining small streams as it approaches Wyoming Trail 1101 at the Continental Divide.

ELEVATION PROFILE

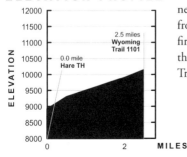

Soon after leaving Hare Trailhead, an old road heads to the south, and a sign marks the continuation of Hare Trail 1199 to the east. At 0.5 miles, the path comes near a stream and follows it for the climb to the Divide.

At 1.4 miles, the trail enters a large meadow in which you'll remain for the rest of the hike. The meadow offers plenty of campsites that meet U.S. Forest Service regulations and Leave No Trace guidelines. While this trail lies outside the wilderness, it's still a good idea to follow wilderness regulations and Leave No Trace guidelines while on National Forest land. The path leaves the course of the stream it has followed at 2.0 miles, heading for the Wyoming Trail.

The last water source along Hare Trail 1199 is a spring at 2.4 miles. The path continues past the spring and meets with Wyoming Trail 1101 at 2.5 miles, a junction marked with a sign.

Meadow along Hare Trail 1199

Main Fork Trail 1152

Main Fork Trail 1152 runs south to north from its origin at Diamond Park Trailhead to its terminus at the second junction with West Fork Trail near the Encampment Trailhead.

Main Fork Trail 1152 meets West Fork Trail twice, allowing a loop hike of the Main and West Forks of the Encampment River. Beaver Creek Stump Park Trail and Big Creek Trail also join with the Main Fork Trail 1152 and allow access to the trail network and trailheads in the northeast section of the wilderness. Main Fork Trail 1152 and the northern section of Wyoming Trail connect the network of trails in northern portion of the wilderness with the network of trails in the Elk River drainage via Wyoming Trail 1101.

DIFFICULTY
Below Average, 800-foot climb in 2.1 miles, easy to follow

TOTAL LENGTH
18.3 miles

SCENERY
Below Average, but you'll have nice views of the Sawtooth Range near the Continental Divide

USAGE
Moderate, with more use between the trail junctions with West Fork Trail

ALLOWED USES
Hikers and pack stock are allowed all along this trail. Single- and double-track motorized vehicles are allowed from Diamond Park Trailhead as far as Wyoming Trail 1101 only. Motorized vehicles are not allowed east of Wyoming Trail. Mountain bikers can ride east of the Diamond Park Trailhead as far as the Mount Zirkel Wilderness boundary.

ACCESS
Main Fork Trail 1152 begins at the Diamond Park or North Fork Trailhead (see page 162) and ends where it intersects West Fork Trail 1153 the second time, 1.1 miles south of the Encampment Trailhead.

MAPS
Trails Illustrated: #116 Hahns Peak Steamboat Lake
USGS 7.5' Quadrangles: Farwell Mountain Mount Zirkel, Davis Peak, West Fork Lake

ELEVATION PROFILE

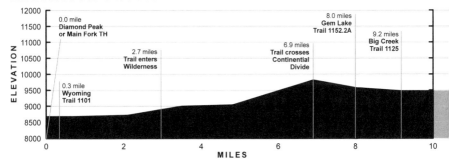

WAYPOINTS

Diamond Park or Main Fork Trailhead marks the beginning of the trail at 0 miles
Wyoming Trail 1101 (Northern section) — 0.3 miles
Mount Zirkel Wilderness boundary — 2.7 miles
Continental Divide (Encampment Meadows) — 6.9 miles
Gem Lake Trail 1152.2A — 8.0 miles
Big Creek Trail 1125 — 9.2 miles
West Fork Trail 1153 (first encounter) — 10.7 miles
Beaver Creek Stump Park Trail 1124 — 11.3 miles
The second encounter with West Fork Trail 1153 marks the end of the trail at 18.3 miles

TRAIL DESCRIPTION

Main Fork Trail 1152 begins at Diamond Park Trailhead and heads east, then north toward its terminus at the second junction with West Fork Trail near the old Hog Park Guard Station. Campsites meeting U.S. Forest Service regulations and Leave No Trace guidelines are easy to find along much of this trail, with some exceptions near Diamond Park and where the Encampment valley narrows north of Beaver Creek Stump Park Trail.

The trail begins at low elevation, traveling through sagebrush meadows and aspen groves near Diamond Park. The path is very hard to find in some sections as it travels along the hillside north of Diamond Park. The trail then works its way adjacent to the wetlands along the North Fork of the Elk River. After climbing north to the Continental Divide, the path generally travels in spruce-fir forest. The spruce-fir forest near the headwaters of the Encampment River is punctuated by the expansive sub-alpine meadows of Encampment Meadows.

A sign marks the beginning of Main Fork Trail 1152 at the North Fork or Diamond Park Trailhead, and you can find camping opportunities near the trailhead. But you'll have a difficult time finding campsites that meet U.S. Forest Service regulations and Leave No Trace guidelines again until the trail reaches the Continental Divide near Encampment Meadows.

The trail is initially a double-track ATV path that provides access to Wyoming Trail 1101. Soon after it begins, the trail crosses a bridge over Trail Creek. The path intersects

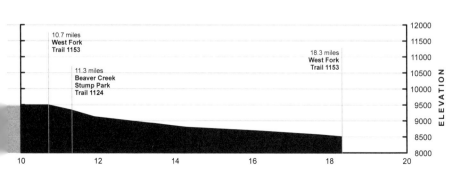

Wyoming Trail 1101 at 0.3 miles where signs mark the junction. Motorized use is not allowed on Trail 1152 past the trail junction with Wyoming Trail 1101.

Main Fork Trail 1152 becomes single-track trail east of Wyoming Trail. The faint path initially treks along the hillside on the north side of Diamond Park. You can see a road that winds through private property within Diamond Park below the trail. This road is not open to the public. Anyone traveling on this road or hiking on the private property in Diamond Park without the permission of the landowners is trespassing, and violators will be prosecuted.

Along the first two miles of the trail, if you stay on the hillside north of Diamond Park, you will stay on National Forest land and avoid potential conflicts with the property owner. As you approach the head of the valley, private property appears to extend to some of the low hills north of the valley floor. Here, the trail turns to a heading of north-northeast and enters an aspen stand where the tread is distinct. You'll have to find the trail in the aspens here to avoid trespassing on the low hills adjacent to the valley floor.

Main Fork Trail 1152 continues northeast past its intersection with Wyoming Trail. The trail becomes very faint as it heads toward the aspens lining the north side of Diamond Park. The path soon enters the aspen. It helps to have a keen eye to find the tread in this section. An active imagination doesn't hurt either. The path crosses a small stream in the aspens at 0.7 miles. You'll see the tread near the stream crossing, as well as fallen trees that have been sawed on the east side of the stream.

The path exits the aspens at 0.8 miles to traverse sagebrush meadow. The trail becomes very difficult to follow as the tread dissolves into a maze of game trails upon entering the sagebrush meadow. Some map and compass work may be necessary to retain your bearings here.

A fairly distinct path emerges from a shallow grassy basin not far from the edge of the aspens that may be the trail. If this isn't the trail, it's a very nice game path that leads to the trail anyway as it enters the forest at the head of the valley.

The path continues east, rising over a low ridge (that extends south from the hillside north of Diamond Park) before descending the opposite side. After you cross the first ridge, the path settles into tracking about 100 yards or so above the valley floor.

As the path approaches the head of Diamond Park, a tree line and a very low string of hills come into view ahead. As you approach the head of the park, the bearing of the trail shifts to north-northeast. The trail heads toward the aspens near the foot of the steeper hillside north of the valley (these trees were likely burned by the Hinman Fire in 2002, after this description was written).

At 2.1 miles, the path enters the aspen at the head of Diamond Park. The trail soon passes to the north of a small pool in the forest. You can see the tread along this section of the trail as the path travels through the aspens for about a half-mile.

A short distance after leaving the aspens and entering a sagebrush meadow, the path joins with a much more distinct trail leading to the Diamond Park Road. The trails merge about 50 yards west of the sign marking the wilderness boundary.

If you're traveling from east to west, the trail is hard to spot where it separates from the more distinct tread going to the Diamond Park Road. It's very easy to continue on the much more distinct path toward the road. If the trail you are following turns to double-track road, you have missed the point where Main Fork Trail 1152 separates from the path leading to the road and you will soon be trespassing on private property. The two paths separate about 50 yards west of the wilderness boundary sign.

At 2.7 miles, you'll reach a sign that marks the **Mount Zirkel Wilderness boundary.** Mountain bikes are not allowed east of the wilderness boundary on this trail. The trail continues east across sagebrush meadows, entering the canyon of the North Fork of the Elk River. Private property is no longer a concern as you hike east from here.

The trail initially travels along the north side of the canyon out of sight of the North Fork. But you come within view of the North Fork at 3.7 miles where the river forms a series of pools along its course. The trail continues toward the east within sight of the river, which threads its way through willow thickets along this section (excellent moose habitat).

At 4.8 miles, the trail turns north to begin its climb to the Continental Divide soon after you enter a spruce-fir forest. The topography in this area appears favorable for finding a campsite, but wind-thrown trees and undergrowth make it more difficult than you think.

The trail makes the 800-foot climb to the Divide through a series of switchbacks. As the path rises, views of Big Agnes Peak and the Sawtooth Range to the south continue to improve.

At about 6.9 miles, the path crests the **Continental Divide.** As you near the Divide, the first of a series of meadows that make up **Encampment Meadows** appears to the east of the trail. Campsites meeting U.S. Forest Service regulations and Leave No Trace guidelines become easy to find from this point until the trail junction with Beaver Creek Stump Park Trail 1124 at 11.3 miles.

Soon after cresting the Divide, the path begins to travel through subalpine meadows. The trail enters a large meadow at 7.4 miles where the view south of the Sawtooth Range is quite nice.

A short distance after entering the thin forest at the north edge of the first large meadow, the trail meets with **Gem Lake Trail 1152.2A** at 8.0 miles. The trail junction is not marked. Trail 1152.2A treks to the west toward Gem Lake, and the tread is clearly visible where it intersects with the tread of Main Fork Trail 1152.

Main Fork Trail 1152 continues north through a series of small meadows along the floor of the Encampment River valley. At 8.6 miles, the path enters the second large meadow of the chain of grassy clearings that constitute Encampment Meadows.

Soon after you enter the forest at the north end of the second large meadow, the trail meets **Big Creek Trail 1125** at 9.2 miles. The trail junction sign indicates the direction to Seven Lakes.

The path crosses a stream just after the trail junction and then encounters a small meadow as you continue north, the last of the series of Encampment Meadows. The trail then travels through spruce-fir forest.

At 10.2 miles, the path crosses to the west bank of the Encampment River and continues north, following the course of the river through the forest.

The path meets with **West Fork Trail 1153** for the first time at 10.7 miles. The trail junction is marked with a sign. Main Fork Trail 1152 continues to follow the Main Fork of the Encampment to the north here.

At 11.3 miles, the trail meets **Beaver Creek Stump Park Trail 1124,** but no sign marks this junction. Instead, an uprooted tree marks the location of the trail junction. Main Fork Trail 1152 treks to the north here, and the trail enters a section where the valley narrows considerably. You'll be hard-pressed to find campsites that meet U.S. Forest Service regulations and Leave No Trace guidelines north of the junction with Beaver Creek Stump Park Trail 1124 for about the next 4.3 miles.

At 11.9 miles, the trail crosses to the east side of the Encampment River. This river crossing is a definite swiftwater drowning hazard during spring runoff. An unfortunate swimmer would probably be seriously injured or worse on the rocks in the swift water below this crossing. If you must cross the river in this area during periods of high flow, you're better off trying a more suitable crossing to the north where the river gradient is less and the rocks are fewer.

The trail continues north, following the course of the Encampment River through a narrow section of the canyon. The trail alternates between traveling near the level of the river and on the hillside east of the river through this long section.

At 14.3 miles, the trail crosses a fair-sized stream flowing to the Encampment. The valley begins to widen again, and you'll have luck finding campsites that meet U.S. Forest Service regulations and Leave No Trace guidelines again at about 15.6 miles.

At 16.1 miles, the trail reaches the south edge of a long narrow meadow. The path continues through this meadow until reaching the north edge at 16.5 miles.

As the trail continues, signs marking the old Boundary Stock Driveway are posted along the way. The path skirts the west edge of a small sagebrush meadow at 16.9 miles.

At 17.3 miles, the path skirts the west edge of a small meadow. The trail turns west into the forest at the edge of this small sagebrush meadow. As the trail makes its way toward the Encampment River through the forest, yellow signs marking the old Center Stock Driveway let you know you're on the right path.

The trail crosses to the west side of the Encampment River at 17.7 miles, yet another swiftwater drowning hazard during periods of high flow. Cairns mark the path upstream on the west bank of the river before the trail turns to follow it downstream.

A sign marks the trail's end at its second junction with **West Fork Trail 1153** at 18.3 miles.

Manzanares Trail 1204

Manzanares Trail 1204 runs west to east from its origin at Wyoming Trail 1101 at the Continental Divide until it reaches West Fork Trail 1153.

Providing the northernmost access point to the wilderness from the west side, Manzanares Trail 1204 passes by Manzanares Lake on its way to the West Fork of the Encampment River.

DIFFICULTY
Above Average, 1,100-foot descent in 2.1 miles, two very steep rocky pitches

TOTAL LENGTH
2.1 miles

SCENERY
Average

USAGE
Light

ALLOWED USES
Hikers and pack stock only are allowed on this trail.

ACCESS
Manzanares Trail 1204 intersects Wyoming Trail 0.9 miles south of where Forest Road 499 ends and 12.6 miles north of Diamond Park Trailhead.

MAPS
Trails Illustrated: #116 Hahns Peak Steamboat Lake
USGS 7.5' Quadrangle: West Fork Lake

WAYPOINTS
Wyoming Trail 1101 marks the beginning of the trail at 0 miles
Spur trail to Trail Creek Trail — 0.7 miles
Manzanares Lake — 1.1 miles
West Fork Trail 1153 marks the end of the trail at 2.1 miles

TRAIL DESCRIPTION
Manzanares Trail 1204 is a good place to contemplate the role of Colorado's wilderness areas in preserving and protecting the quality of our water sources. Water literally springs from the ground on the bench where Manzanares Lake is located, and this water insures the health of the West Fork of the Encampment River during the dry months of late summer.

I hiked this trail during the summer of 2002, the driest on record, and water still flowed from this bench, down a number of small streams, and into the West Fork of the Encampment River. The area functions as a natural ground water reservoir, keeping the river alive and flowing in the summer months for all downstream users.

Manzanares Trail 1204 begins where it intersects Wyoming Trail 1101 at the Continental Divide and heads east towards its terminus at West Fork Trail 1153. The trail descends in two pitches, the first pitch delivering you to the elevation of Manzanares Lake, the second to the elevation of the West Fork of the Encampment River. You can find campsites that meet U.S. Forest Service regulations and Leave No Trace guidelines on the Manzanares Lake bench. The trail generally travels in spruce-fir forest.

A spur trail from Manzanares Trail 1204 leads from the bench near Manzanares Lake to Trail Creek Trail 1184 (near its intersection with West Fork Trail). A separate description of this trail follows the description of Manzanares Trail 1204.

Soon after leaving Wyoming Trail 1101, you'll encounter what's left of a sign marking the Mount Zirkel Wilderness boundary and begin a steep, rocky, exposed, and treacherous descent to Manzanares Lake. The trail drops about 500 vertical feet in roughly a half-mile.

At 0.7 miles, a spur trail to Trail Creek Trail 1154 intersects Manzanares Trail 1204, which is marked with a sign. Manzanares Trail 1204 heads northeast toward Manzanares Lake and becomes indistinct as it crosses marshy meadows.

Since this area stays wetter than others in the wilderness throughout most of the hiking season, you can expect the mosquitoes to be a little worse. If you are planning to spend any time here, remember the bug juice.

At 1.1 miles, you'll find Manzanares Lake nestled in a spruce-fir forest. This marks the beginning of a trail section where it's easy to find campsites meeting U.S. Forest Service regulations and Leave No Trace guidelines. The path continues around the lake, crossing the stream flowing out of it.

ELEVATION PROFILE

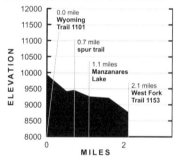

The trail leaves the lake on an easterly heading, shifting to a northeast heading. At 1.6 miles, the descent to the West Fork of the Encampment River begins (and hopes for finding suitable camping end).

You'll have a chance to enjoy pleasant views of West Fork Meadows through the trees soon after beginning the drop toward the river, courtesy of the Routt Divide Blowdown. The path to the river is steep, rocky, and treacherous, although it doesn't have the kind of exposure you encounter on the first drop. At 2.1 miles, Manzanares Trail ends where it intersects West Fork Trail 1153.

TRAIL DESCRIPTION for spur trail to Trail Creek Trail 1154

Not far after leaving Manzanares Trail 1204, the spur trail to Trail Creek Trail 1154 crosses a small stream issuing from a spring. The path continues through spruce-fir forest a short distance west of a small meadow.

At 0.3 miles, the path enters a large meadow, crossing along its north edge. This marks the beginning of a section of the trail where you can find campsites that meet U.S. Forest Service regulations and Leave No Trace guidelines. You'll reach a large spring pool at 0.5 miles in this meadow. The path continues through the open area, ducking in and out of small clumps of forest along the meadow's edge. Remember to avoid camping on soft marshy ground.

At 0.9 miles, the trail leaves the meadow and begins descending toward the West Fork of the Encampment following the stream that comes from the large spring pool. This marks the end of acceptable camping possibilities along this trail.

The descent toward the river is (once again) steep, rocky, and treacherous. The path crosses the stream it has been following at 1.1 miles, and the descent continues until you cross another stream just before reaching the sign marking Trail Creek Trail at 1.5 miles. Where it meets the spur trail, Trail Creek Trail 1154 is only 100 yards from its intersection with West Fork Trail 1153, which is also marked with a sign.

Spring pool along Manzanares Trail 1204

Trail Creek Trail 1154

Trail Creek Trail 1154 runs south to north from its origin where it intersects Wyoming Trail 1101 to its terminus at West Fork Trail 1153 near the West Fork of the Encampment River. Trail Creek Trail 1154 provides access to West Fork Trail 1153 from Wyoming Trail 1101.

DIFFICULTY
Average, 900-foot decent in 1.5 miles, trail is indistinct through meadows along Trail Creek

TOTAL LENGTH
3.8 miles

SCENERY
Below Average

USAGE
Light

ALLOWED USES
Hikers and pack stock are allowed on this trail. Mountain bikes are allowed from the beginning of the trail to the wilderness boundary.

ACCESS
Trail Creek Trail 1154 begins at Wyoming Trail 1101, 4.0 miles north of Diamond Park or Main Fork Trailhead and 4.6 miles south of where Forest Road 499 ends.

MAPS
Trails Illustrated: #116 Hahns Peak Steamboat Lake
USGS 7.5' Quadrangle: West Fork Lake

WAYPOINTS
The intersection with Wyoming Trail 1101 marks the beginning of the trail at 0 miles
Continental Divide marks the end of camping opportunities — 2.4 miles
West Fork Trail marks the end of the trail at 3.8 miles

TRAIL DESCRIPTION
Trail Creek Trail 1154 begins where it intersects Wyoming Trail 1101 and heads northeast toward its terminus at West Fork Trail 1153. The path initially travels through spruce-fir forest and meadows adjacent to Trail Creek. The tread is hard to find in some sections, particularly when you travel through meadows adjacent to Trail Creek.

The trail rises modestly before beginning its descent into the West Fork of the Encampment Valley. You won't have a hard time finding campsites that meet U.S. Forest Service regulations and Leave No Trace guidelines along the initial section through the meadows before the wilderness boundary sign at the Continental Divide. However, you won't find camping opportunities north of the wilderness boundary along this trail, which enters a spruce-fir forest at the Divide before it begins to drop toward the West Fork of the Encampment River.

I was not able to use my measuring wheel on the section of this trail south of the Continental Divide when I hiked it in October 2002. The snow was too deep at the time, but I did hike the trail to identify landmarks mentioned in this trail description. The distances quoted in this description were determined using a mapping program. The trail section is short and relatively flat, so the distances should be reasonably accurate.

The trail begins with a sign marking the intersection with Wyoming Trail 1101. You'll initially head east over a low knoll, then turn north and cross a tributary to Trail Creek.

At about 0.3 miles you'll cross another tributary about 100 yards west of the creek. The path continues north, following the course of the creek. In fact, you'll hike within about 100 yards west of Trail Creek all the way to the Continental Divide. Soon after crossing the tributary to the creek, the path enters a thin spruce-fir forest.

At about 1.0 miles, the trail moves very close to Trail Creek and crosses a small feeder stream. The path then resumes its former spacing from the creek, about 100 yards to the west.

At about 1.3 miles, the trail enters a large meadow. Be careful when you cross this meadow because small feeder streams are entrenched (and well hidden) in the thick grasses that cover the meadow, making for potentially hazardous footing for people and horses alike.

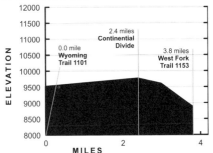

ELEVATION PROFILE

Some map and compass work may be necessary to find where the trail leaves the meadow. The point where it re-enters the forest is on an approximate heading of north-northeast, but the trail doesn't travel directly across the meadow.

For those traveling south to north, a cairn marks where the trail leaves the meadow, not far west of Trail Creek. Another cairn marks the trail on a small mound in the middle of the meadow on a due north heading from where the path enters the meadow. A third cairn at the north edge of the meadow marks the trail on a northeast heading from the cairn in the middle of the meadow. Remember that the trail leaves the meadow following west of the main feeder stream for Trail Creek.

At about 2.4 miles, the trail reaches the Continental Divide where a sign marks the Mount Zirkel Wilderness boundary, and the end of camping opportunities and water sources along this trail. The path enters the forest here, and you'll soon find yourself traveling on a hillside, descending moderately toward the West Fork of the Encampment River.

At 3.0 miles, you can see the West Fork of the Encampment River Valley through the trees ahead. The drop into the valley accelerates here. As the descent continues to grow steeper toward the valley floor below, the path enters a series of switchbacks.

At 3.8 miles, a sign marks the intersection with a spur trail from Manzanares Trail 1204.

Only 100 yards beyond the spur trail junction, Trail Creek Trail 1154 ends at West Fork Trail 1153, a junction also marked with a sign.

West Fork Trail 1153

West Fork Trail 1153 runs north to south from its origin at Encampment Trailhead to its second trail junction with Main Fork Trail near West Fork Lake. The trail follows the course of an old jeep road along the West Fork of the Encampment River.

From Encampment Trailhead near Commissary Park, West Fork Trail 1153 provides you access to the northernmost parts of the wilderness. West Fork Trail 1153 meets Main Fork Trail twice, which means you can hike the West and Main Forks of the Encampment River loop.

You can also access trails to the south through the trail junctions with Trail Creek Trail, Manzanares Lake Trail, and Main Fork Trail, all of which lead to Wyoming Trail 1101 outside of the wilderness. Wyoming Trail 1101 links trails in the northern part of the wilderness with the central and southern wilderness trails. In addition, Main Fork Trail 1152 also provides access to the trail network in the northeast part of the wilderness through Beaver Creek Stump Park Trail and Big Creek Trail.

DIFFICULTY
Below Average, with 1,100-foot climb in 8.7 miles, easy to follow

TOTAL LENGTH
8.7 miles

SCENERY
Below Average, with views of West Fork Meadows and West Fork Lake

USAGE
Moderate to Heavy

ALLOWED USES
Hikers and pack stock only are allowed on this trail.

ACCESS
 West Fork Trail 1153 begins at the Encampment Trailhead, see page 163.

MAPS
Trails Illustrated: #116 Hahns Peak Steamboat Lake
USGS 7.5' Quadrangles: Davis Peak, West Fork Lake

ELEVATION PROFILE

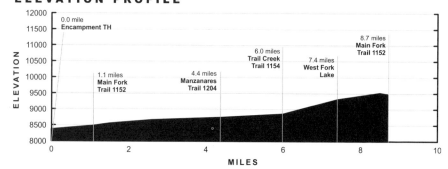

WAYPOINTS

Encampment Trailhead marks the beginning of the trail at 0 miles
Main Fork Trail 1152 (first meeting) — 1.1 miles
West Fork Meadows entered — 2.9 miles
Manzanares Trail 1204 — 4.4 miles
Trail Creek Trail 1154 — 6.0 miles
West Fork Lake — 7.4 miles
Main Fork Trail 1152 (second meeting) marks the end of the trail at 8.7 miles

TRAIL DESCRIPTION

West Fork Trail 1153 begins at Encampment Trailhead and heads south to where it ends at the second junction with Main Fork Trail 1152, near West Fork Lake. Campsites meeting U.S. Forest Service regulations and Leave No Trace guidelines are easy to find along most of its course, with one exception west of West Fork Lake. The trail begins at low elevation, traversing sagebrush meadows and willow thickets near Commissary Park. The path then works its way through stands of lodgepole pine and, as it makes its way to higher elevation, spruce-fir forest. You'll pass through West Fork Meadows, one of the largest subalpine meadows in the wilderness.

From the start, you'll follow the double tracks of the remnants of a jeep road from the old Hog Park Ranger Station. After you cross a small stream, the path works its way across a sagebrush meadow adjacent to the West Fork of the Encampment River.

At 0.7 miles, the trail crosses to the east side of the West Fork and enters the lodgepole forest between the two forks of the river. The crossing of the West Fork of the Encampment River could be a swiftwater drowning hazard during periods of high flow.

You'll meet up with Main Fork Trail 1152 for the first time at 1.1 miles, seeing a sign here that marks the northern terminus of the Main Fork Trail.

West Fork Trail 1153 continues to the south past the trail junction, following the course of the West Fork along the west side of Black Mountain. You'll reach the Mount Zirkel Wilderness boundary sign at 1.5 miles. When you cross to the west side of the West Fork, you'll be 2.6 miles from the trailhead.

At 2.9 miles, the trail reaches the northern edge of West Fork Meadows, and you'll continue south across the meadow until you reach the south edge of West Fork Meadow, at 3.7 miles, where the path re-enters the forest.

The trail meets with Manzanares Trail 1204 at 4.4 miles where a sign marks the trail junction. West Fork Trail 1153 continues south here, crossing a series of boardwalks along its way.

At 6.0 miles, the trail meets Trail Creek Trail 1154. A sign indicating the direction to Manzaneres Lake and West Fork Lake marks this trail junction.

West Fork Trail 1153 continues toward West Fork Lake, its bearing shifting toward the east. Soon after you pass the Trail Creek Trail junction, the West Fork valley narrows considerably until it nears West Fork Lake, which makes it hard to find a campsite 100 feet from the river and trail.

At 7.4 miles, you'll come upon West Fork Lake, which lies to the south of the trail here. You won't have a problem finding campsites that meet U.S. Forest Service regulations and Leave No Trace guidelines in this area. The trail continues east along the hillside to the north of the lake before it climbs over the low divide separating the main and west forks of the Encampment River.

At 8.7 miles, the trail concludes at its second junction with the Main Fork Trail 1152 where a sign marks the end of the trail.

Wyoming Trail 1101—
North of Seedhouse Road

The northern section of the Wyoming Trail 1101 runs south to north from the Seedhouse Trailhead on Forest Road 400 to the end of Forest Road 499, and it continues north on Forest Road 499 to points beyond in Wyoming. This is the northernmost section of the Continental Divide Trail (CDT) described in this book. To continue southward on the CDT from Seedhouse Trailhead, go 0.4 miles east on Forest Road 400 until it meets Forest Road 443. Then go 4.8 miles south on Forest Road 433 to North Lake Trailhead where the CDT continues south on North Lake Trail 1164.

This trail description covers the Wyoming Trail 1101 from Seedhouse Road to the southern end of Forest Road 499, which is the jeep road that follows a portion of the Fireline Trail (cleared by tie hacks almost 100 years ago) atop the Sierra Madre Range just north of Manzanares Trail. Manzanares Trail provides the northernmost access route into the Mount Zirkel Wilderness from the West.

The northern section of Wyoming Trail 1101 intersects Main Fork Trail 1152, Trail Creek Trail 1154, and Manzanares Trail 1204. All these trails provide access into the Mount Zirkel Wilderness from the west, which creates a variety of loop hiking opportunities.

The Wyoming Trail, Seedhouse Road, and FR 443 provide a link that connects the trails in the northern section of the wilderness to the trails in the central and southern sections.

The southern section of Wyoming Trail 1101 runs from Buffalo Pass to where it intersects Gold Creek Lake Trail near Gold Creek Lake. Gold Creek Trail begins not far from the Slavonia Trailhead, about 2.9 miles east (on FR 400) of where the northern section of Wyoming Trail 1101 begins.

DIFFICULTY
Below Average, relatively small elevation gains, easy to follow

TOTAL LENGTH
13.5 miles

SCENERY
Above Average, beautiful valley meadows along the North Fork of the Elk River, nice views near the Continental Divide at the south edge of the Sierra Madre Range

USAGE
Moderate, Heavy motorized use north of Diamond Park

ALLOWED USES
Hikers, mountain bikes, and pack stock are allowed all along the trail. Single-track motorized use only is allowed from Seedhouse Trailhead north to the trail junction with Main Fork Trail 1152. Single- or double-track motorized use is allowed from the trail junction with Main Fork Trail 1152 north to the junction with Forest Road 500.

ACCESS
This trail section begins at Seedhouse Trailhead (see page 164), then passes Stiletto Road (FR 44.1, see page 165), and Diamond Park or North Fork Trailhead (see page 162), and finally meets Forest Road 499 (see page 165).

MAPS

Trails Illustrated: #116 Hahns Peak Steamboat Lake

USGS 7.5' Quadrangles: Farwell Mountain (Wyoming Trail 1101 from Seedhouse Road to Diamond Park is not marked on this map), West Fork Lake

WAYPOINTS

Seedhouse Trailhead marks the beginning of the trail at 0 miles

Lost Dog Road spur trail — 0.9 miles

Stiletto Road (near bridge over North Fork of the Elk River) — 3.7 miles

Bridge over the North Fork of the Elk River — 4.2 miles

Main Fork Trail 1152 — 5.2 miles

Trail Creek Trail 1154 — 8.9 miles

Hare Trail 1199 — 10.4 miles

Manzanares Trail 1204 — 12.6 miles

Forest Road 499 marks the end of the trail at 13.5 miles

TRAIL DESCRIPTION

Wyoming Trail 1101 initially follows the course of the North Fork of the Elk River before following Trail Creek north of Diamond Park. The trail is relatively flat and easy to follow. As it works its way up the river valley, you'll travel through a variety of terrains ranging from forests to sagebrush meadows and willow thickets. You'll also encounter aspen and spruce-fir forests separated by subalpine meadows or willow thickets on the valley floor adjacent to streams.

Before leaving Diamond Park, this trail passes through an area heavily affected by the Hinman Fire in 2002. This description was written about a month before the fire swept across this trail section, but it has not been updated because I haven't hiked through the area to learn the extent of the damage. So this description provides a record of what the valley of the North Fork of the Elk River south of Diamond Park looked like before the fire. Remember to exercise caution when using trails in recently burned areas.

Campsites that meet U.S. Forest Service regulations and Leave No Trace guidelines are never far away when traveling along this trail.

Wyoming Trail 1101 begins near the Seedhouse Campground and treks northward. The trail begins in aspen groves (burned by the Hinman Fire) above the valley floor for the first 0.3 miles. The path then enters a spruce-fir forest above the river and continues north.

ELEVATION PROFILE

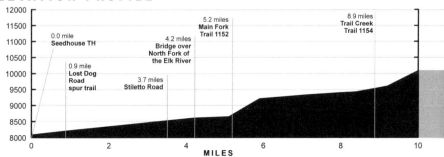

After descending to the elevation of the river, the path enters a meadow adjacent to the river where a **spur trail** connects it **to Lost Dog Road.**

At 0.9 miles, a sign marks the trail through a meadow. After leaving the meadow, the way continues north through thin spruce-fir forest interspersed with small pocket meadows.

At 1.5 miles, you'll cross Lost Dog Creek and then follow the course of the creek upstream, climbing for 0.2 miles before turning north again. The path continues north through spruce forests above the elevation of the river.

As you descend once again to the elevation of the river, the forest begins to thin and you'll encounter small pocket meadows again. At 2.3 miles, the path crosses a slightly larger meadow before traveling through an aspen grove.

At 2.5 miles, you'll enter a large beautiful meadow that covers the valley floor. The trail travels through this meadow for the next 0.7 miles before entering spruce-fir forest once again, where the path continues north through the forest adjacent to the river.

At 3.7 miles, **Stiletto Road (FR 44.1)** intersects the trail about 50 yards east of the bridge over the North Fork of the Elk River. The path continues north, across the road and into spruce-fir forest.

At this point, the trail enters an area heavily affected by the Routt Divide Blowdown. This section of trail was closed for four years after the blowdown while salvage logging operations were carried out in the area.

At 4.2 miles, the trail crosses to the west side of the **North Fork of the Elk River** on a bridge. Soon after crossing the bridge, the trail enters an area where salvage logging has removed most of the felled trees.

At 5.0 miles, the trail intersects the private road through Diamond Park. Remember to stay on either Wyoming or Main Fork Trail in Diamond Park, avoiding the road that goes east through private property in the park (where trespassers are prosecuted). After passing the road in Diamond Park, the trail begins to climb north.

At 5.2 miles, the trail intersects **Main Fork Trail 1152** while climbing out of Diamond Park. In addition to the trail junction sign, other signs here also indicate that Wyoming

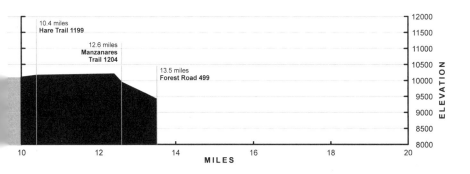

Trail 1101 is double-track motorized trail north of here and single-track motorized trail south of this trail junction. Wyoming Trail 1101, now double-track and well worn, continues to climb the hillside north of Diamond Park.

At 5.4 miles, the path enters a burned-out aspen grove from the Hinman Fire during the summer of 2002. The trail continues traveling through burned-out timber until cresting the hill north of Diamond Park. Views into the North Fork of the Elk River valley and beyond to The Dome continue to improve along the climb.

At 5.9 miles, the path leaves burned forest soon after topping the hill. The trail continues north through thin spruce-fir forest and large sage meadows.

At 7.1 miles, the trail comes within 50 yards of Trail Creek and begins to follow the course of the creek more closely. The path continues to travel through spruce-fir forest and meadows.

At 8.4 miles, the trail crosses to the west side of Trail Creek. The path then begins to skirt the east edge of a large meadow. Signs mark the path as an old stock driveway.

At 8.9 miles, the path meets a sign marking **Trail Creek Trail 1154**. Wyoming Trail 1101 continues toward the base of a hill that it soon begins to climb.

At 9.2 miles, the path begins a traversing climb out of the Trail Creek drainage toward the Continental Divide atop the Sierra Madre Range. The climb is steep and rocky, but views back down the Trail Creek drainage continue to improve along the way.

At 9.8 miles, the trail nears the crest of the Divide and yields very nice views of the wilderness. From here, you can see much of the Sawtooth Range, as well as The Dome, Lost Ranger Peak, and Mount Ethel. This is a good place to see the course and magnitude of the glaciers that once flowed on both sides of the Sawtooth Range from cirques below Mount Zirkel, as well as the glaciers the flowed into the South Fork of the Elk River valley from as far south as The Dome, all converging into the Elk River drainage. This site also offers a good look at areas affected by the Burn Ridge and Hinman Fires during the summer of 2002, as well as much of the Routt Divide Blowdown damage.

The path continues north through meadows dotted with clumps of spruce-fir forest. At 10.4 miles, a sign marks the intersection with **Hare Trail 1199** at the Continental Divide. Water is available from a spring that crosses Hare Trail 0.1 miles west of the trail junction. Wyoming Trail 1101 continues north here, following the course of the Continental Divide through a narrow meadow. At about this point, the trail begins to follow the Fireline Trail (cleared by tie hacks almost 100 years ago) as it continues northward.

At 10.5 miles, the trail enters a spruce-fir forest as it skirts the east side of a small peak along the Divide. The path leaves the forest to return to a narrow meadow that marks the summit of the Continental Divide at 11.1 miles.

The path continues through the long narrow meadow that marks the crest of the Sierra Madre Range until it returns to the forest for a short time at 11.8 miles. You'll enter a narrow meadow once again at 11.9 miles where you can see Hahns Peak to the west.

Soon after entering this small meadow, the trail climbs a low hill where the forest closes in once again. At the crest of the hill, you can take in views down the West Fork of the Encampment Valley.

The path then descends the north side of the hill through a series of switchbacks. The trail is steep and rocky here, and the switchbacks appear to have been constructed to address erosion damage to the previous, more direct, trail route that is still visible. Stay on the new trail route through the switchbacks to give the forest a chance to heal. Remember that short cutting switchbacks is illegal in National Forest.

At 12.6 miles, you'll see a sign where the trail meets the east branch of **Manzanares Trail 1204.** The view into the West Fork of the Encampment River is quite nice here.

Wyoming Trail 1101 continues north, following the course of the Continental Divide. At 12.7 miles, the trail meets the west branch of Manzanares Trail 1204. You can find water 0.9 miles west and about 600 vertical feet down along the Manzanares Trail 1204. The trail is steep, rocky, and heavily eroded on the way to the water source. You won't find campsites until 2.2 miles west of here along Manzanares Trail.

Wyoming Trail 1101 continues north beyond Manzanares Trail 1204 and climbs a small hill. The path begins to descend after cresting the hill, and you'll notice a spring at 13.0 miles. The trail continues down the hill past the spring.

At 13.5 miles, Wyoming Trail 1101 meets **Forest Road 499,** a jeep trail that also follows the Continental Divide (and the Fireline Road). A post marks the end of the jeep trail coming in from the north. Forest Road 499 is the continuation of Wyoming Trail 1101 and the Continental Divide Trail to the north. Forest Road 500 (Big Red Park Road) intersects Forest Road 499 2.3 miles to the north.

Appendix A: Contact Information

U.S. Forest Service Contacts / Information

Medicine Bow-Routt National Forests
http://www.fs.fed.us/r2/mbr/resourcemgmt/wilderness/

For visits to the west side of the Continental Divide
Hahns Peak / Bears Ears Ranger District
925 Weiss Drive
Steamboat Springs, CO 80487
(970) 879-1870
http://www.fs.fed.us/r2/mbr/rd-hpbe/

For visits to the east side of the Continental Divide
Parks Ranger District
P.O. Box 158
100 Main Street
Walden, CO 80480
(970) 723-8204
http://www.fs.fed.us/r2/mbr/rd-parks/

Local Sheriff's offices who manage search and rescue
Routt County Sheriff's office: (970) 879-1090 or 911 for emergencies
Jackson County Sheriff's office: (970) 723-4242 or 911 for emergencies

Colorado Division of Wildlife
(for hunters who need to contact DOW, or anyone reporting mountain lion or bear)

For the west side of the Continental Divide
On the west side of the Continental Divide, call the Colorado Division of Wildlife Steamboat Springs office at (970) 870-2197

For the east side of the Continental Divide
On the east side of the Continental Divide, call the Colorado Division of Wildlife Walden Work Center at (970) 723-4625

Swiftwater rescue training classes and information
Rescue3 International
9075 Elk Grove Boulevard, #200
PO Box 519
Elk Grove, CA 95759-0519
(800) 45-RESCU
http://www.rescue3.com

Colorado Search and Rescue Fund
(to obtain information about the Fund and learn where to purchase
a Colorado Outdoor Recreation Search and Rescue Card)
Sue Schneider (sue.schneider@state.co.us)
Colorado Department of Local Affairs
222 S. 6th St., Room 409
Grand Junction, CO 81501
(970) 248-7310
http://www.state.co.us/searchandrescue

Appendix B: Bibliography

Alden, Peter, Grassy, John, *National Audubon Society Field Guide to the Rocky Mountain States: Idaho, Montana, Wyoming, Colorado,* New York, New York, Alfred A. Knopf Publishers, 1999.

Atwood, Wallace W., *Records Of Pleistocene Glaciers In The Medicine Bow And Park Ranges, The Journal of Geology,* Chicago, Illinois, University of Chicago Press, Volume XLV, Number 2, February – March 1937.

Benedict, Audrey DeLella, *A Sierra Club Naturalist's Guide, The Southern Rockies: The Rocky Mountain Regions of Southern Wyoming, Colorado, and Northern New Mexico,* San Francisco, California, Sierra Club Books, 1991.

Cooney, David O., PhD, *Purification Of Wilderness Waters: A Practical Guide,* Laramie, Wyoming, Balsam Books, 1998.

Emmitt, Robert, *The Last War Trail: The Utes And The Settlement of Colorado,* Norman, Oklahoma, University of Oklahoma Press, 1954.

Forgey, William W., *Wilderness First Aid Manual, A Reference Guide to Backcountry First Aid,* Seattle, Washington, Hart Health and Safety, 1996.

Hopkins, Ralph Lee, Hopkins, Lindy Birkel, *Hiking Colorado's Geology,* Seattle, Washington, The Mountaineers, 2000.

Langendorf, Patricia, *Logging The Rockies The Langendorf-Olson Story,* Rome, New York, Spruce Gulch Press, 1992.

Marsh, Charles S., *People of the Shining Mountains,* Boulder, Colorado, Pruett Publishing, 1982.

Sabel, Gerald (editor), *First Aid, Quick Information for Mountaineering and Backcountry Use,* Seattle, WA, The Mountaineers, 1988.

Schmid, J. M., Frye, R. H., *Spruce Beetles in the Rockies, USDA Forest Service General Technical Report RM-49,* Fort Collins, Colorado, US Department of Agriculture, 1977.

Snyder, George L, *Mineral resources of the Mount Zirkel Wilderness and northern Park Range vicinity, Jackson and Routt Counties, Colorado, US Geological Survey Bulletin 1554, Supt. Of Docs. No.:I* 19.3:1554, Denver Colorado, US Geological Survey, 1980.

Stevenson, Thelma V., *Historic Hahns Peak,* Fort Collins, Colorado, Robinson Press Inc., 1976.

Thybony, Scott, Rosenberg, Robert G., Rosenburg, Elizabeth Mullet, *The Medicine Bows: Wyoming's Mountain Country,* Caldwell Idaho, The Caxton Press, 1986.

Veblen, Thomas T., Hadley, Keith S., Nel, Elizabeth M., Kitzberger, Thomas, Reid, Marion, and Villalba, Ricardo, Disturbance regime and disturbance interactions in a Rocky Mountain subalpine forest, *Journal of Ecology,* London, United Kingdom, British Ecological Society, 82, 125-135,1994.

Appendix C: Fishing Information
West side of the Continental Divide

Name	Acreage	Max Depth (feet)	Fish Species Present (trout)	Last Stock	Fish Stocked (trout)
Porcupine Lake (south of Lake Elbert)	4.2	17	Cutthroat	1993	Cutthroat
Lake Elbert	11.0	35	Cutthroat (some rainbows historically)	1993	Cutthroat
Luna Lake*	38.6	55	Cutthroat	Not since 1973*	
Lake of the Crags	4.8	11	Cutthroat	1993	Cutthroat
Big Creek Lake	8.2	41	Cutthroat	1993	
Fish Hawk Lake*	3.7	24	Brook, Cutthroat	Not since 1973*	
Snowstorm Lake*	8.3	45	Brook, Cutthroat	Not since 1973*	Cutthroat
Lake Edward*	14.7	40	Cutthroat, Brook	1993	Cutthroat
Lake Margaret	33.1	50	Cutthroat, Rainbow	1993	Cutthroat
North Lake*	5.5	9	Brook	Not since 1973*	Cutthroat
Three Island Lake*	23.2	40	Brook	Not since 1973*	Cutthroat
Beaver Lake (SE of Three Island Lake)*	7.0	20	Brook	Not since 1973*	Cutthroat
Gold Creek Lake*	7.7	34	Brook	Not since 1973*	
Gilpin Lake*	18.4	> 55	Brook	Not since 1973*	Cutthroat
Mica Lake	5.5	11	Rainbow	1995	Cutthroat
Lake Diana	9.2	16	Cutthroat	1993	

The stocking database goes back to 1973, the earliest records. Several lakes were stocked historically with Brook Trout.

East side of the Continental Divide

Name	Acreage	Max Depth (feet)	Fish Species Present (trout)	Last Stock	Fish Stocked (trout)
Jonah Lake	8.6	12	Greenback	2001	Greenback
Whale Lake	11	37	Greenback	2001	Greenback
Martha Lake	9.5	32	Brook		
Shoestring Lake*	7.2	7	Greenback, Brook	2001	Greenback
Round Mtn.Lake*	10	12	Brook		
Aqua Fria Lake*	27.6	59	Brook, Mackinaw (Lake Trout)		
Lower Rainbow Lake	9	29	Greenback	2001	Greenback
Middle Rainbow Lake	9	33	Greenback	2001	Greenback
Rainbow Lake	96	91	Greenback	2001	Greenback
Slide Lake*	27.2	65	Greenback, Brook	2001	Greenback
Upper Slide Lake*	8.6	35	Greenback, Brook	2001	Greenback
Roxy Ann Lake	63	126	Greenback	2001	Greenback
Lake Katherine*	23	not available	Brook, Mackinaw (Lake Trout)		
Bighorn Lake	13.8	59	Greenback	2001	Greenback
Bear Lakes	10.1,15.8,5.7	37	Greenback	2001	Greenback
Twin Lakes*	4.3,5.7	22	Brook, Mackinaw (Lake Trout)		
Blue Lake*	21.4	132	Brook		
Seven Lakes	14.0,2.9	25	Greenback	2001	Greenback
Big Creek Lakes*	350,105	65	Grayling, Mackinaw (Lake Trout), Tiger Muskie, Rainbow, Cutthroat, and Brook	2001	Greenback
Manzanares Lake*	4.2	12	Brook		
West Fork Lake*	13	26	Brook		
Ute Lake	5.6	15	Rainbow		

* Several lakes were historically stocked with Brook Trout, and some were later stocked with Lake Trout by the Colorado Division of Wildlife.

Index

Page numbers in **bold** refer to photographs.
Page numbers in *italics* refer to illustrations.

A

Acute Mountain Sickness 39
Altitude Sickness. *See* Acute Mountain
    Sickness
Aqua Fria Lake *4–5*
    fishing information 201
Aspen forests 19

B

Bear Creek Trail 1180 *4–5, 127*, 132–133
Bear encounters 41–43
Bear Lakes *127*
    access from Bear Lakes Trail 1159 135
    fishing information 201
    geology 29
Bear Lakes Trail 1159 *4–5, 127*, 134–135
Beaver Creek Stump Park Trail 1124 *4–5,
    158–159*, 166–167
    access from Beaver Creek Trailhead 162
Beaver Creek Trailhead *4–5, 158–159*, 162
Beaver Lake
    access from Three Island Trail 1163 119
    fishing information 200
Beetles. *See* Spruce beetle epidemic
Bighorn Lake *4–5, 50–51*
    access from Bighorn Lake Trail 1040 65
    fishing information 201
    glacial origin 27
Bighorn Lake Trail 1040 *4–5, 50–51*,
    64–65
Big Creek Falls
    access from Big Creek Trail 1125 169
    glaciers and 28
Big Creek Lakes (east side of the Continen-
    tal Divide) *4–5, 158–159*
    fishing information 201
    geology and origin 28
Big Creek Lake (west side of the Continen-
    tal Divide) *4–5, 50–51*
    access from Big Creek Lake Trail 1184 63
    fishing information 200

Big Creek Lake Trail 1184 *4–5, 50–51*,
    62–63
    access from Luna Lake Trail 1168 89
    Big Creek Trail 1125 *4–5, 158–159*,
    168–170, **170**
Black Bear encounters 41–43
Blue Lake *4–5, 127*
    access from Blue Lake Trail 1178 137
    fishing information 201
    glacial origins 27
Blue Lake Trail 1178 *4–5, 127*, 136–137
Browns Creek Road *4–5*
    ATV usage and 146
Buckskin Network 46
Buffalo Pass Trailhead *4–5, 50–51*, 54
Buffalo Ridge **172**
Buffalo Ridge Trailhead *4–5, 158–159*,
    162
Buffalo Ridge Trail 1151 *4–5, 158–159*,
    171–174
    access from Buffalo Ridge Trailhead 162
Burn Ridge Fire (2002) *4–5*
    fire affected trails
        Lost Ranger Trail 1131 85
        North Lake Trail 1164 95
        Swamp Park Trail 1100 115
    Hazards in Recently Burned Areas 40
    spruce beetle epidemic and 24
Burn Ridge Trailhead *4–5, 50–51*, 54

C

Carbon Timber Company 16–17
Central Wilderness
    Overview *127*
    Trails At-a-Glance 128
Chilton Trailhead *4–5, 50–51*, 55
Chilton Trail 1170 *50–51*, 66–67
Colorado Division of Wildlife
    Contact Information 198
Colorado Search and Rescue Fund 43, 198
Commissary Park
    timber harvesting 16
Crags Trail 1182 *4–5, 50–51*, 68–69

D

Davis Peak *4–5*
  peak-bagging safety and ethics 41
  route to summit from Buffalo Ridge Trail
    1151 174
Diamond Park
  private property and tresspassing in 182,
    183, 195
Diamond Park Trailhead *4–5, 158–159,*
    162
Ditch Creek Trail 1099 *4–5, 50–51,*
    70–71
Dogs in the Routt National Forest 31
Drinking Water Treatment 39–40
Dry Lake Campground *4–5*

E

Ecosystems 19–20
Elkhead Mountains geology 26
Elk Park Trailhead *4–5, 50–51,* 55
Elk Park Trail 1118 *4–5, 50–51,* 72–73
Emergencies. *See* Search and Rescue
  contact information 198
Encampment Meadows
  access from Main Fork Trail 1152 183
Encampment Trailhead *4–5, 158–159,*
    163
Englemann spruce forests 20
  beetles 20–25

F

Fire. *See* Burn Ridge Fire (2002); *See
    also* Hinman Fire (2002); *See
    also* Mad Creek Fire (2001)
  and spruce beetles 20–25
Fireline Trail
  history of 17
  Wyoming Trail 1101 and 196
Fishing Information 45, 200
Fish Hawk Lake
  fishing information 200

Fish Hawk Lake Trail 1168.1A
  access from Luna Lake Trail 1168 89
Flat Tops Wilderness
  spruce beetle epidemic 20, 23
Forest Road 499 Trailhead *4–5, 158–
    159,* 165
Fryingpan Basin
  rock glaciers 28
Fryingpan Basin Trail 1127 *4–5, 127,*
    138–139

G

Gem Lake *4–5, 158–159*
  access from Gem Lake Trail 1152.2A 177
Gem Lake Trail 1152.2A *4–5, 158–159,*
    176–177
  intersection with Main Fork Trail 1152
    183
Geology of the Mount Zirkel Wilderness
    25–30
  geologic map 28
Gilpin Lake *4–5, 127*
  access from Gilpin Trail 1161 141
  fishing information 200
  restricted camping zone 31, 141
Gilpin Trail 1161 *4–5, 127,* 140–141
  access from Slavonia Trailhead 131
  pack stock use and 140
Glaciers in the Mount Zirkel Wilderness
    26–28
Gold Creek Lake *127*
  access from Gold Creek Trail 1150 143
  fishing information 200
  restricted camping zone 31, 143
Gold Creek Trail 1150 *4–5, 127,*
    142–144
  pack stock use and 143
Grizzly Creek Campground *4–5*
Grizzly Helena Trail 1126 Northern Sec-
    tion *4–5, 127,* 145–149, **148**
  access from Helena Trailhead 130
  access from Lone Pine North Trailhead
    130
  ATV usage and 146

Grizzly Helena Trail 1126 Southern Section
   4–5, 50–51, 74–79
   trailhead access
      Grizzly Trailhead 56
      Lone Pine South Trailhead 57
      Pitchpine Trailhead 58
      Rainbow Trailhead 58
      Red Canyon Trailhead 59
Grizzly Trailhead *4–5, 50–51,* 56

H

Hahns Peak *4–5*
   geology 26
   history 15
Hahns Peak Village
   history 15
Hahn, Joseph 15
Hare Trailhead *4–5,* 164
Hare Trail 1199 *4–5, 158–159,* 178–179,
   179
   access from Hare Trailhead 164
Helena Trailhead *4–5, 127,* 130
High Altitude Pulmonary Edema 39
Hinman Campground *4–5*
Hinman Fire (2002) *4–5*
   affect on Wyoming Trail 1101 196
   hazards in recently burned areas 40
   spruce beetle epidemic and 24
Historic Preservation on Public Lands 18
History of Northwest Colorado 13–18
Hog Park
   timber harvesting 16
Hog Park Guard Station
   history 17
Hunting 45, 46
Hypothermia 37–39

J

Jackson County Sheriff's office 198
Jonah Lake
   fishing information 201

K

Katherine Trailhead *4–5, 50–51,* 56
Krummholz 20

L

Lake Diana
   fishing information 200
Lake Edward
   fishing information 200
Lake Elbert
   access from Luna Lake Trail 1168 89
   fishing information 200
Lake Katherine *4–5, 50–51*
   fishing information 201
   geology and glacial origins 27, 29
Lake Katherine Trail 1157 *4–5, 50–51,*
   80–81
   access from Lone Pine Trail 1129 83
Lake Margaret *4–5*
   access from Luna Lake Trail 1168 89
   fishing information 200
Lake of the Crags *4–5*
   fishing information 200
Leave No Trace 32–33
Livingston Park
   glaciers and 27
lodgepole pine 20
Lone Pine North Trailhead *4–5, 127,* 130
Lone Pine South Trailhead *4–5, 50–51,* 57
Lone Pine Trail 1129 *4–5, 50–51,* 82–83
   access from Katherine Trailhead 56
Lost Ranger Peak *4–5, 50–51*
   access from Wyoming Trail 1101 123
   peak-bagging safety and ethics 41
Lost Ranger Trail 1131 *4–5, 50–51,* 84–86
Lumber camps. *See* Carbon Timber Company
   pany
Luna Lake *4–5, 50–51,* **125**
   access from Luna Lake Trail 1168 89
   fishing information 200
Luna Lake Trail 1168 *4–5, 50–51,* 87–89
   Routt Divide Blowdown and 88

M

Mad Creek Fire (2001) *4–5*
   Hazards in recently burned areas 40
   spruce beetle epidemic and 24
Mad Creek Trailhead *4–5, 50–51,* 57

Main Fork Trail 1152 *4–5, 158–159,*
      180–184
   access from Diamond Park Trailhead 162
   Diamond Park private property and tress-
      passing 182, 183
   tie hacks and 17
Manzanares Lake *158–159*
   access from Manzanares Trail 1204 186
   fishing information 201
Manzanares Trail 1204 *4–5, 158–159,*
      185–187, **187**
   spur trail to Trail Creek Trail 1154
      186–187
Martha Lake
   fishing information 201
Meeker, Nathan 14–15
Mica Basin Trail 1162 *4–5, 127,*
      150–151
   access from Gilpin Trail 1161 141
   glaciers and 150
   pack stock use and 150
Mica Lake *127*
   access from MIca Basin Trail 1162 151
   fishing information 200
   glacial origins 27
Milk Creek battle 14
Mining history 15–18
Mirror Lake
   access from Luna Lake Trail 1168 89
Mosquitoes 44–45
Mountain Lion encounters 41–43
Mount Ethel Pluton
   description along Wyoming Trail 1101
      122
   geology 29
Mount Zirkel Summit *4–5*
   peak-bagging safety and ethics 41
   route from Red Dirt Pass 153
Mount Zirkel Wilderness
   geology 25–30
   history 18
   Overview *4–5*
   regulations and travel restrictions 31–32

N

Natural Setting 19–30
Never Summer mountain range
      geology 25

Newcomb Creek **92**
Newcomb Creek Trail 1132 *4–5, 50–51,*
      90–93
   access from Newcomb Trailhead 57
Newcomb Trailhead *4–5, 50–51,* 57
Northern Wilderness
   Overview *158–159*
   Trails At-a-Glance 160–161
North Fork Trailhead. *See* Diamond Park
      Trailhead
North Lake *4–5, 50–51*
   access from North Lake Trail 1164 95
   fishing information 200
North Lake Trailhead *4–5, 50–51,* 58
North Lake Trail 1164 *4–5, 50–51,*
      94–95
   access from North Lake Trailhead 58

P

Packstock use 31–32, 43–44
Peak-bagging safety and ethics 41
Pearl mining history 16
Pets in the Routt National Forest 31
Pitchpine Trailhead *4–5, 50–51,* 58
Porcupine Lake
   fishing information 200
Poverty Flats. *See* Hahns Peak Village

R

Rabbit Ears mountain range geology 25
Rainbow Lake (Lower)
   fishing information 201
Rainbow Lake (Middle)
   fishing information 201
Rainbow Lake (Upper) *4–5, 50–51*
   fishing information 201
   restricted camping zone 97
Rainbow Lake Trail 1130 *4–5, 50–51,*
      96–98
   access from Rainbow Trailhead 58
Rainbow Trailhead *4–5, 50–51,* 58
Red Canyon **79**
   glacial features 27, 78, 84
Red Canyon Trailhead *4–5, 50–51,* 59
Red Dirt Pass *4–5, 127*
   route to Mount Zirkel summit from 153

Red Dirt Pass Trail 1142 *4–5, 127,*
    152–153
  pack stock use and 152
Red Dirt Trailhead *4–5, 50–51,* 59
Red Dirt Trail 1171 *4–5, 50–51,* 99–101
  access from Red Dirt Trailhead 59
Regulations and Travel Restrictions 31–32
Rescue3 International
  contact information 198
River crossings. *See* Swiftwater crossings
Roaring Fork Trailhead *4–5, 50–51,* 59
Roaring Fork Trail 1166 *4–5, 50–51,*
    102–103
  access from Roaring Fork Trailhead 59
Rock glaciers 28
Round Mountain Lake *50–51*
  access from Newcomb Creek Trail 1132 93
  fishing information 201
Routt County Sheriff's office 198
Routt Divide Blowdown
  affect on Luna Lake Trail 1168 88
  spruce beetle epidemic and 23
Routt National Forest *4–5*
  history 18
  regulations and travel restrictions 31–32
Roxy Ann Lake *4–5, 50–51,* **105**
  access from Roxy Ann Lake Trail 1179 105
  fishing information 201
Roxy Ann Lake Trail 1179 *4–5, 50–51,*
    104–105
Rules and Travel Restrictions. *See* Regula-
    tions and Travel Restrictions

S

Saddle Trail 1140 *4–5, 50–51,* 106–107
Search and Rescue. *See* Colorado Search
    and Rescue Fund
  contact information 198
Seedhouse Trailhead *4–5, 158–159,* 164
  history of 18
Seven Lakes *158–159*
  access from Big Creek Trail 1125 169–170
  fishing information 201
  geology 29
Seven Lakes Trailhead *4–5, 158–159,* 164

Sheriff's office
  contact information 198
Shoestring Lake
  fishing information 201
Slavonia Mine 16
Slavonia Trailhead *4–5, 127,* 131
  pack stock use and 43
Slide Lake *50–51*
  access from Rainbow Lake Trail 1130 98
  fishing information 201
Snowstorm Lake
  fishing information 200
Southern Wilderness
  Overview *50–51*
  Trails At-a-Glance 52–53
South Fork Trailhead *4–5, 50–51,* 60
South Fork Trail 1100.3A *4–5, 50–51,*
    108–109
  access from South Fork Trailhead 60
Spruce-fir forest 20
Spruce beetle epidemic 20–25
Stiletto Road (FR 44.1) Trailhead *4–5,*
    158–159, 165
Stream crossings. *See* Swiftwater crossings
Stump Park **175**
  access from Beaver Creek Stump Park Trail
    1124 167
  access from Buffalo Ridge Trail 173
Subalpine fir 20
Summit Lake Campground *4–5*
Swamp Park
  geologic origins 28
  natural setting 19
  trail access
    Ditch Creek Trail 1099 71
    Roaring Fork Trail 1166 103
    Swamp Park Trail 1100 113
Swamp Park Trail 1100 *4–5, 50–51,*
    110–116
  access from Burn Ridge Trailhead 54
  access from Mad Creek Trailhead 57
Swiftwater crossings 33–36
Swiftwater Rescue
  training contact information 198

T

Teal Lake Campground 4–5
Ten essentials 33
Three Island Lake 4–5, 50–51
   access from Three Island Trail 1163 118
   fishing information 200
   restricted camping zone 31, 118
Three Island Trailhead 4–5, 50–51, 60
Three Island Trail 1163 4–5, 50–51,
      117–119
   access from Three Island Trailhead 60
Tie hacks 16–17
Timber harvesting. See Carbon Timber
      Company
Topographic maps
   Trails Illustrated maps 47
   USGS quadrangles 46, 47
Trail Creek Trail 1154 4–5, 158–159,
      188–189
   access from Manzanares Trail 1204 spur
      trail 187
Twin Lake 4–5, 127, **155**
   access from Twin Lake Trail 1174 155
   fishing information 201
   glacial origins 27
Twin Lake Trail 1174 4–5, 127, 154–155

U

U.S. Forest Service
   contact information 198
   regulations and travel restrictions 31–32
Upper Slide Lake
   access from Rainbow Lake Trail 1130 98
   fishing information 201
USGS quadrangle index 46
Ute Creek Trail 1128 4–5, 127, 156–157
Ute Indian Tribe 13–15
Ute Lake
   fishing information 201
Ute Pass 4–5, 127
   access from Bear Creek Trail 1180 133
   access from Gold Creek Trail 1150 144
   access from Ute Creek Trail 1128 157
   history 14

W

Water treatment. See Drinking Water
      Treatment
West Fork Lake 158–159
   access from West Fork Trail 1153 192
   fishing information 201
West Fork Meadows
   access from West Fork Trail 1153 191
West Fork Trail 1153 4–5, 158–159,
      190–192
   access from Encampment Trailhead 163
   tie hacks and 17
Whale Lake
   fishing information 201
Wilderness Act 18
Wildfires. See Burn Ridge Fire (2002);
      See also Hinman Fire (2002); See
      also Big Creek Fire (2001)
   and spruce beetles 20–25
Wildlife 41–43
Winter recreation 45
Wyoming Trail 1101 Northern Section
      4–5, 158–159, 193–197
   trailhead access
      Diamond Park Trailhead 162
      Forest Road 499 165
      Seedhouse Trailhead 164
      Stiletto Road (FR 44.1) 165
Wyoming Trail 1101 Southern Section
      4–5, 50–51, 120–125
   access from Buffalo Pass Trailhead 54

About the Author

Raymond Ave has hiked more than 500 miles in and around the Mount Zirkel Wilderness with a measuring wheel, camera, and notebook so he could gather the details for this book. Ray has been an avid hiker and backpacker in the Rocky Mountains for more than seven years (when he could get time away from his "day job" as a chemical engineer). While exploring Colorado's backcountry, Ray saw the need for quality adventure travel information and decided to fill it by writing hiking guidebooks and complementing them with Web sites that provide the knowledge needed to make the most of our valuable leisure time.

Ray would like to know about your experiences using his book. You can leave a message on the bulletin board of his web site www.mountzirkelwilderness.com, or email him comments or suggestions for updates to this book at rayave@mountzirkelwilderness.com. Additional copies of this book can be purchased through the Mountain Jay Media website at www.mountainjaymedia.com